MY FATHER'S HEART

Do Not Lean
on Your Own Understanding

Meditative Study and Contemplative Prayer

By Sharon K. Young

BurgYoung Publishing, LLC

MY FATHER'S HEART
Do Not Lean on Your Own Understanding

By: Sharon K. Young

BurgYoung Publishing, LLC.
c/o H. Court Young
170 S Holman Way
Golden, CO 80401
skytmcco@hotmail.com

First Printing, December, 2017

My Father's Heart - Do Not Lean On Your Own Understanding - Meditative Study and Contemplative Prayer

December, 2017
ISBN: 1-893478-34-3
ISBN: 978-1-893478-34-3

Dedication

This book is dedicated to my husband who never fails to support and challenge and encourage me and has so generously given much of his time, knowledge and skill to bring this project to completion.

And to my children who have so often been God's instruments in growing me and teaching me about his steadfast love.

My Father's Heart

My Father's Heart Title Page

Contents

Note to Fellow Seekers

Dear Fellow Seeker of God's Face,

I invite you to join me in seeking God to discover who God is and who we are by using the prophets' and psalmists' method of conversing and interacting with God. Meditation. Contemplation. Prayer. Heart to heart conversation that moves us to worship.

I appreciate Eugene Peterson's description of the biblical concept of meditation:

*"Meditate (hagah) is a bodily action; it involves murmuring and mumbling words, taking a kind of physical pleasure in making the sounds of the words, getting the feel of the meaning as the syllables are shaped by larynx and tongue and lips. Isaiah used this word "meditate" for the sounds that a lion makes over its prey (Isa 31:4). They purr and growl in pleasurable anticipation of taking in what will make them more themselves, strong, lithe, swift." (*From his book *Answering God, pg 26)*

Getting the *feel* of the meaning… Experience. Experience in body, mind and heart the meaning of God's words through murmuring and mumbling them. I think that means going even deeper than the intellect and the emotions. Going deeper than what we can see and hear and judge with our physical senses. I think it means becoming acquainted with the spirit in us, learning to fellowship with God's Spirit as we murmur and mumble God's words. Experience pleasurable anticipation of taking in what will make us more ourselves, made in the likeness and image of God.

I've discovered that meditating on God's word somehow lets God's word work itself deeper within me, and over time it changes my thoughts and my feelings and my desires and, I think, develops my character and begins to reveal my true self, my whole self, my "made in God's image" self, at one with God and with all. Meditating on God's word re-creates me. That is so much more effective than trying, through sheer willpower, to do and become what and who I *think* God wants me to be.

I've also discovered that God often begins our conversations by raising questions that deeply probe my heart in order to expose what hinders me from drawing close to him so that I can know him and experience him. It seems that humankind is fairly good at questioning, judging and criticizing others, but not so adept at healthy self-criticism. Until we become aware of our deeper self that is wholly identified with God, we don't realize that the "me" we're familiar with is an illusion. We get so caught up with our outer nature that we're unaware of our inner nature. This "me" that is our outer nature, that we're familiar with, needs to be cut away, cast aside, and die in order for us to discover and live in to who we really are (Matthew 10:39, Mark 8:35).

I encourage you to not quickly gloss over Scripture by simply reading the words. Instead, carefully consider God's words. Not just for a minute or two but for hours and days. Pause often as you speak aloud God's words, murmuring and mumbling them. Phrase by Phrase. Word by word. Syllable by syllable. Feel God's words. Chew them. Taste them. Swallow them. It takes time to absorb and digest them. Let them go far deeper than just your thoughts, in anticipation of taking in what will make you more yourself, the self who was created in God's image and likeness.

Pause often to notice thoughts and feelings and memories and questions and responses that arise in you as you speak and hear God's words. Especially when there is negativity or resistance to his word. I've discovered that's often the place where something restricts my fellowship with God, thus hindering me from knowing and being my true self, and so causing a separation between God and me and others.

In those instances when you find yourself resisting God's word, try reading the Scripture text again and again. Read aloud. Emphasize different words each time you read. Refer to a dictionary to better understand the word(s). Seek to feel the meaning of God's word. Use a concordance to look up other Scripture texts that contain the same word over which you're stumbling. Then be silent. Listen. Not with your physical ears, but for a stirring deep within you that confirms the truth of God's word. There is a "you" hidden deep in your core, in the inner sanctuary where God dwells, where you and God are one, where your outer nature cannot connect or influence or know or be known.

You may wonder why we explore the same Scripture text repeatedly in meditation. Much like treading the same ground, the same path through a garden, for example, day by day, even several times during the same day, lets us become intimately familiar with the path, the garden, and the treasures that reside there. Treading the same ground repeatedly allows us to see from different perspectives, to notice any change, to recognize rot or spoilage or contamination, and to spot new buds of growth and fruit. As treading a garden path reveals the secrets of the garden, so repeatedly treading the Scriptures reveals the secrets of our hearts and God's heart.

I think contemplation, to simply sit in silence in God's presence, is the energy and life behind getting to know who God is and who I am. To be silent in God's presence lets me become aware that I am a participant in God's activities of grace and love. God always initiates. And I respond. He is the giver of all good gifts. When I am silent and present I'm in a position to receive what he gives. Though I may not be aware of any activity, especially initially, my stillness gives the Spirit of God uninterrupted access to my heart and mind and soul and body. I open myself to becoming acquainted with God, according to his way and in his time. In my stillness and silence, I am surrendered to God. I am allowing my outer nature to die so I can become awakened to my inner nature.

I urge you to not begin this study/meditation/contemplation with any preconceived ideas of what you'll gain from it. Simply anticipate that what God chooses to give you will be absolutely perfect for you. Think of this meditational study as a time of opening yourself to discovery, to being discovered, and a time of becoming acquainted with the best friend you'll ever encounter. Simply rest and luxuriate in the grace and love and peace and friendship and fellowship of the one who knows and loves you like no other.

I hope that conversing with God will cause you to grow deeply, all-out in love with him, for that is surely how God loves you!

The grace of the Lord Jesus Christ and the love of God and the fellowship of the Holy Spirit be with you all (2 Cor 13:14).

Sharon

P.S. I quote the ESV version of the Bible throughout unless otherwise noted.

Blank spaces have been provided throughout these pages for you to record your thoughts and responses. I encourage you to journal, to track your discoveries and your growth.

Introduction to Contemplation

Contemplation is an activity that helps us become aware of our inner nature, the hidden person of the heart. This practice helps us learn to discern between flesh and spirit, body and soul.

Jesus taught, "God is spirit, and those who worship him must worship in spirit and truth." (John 4:24)

Scripture describes an outward and an inner being. The inner being is where we meet God.

1 Sam 16:7 - But the Lord said to Samuel [when searching for a man to be king over Israel], "Do not look on his appearance or on the height of his stature, because I have rejected him. For the Lord sees not as man sees: man looks on the outward appearance, but the Lord looks on the heart."

Luke 11:39-40 - And the Lord said to him, "Now you Pharisees cleanse the outside of the cup and of the dish, but inside you are full of greed and wickedness. You fools! Did not he who made the outside make the inside also?

Rom 7:22 - For I delight in the law of God, in my inner being, but I see in my members [a limb or part of the body] another law waging war against the law of my mind [thought, feeling, will, meaning]...

1 Peter 3:4 - but let your adorning be the hidden person of the heart with the imperishable beauty of a gentle and quiet spirit, which in God's sight is very precious.

Ps 51:6 - Behold, you delight in truth in the inward being, and you teach me wisdom in the secret heart.

Job 38:36 - Who has put wisdom in the inward parts or given understanding to the mind?

Job 32:8 - But it is the spirit in man, the breath of the Almighty, that makes him understand.

Ps 142:3a - When my spirit faints within me, you know my way!

John 3:6 - That which is born of the flesh is flesh, and that which is born of the Spirit is spirit.

John 6:63 - It is the Spirit who gives life; the flesh is of no avail. The words that I have spoken to you are spirit and life.

How do we become acquainted with the hidden person of the heart, our inner being, our spirit?

Acts 17:24-28 - The God who made the world and everything in it, being Lord of heaven and earth, does not live in temples made by man, nor is he served by human hands, as though he needed anything, since he himself gives to all mankind life and breath and everything. And he made from one man every nation of mankind to live on all the face of the earth, having determined allotted periods and the boundaries of their dwelling place, that they should seek God, in the hope that they might feel their way toward him [look for, grope, reach out, search all around for; verify by contact] and find him. Yet he is actually not far from each one of us, for "'In him [fixed position in place, time or state, i.e. a relation of rest] we live and move and have our being'; as even some of your own poets have said, "'For we are indeed his offspring.'

John 12:25 - Whoever loves his life loses it, and whoever hates [loves less] his life in this world will keep it for eternal life. If anyone serves me, he must follow me; and where I am, there will my servant be also.

John 17:22-23 - The glory that you [Father] have given me [Christ Jesus] I have given to them, that they may be one even as we are one, I in them and you in me, that they may become perfectly one, so that the world may know that you sent me and loved them even as you loved me.

I encourage you to develop a practice of contemplation. I share mine in case you'd like to try it.

I find that contemplation is an exercise in surrender. Surrender (death) of my outer nature (even if it's only for seconds at a time) in order to find and live from my inner self, my spirit that identifies with and unites with God's Spirit.

Contemplation is a tool or channel to experience oneness and a relationship of love with God.

God doesn't need anything from me. I *am* nothing and *have* nothing apart from God. It is in this discovery and acknowledgement that I begin to find my true self, my inner self.

If you'd like to try this practice, I suggest you begin by taking just five minutes to surrender to God each day. Gradually increase to twenty minutes.

Find a quiet location where you can be alone and uninterrupted. Choose a word or very short phrase from the Scripture text you've meditated on today. You will use this word/phrase to draw you back to God and your inner being whenever your outer nature distracts you and draws you away.

Find a comfortable place to sit. Close your eyes. Inhale deeply. Then exhale. Notice your body. Notice any discomfort. Flex and relax your muscles. Get as comfortable as you can so your body won't be a distraction. Sit tall and straight, alert and committed to being present to this moment. Inhale deeply then exhale. Notice what your physical senses are aware of. Quietly say the word/phrase you've chosen and turn to God, intentionally placing the distractions in the background.

Take in a deep breath and hold it for a second, aware that this breath, this moment, this place is a precious gift from God. Then exhale, aware that you are giving God's breath, this moment, this place back to him.

Again inhale deeply, aware that God *is* in your hidden parts, that it is *his* breath that makes you understand his word. Then deeply and completely exhale, aware that you are completely emptying yourself while trusting that God will fill you with his breath and with himself once again.

Be still. Be silent. Don't expect anything. Don't think. Don't analyze. Don't judge. Don't plan. Simply be. Simply know. In this moment, in this state, you are giving God the gift that he most desires from you, your exposed and surrendered heart, mind, soul, spirit, and body, your whole self, both outer and inner.

Your outer nature won't like this. You'll find your body wants to fidget, and thoughts will race through your head, and urges of all kinds will prod you. Quietly and gently say the word or phrase that you chose for today. Allow your outer self to do what it will, but don't set your heart (desire) and mind (attention) on what it is doing and saying. Rather, dive down deep to the hidden person of your heart. Settle in and rest there in God's presence. Let your outer self be muted in the background.

Lay your hands on your thighs, palms up, signifying that you are open to God, totally surrendered.

Each time you find that your outer self has pulled your attention away, quietly and gently say the word or phrase you chose and then dive back down deep to the hidden person of your heart to return to the Lord. He is not far from you. Feel your way toward him in your spirit, your consciousness, your intuition. Reach out. Find him. Your own thoughts can't help you find him. In him, you live and move and have your being (in him you are, in him you exist). Bask in him.

Be still. Be silent. Wait. Listen. Anticipate with pleasure that you will experience being in the presence of God in this fixed position in place, time and state as you rest in Christ Jesus. Rest in perfect love. Simply exist. Be.

At the end of your contemplation, inhale deeply and hold it for a second, aware that you exist in God's abounding grace. Only in God's abounding grace do you exist. In God's abounding grace you are you, the real you.

*2 Cor 9:8 - And **God is able** to make all grace abound to you, so that having all sufficiency in all things at all times, **you may** abound in every good work.*

Exhale slowly and deeply, anticipating that God's abounding grace, in which you exist and are, will flow around you and through you to love as you have been loved so that you may abound in every good work this day.

1 – The Heart is Deceitful

Pray: Ask God to prepare your heart and mind and soul to receive his words, to receive truth that will set you free, which will heal and perfect your understanding and knowledge of who God is and who you are.

Ps 119:25-32 - My soul clings to the dust; give me life according to your word! When I told of my ways, you answered me; teach me your statutes! Make me understand the way of your precepts, and I will meditate on your wondrous works. My soul melts away for sorrow; strengthen me according to your word! Put false ways far from me and graciously teach me your law! I have chosen the way of faithfulness; I set your rules before me. I cling to your testimonies, O Lord; let me not be put to shame! I will run in the way of your commandments when you enlarge my heart! (ESV)

[Murmur and mumble the words. Phrase by phrase. Word by word. Syllable by syllable. Pause. Breathe. Inhale and exhale. Reflect. Listen.]

Journal:

Note how this prayer stirs you today and what you hear God saying to you.

Jer 17:9 - The heart is deceitful above all things, and desperately sick; who can understand it?

The heart.

What is the heart?

…the heart; also used (figuratively) very widely for the feelings, the will and even the intellect; likewise for the centre of anything[1]

The heart. The most interior organ. The feelings, the will, the intellect. The center of anything.

The ***heart***

Your heart

The heart is ***deceitful*** [apt to lie or cheat, or be dishonest]

The heart is ***desperately sick*** [unwell, deeply disturbed, distressed, unsound]

Who can understand it?

[Murmur and mumble the words. Phrase by phrase. Word by word. Syllable by syllable. Take pleasure in making the sounds of the words, getting the feel of the meaning. Experience pleasurable anticipation of taking in what will make you more yourself, the self that God made in his own image and likeness. The self that God made for intimate communion with him. The self that God created for good works, that you should walk in them. Eat God's words. Let God's words become a joy and the delight of your heart.]

Journal:

Consider *your* heart, *your* center. Offer it to God, fully opened. Are you aware of its deceit and sickness in some specific ways? Describe.

Do you agree with God when he says that the heart is deceitful? Do you agree that the heart is desperately sick? Do you agree that you can't understand your heart? Why or why not?

Are you willing to take God at his word? Are you willing to let God probe and seek out the root of the deceit and sickness in your heart?

Jer 17:9 - The heart is deceitful above all things, and desperately sick; who can understand it?

[Pause. Breathe. Inhale and exhale. Reflect. Listen.]

Give me life according to your word, God!

Journal:

What do you hear God saying to you in these Scripture texts? What do they reveal about God and about you? Converse with God about what you're hearing him say. Verbalize and describe your thoughts, memories that come to mind, questions and emotions, concerns, desires.

Is there a particular word or phrase that disturbs or soothes you?

Do the Scripture texts create a picture or an impression that draws you to linger in exploring and experiencing it?

Choose a word or a phrase from your meditation to write on a slip of paper to carry with you today. Refer to it often throughout the day to remind you of your conversation with God and to continue the conversation all day long. Throughout the day pause to become aware of your thoughts and feelings and will. Ask yourself, "What drives me in this moment? Life according to God's word? Or life according to someone else's word?"

Anticipate that God's words stirred your heart for a reason. He's conversing with you through them. Anticipate that God will bring his word to life in you, to bear fruit in your heart and mind and soul and body. Anticipate that God will reveal the secrets of your heart, for anything that is visible is light. And anticipate that God will cause his words to become a joy and the delight of your heart.

CONTEMPLATE

God is spirit, and those who worship him must worship in spirit and truth. Seek him. Feel your way to him. Reach out. Find him.

Take in a deep breath and hold it for a second, aware that this breath, this moment, this place is a precious gift from God. Then exhale, aware that you are giving God's breath, this moment, this place back to him.

Again inhale deeply, aware that God *is* in your hidden parts, that it is *his* breath that makes you understand his word. Then deeply and completely exhale, aware that you are completely emptying yourself while trusting that God will fill you with his breath and with himself once again.

Be still. Be silent. Simply be. Simply know. In this moment, in this state, you are giving God the gift that he most desires from you, your exposed and surrendered heart, mind, soul, spirit, and body, your whole self, both outer and inner.

Each time you find that your outer self has pulled your attention away, quietly and gently say the word or phrase you chose and then dive back down deep to the hidden person of your heart to return to the Lord. He is not far from you. Feel your way toward him in your spirit, your consciousness, your intuition. Your own thoughts can't help you find him. In him, you live and move and have your being (in him you are, in him you exist). Bask in him.

Be still. Be silent. Wait. Listen. Anticipate with pleasure that you will experience being in the presence of God in this fixed position in place, time and state as you rest in Christ Jesus. Rest in perfect love. Simply exist. Be.

At the end of your contemplation, inhale deeply and hold it for a second, aware that you exist in God's abounding grace. Only in God's abounding grace do you exist. In God's abounding grace you are you, the real you.

2 Cor 9:8 - And ***God is able*** *to make all grace abound to you, so that having all sufficiency in all things at all times,* ***you may*** *abound in every good work.*

Exhale slowly and deeply, anticipating that God's abounding grace, in which you exist and are, will flow around you and through you to enlighten and empower you to love as you have been loved so that you may abound in every good work this day.

Resources:

[1]Heart: OT:3820 <START HEBREW>bl@<END HEBREW> leb

(labe); a form of OT:3824; the heart; also used (figuratively) very widely for the feelings, the will and even the intellect; likewise for the centre of anything: (Biblesoft's New Exhaustive Strong's Numbers and Concordance with Expanded Greek-Hebrew Dictionary. Copyright © 1994, 2003, 2006, 2010 Biblesoft, Inc. and International Bible Translators, Inc.)

2 – The Lord Has Searched Me and Known Me

Pray: Ask God to prepare your heart and mind and soul to receive his words, to receive truth that will set you free, which will heal and perfect your understanding and knowledge of who God is and who you are.

Ps 119:25-32 - I'm feeling terrible — I couldn't feel worse! Get me on my feet again. You promised, remember? When I told my story, you responded; <u>train me well in your deep wisdom</u>. Help me understand these things inside and out so I can <u>ponder</u> your miracle-wonders. My sad life's dilapidated, a falling-down barn; <u>build me up again by your Word</u>. Barricade the road that goes Nowhere; <u>grace me with your clear revelation</u>. I choose the true road to Somewhere, I post your road signs at every curve and corner. I grasp and cling to whatever you tell me; God, don't let me down! <u>I'll run the course you lay out for me if you'll just show me how.</u> (MSG)

[Murmur and mumble the words. Phrase by phrase. Word by word. Syllable by syllable. Pause. Breathe. Inhale and exhale. Reflect. Listen.]

Journal:

Note how this prayer stirs you today and what you hear God saying to you.

Jer 17:9 - The heart is deceitful above all things, and desperately sick; who can understand it?

Ps 139:1 - O Lord, you have searched me and known me!

O ***Lord***,

You ***have***

You have ***searched***

You have searched ***me***

And known me!

[Murmur and mumble the words. Phrase by phrase. Word by word. Syllable by syllable. Take pleasure in making the sounds of the words, getting the feel of the meaning. Experience pleasurable anticipation of taking in what will make you more yourself, the self that God made in his own image and likeness. The self that God made for intimate communion with him. The self that God created for good works, that you should walk in them. Eat God's words. Let God's words become a joy and the delight of your heart.]

Journal:

Are you aware that God has searched you? Are you aware that God knows you? How does this discovery make you feel?

What do you think God's purpose is in searching you?

Is it important to you that God knows you? Are you willing to accept his diagnosis that the heart, the will, the thoughts, the feelings, the very center of you is deceitful and desperately sick? What would you like to do about your deceitful and desperately sick heart? What would you like God to do about it?

Why do you think it's important to God to search you and know you?

Do you feel like you know yourself?

Do you search to know God as he searches to know you?

Do you feel like you know God? Who is God to you? How do you perceive him? What words come to mind?

What reactions, what thoughts, and what emotions does hearing the word or name or title "God" bring out in you? Why do you react the way you do?

Jer 17:9 - The heart is deceitful above all things, and desperately sick; who can understand it?

Ps 139:1 - O Lord, you have searched me and known me!

[Pause. Breathe. Inhale and exhale. Reflect. Listen.]

Give me life according to your word, God!

Journal:

What do you hear God saying to you in these Scripture texts? What do they reveal about God and about you? Converse with God about what you're hearing him say. Verbalize and describe your thoughts, memories that come to mind, questions and emotions, concerns, desires.

Is there a particular word or phrase that disturbs or soothes you?

Do the Scripture texts create a picture or an impression that draws you to linger in exploring and experiencing it?

Choose a word or a phrase from your meditation to write on a slip of

paper to carry with you today. Refer to it often throughout the day to remind you of your conversation with God and to continue the conversation all day long. Throughout the day pause to become aware of your thoughts and feelings and will. Ask yourself, "What drives me in this moment? Life according to God's word? Or life according to someone else's word?"

Anticipate that God's words stirred your heart for a reason. He's conversing with you through them. Anticipate that God will bring his word to life in you, to bear fruit in your heart and mind and soul and body. Anticipate that God will reveal the secrets of your heart, for anything that is visible is light. And anticipate that God will cause his words to become a joy and the delight of your heart.

CONTEMPLATE

God is spirit, and those who worship him must worship in spirit and truth. Seek him. Feel your way to him. Reach out. Find him.

Take in a deep breath and hold it for a second, aware that this breath, this moment, this place is a precious gift from God. Then exhale, aware that you are giving God's breath, this moment, this place back to him.

Again inhale deeply, aware that God *is* in your hidden parts, that it is *his* breath that makes you understand his word. Then deeply and completely exhale, aware that you are completely emptying yourself while trusting that God will fill you with his breath and with himself once again.

Be still. Be silent. Simply be. Simply know. In this moment, in this state, you are giving God the gift that he most desires from you, your exposed and surrendered heart, mind, soul, spirit, and body, your whole self, both outer and inner.

Each time you find that your outer self has pulled your attention away, quietly and gently say the word or phrase you chose and then dive back down deep to the hidden person of your heart to return to the Lord. He is not far from you. Feel your way toward him in your spirit, your consciousness, your intuition. Your own thoughts can't help you find him. In him, you live and move and have your being (in him you are, in him you exist). Bask in him.

Be still. Be silent. Wait. Listen. Anticipate with pleasure that you will experience being in the presence of God in this fixed position in place, time and state as you rest in Christ Jesus. Rest in perfect love. Simply exist. Be.

At the end of your contemplation, inhale deeply and hold it for a second, aware that you exist in God's abounding grace. Only in God's abounding grace do you exist. In God's abounding grace you are you, the real you.

2 Cor 9:8 - And ***God is able*** *to make all grace abound to you, so that having all sufficiency in all things at all times,* ***you may*** *abound in every good work.*

Exhale slowly and deeply, anticipating that God's abounding grace, in which you exist and are, will flow around you and through you to enlighten and empower you to love as you have been loved so that you may abound in every good work this day.

3 – God Knows the Secrets of Your Heart

Pray: Ask God to prepare your heart and mind and soul to receive his words, to receive truth that will set you free, which will heal and perfect your understanding and knowledge of who God is and who you are.

Ps 119:25-32 - My soul clings to the dust; give me life according to your word! When I told of my ways, you answered me; teach me your statutes! Make me understand the way of your precepts, and I will meditate on your wondrous works. My soul melts away for sorrow; strengthen me according to your word! Put false ways far from me and graciously teach me your law! I have chosen the way of faithfulness; I set your rules before me. I cling to your testimonies, O Lord; let me not be put to shame! I will run in the way of your commandments when you enlarge my heart! (ESV)

[Murmur and mumble the words. Phrase by phrase. Word by word. Syllable by syllable. Pause. Breathe. Inhale and exhale. Reflect. Listen.]

Journal:

Note how this prayer stirs you today and what you hear God saying to you.

Ps 44:20-21 - If we had forgotten the name of our God or spread out our hands to a foreign god, would not God discover this? For he knows the secrets of the heart.

If

If ***we***

If we had ***forgotten***

If we had forgotten ***the name*** of our God

If we had forgotten the name of ***our God***

Or if we had spread out our hands to ***a foreign god***

Would not God ***discover*** this?

For ***he knows***

For he knows ***the secrets***

For he knows the secrets ***of the heart***.

For God knows the secrets of your ***deceitful and desperately sick*** heart.

[Murmur and mumble the words. Phrase by phrase. Word by word. Syllable by syllable. Take pleasure in making the sounds of the words, getting the feel of the meaning. Experience pleasurable anticipation of taking in what will make you more yourself, the self that God made in his own image and likeness. The self that God made for intimate communion with him. The self that God created for good works, that you should walk in them. Eat God's words. Let God's words become a joy and the delight of your heart.]

Journal:

What secrets in your deceitful and desperately sick heart does God know?

Might God's purpose in searching you be to discover whether you've forgotten the name of your God? Might his purpose be to know whether you serve or love some god other than your Creator and Helper and Giver of everything? If he does search you for these purposes, do you think he searches you for your good or for your harm?

Are you aware that you are serving or loving a foreign god?

Have you considered that there might be secrets in your heart that God alone knows? Might those secrets hinder you from knowing and loving God? Might those secrets hinder your relationships with your fellow human beings? Might those secrets interfere with your discovering and being the best you that you can be?

As you reflect on your understanding of God, consider what or who is the source of your understanding and knowledge about God? Are your friends your source? Your pastor? Theologians? Skeptics? Your own experiences and observations and judgments? Religious books? Are your sources reliable?

Do you know what God himself wants you to know about him? And about you?

Ps 44:20-21 - If we had forgotten the name of our God or spread out our hands to a foreign god, would not God discover this? For he knows the secrets of the heart.

[Pause. Breathe. Inhale and exhale. Reflect. Listen.]

Give me life according to your word, God!

Journal:

What do you hear God saying to you in these Scripture texts? What do they reveal about God and about you? Converse with God about what you're hearing him say. Verbalize and describe your thoughts, memories that come to mind, questions and emotions, concerns, desires.

Is there a particular word or phrase that disturbs or soothes you?

Do the Scripture texts create a picture or an impression that draws you to linger in exploring and experiencing it?

Choose a word or a phrase from your meditation to write on a slip of paper to carry with you today. Refer to it often throughout the day to remind you of your conversation with God and to continue the conversation all day long. Throughout the day pause to become aware of your thoughts and feelings and will. Ask yourself, "What drives me in this moment? Life according to God's word? Or life according to someone else's word?"

Anticipate that God's words stirred your heart for a reason. He's conversing with you through them. Anticipate that God will bring his word to life in you, to bear fruit in your heart and mind and soul and body. Anticipate that God will reveal the secrets of your heart, for anything that is visible is light. And anticipate that God will cause his words to become a joy and the delight of your heart.

CONTEMPLATE

God is spirit, and those who worship him must worship in spirit and truth. Seek him. Feel your way to him. Reach out. Find him.

Take in a deep breath and hold it for a second, aware that this breath, this moment, this place is a precious gift from God. Then exhale, aware that you are giving God's breath, this moment, this place back to him.

Again inhale deeply, aware that God *is* in your hidden parts, that it is *his* breath that makes you understand his word. Then deeply and completely exhale, aware that you are completely emptying yourself while trusting that God will fill you with his breath and with himself once again.

Be still. Be silent. Simply be. Simply know. In this moment, in this state, you are giving God the gift that he most desires from you, your exposed and surrendered heart, mind, soul, spirit, and body, your whole self, both outer and inner.

Each time you find that your outer self has pulled your attention away, quietly and gently say the word or phrase you chose and then dive back down deep to the hidden person of your heart to return to the Lord. He is not far from you. Feel your way toward him in your spirit, your consciousness, your intuition. Your own thoughts can't help you find him. In him, you live and move and have your being (in him you are, in him you exist). Bask in him.

Be still. Be silent. Wait. Listen. Anticipate with pleasure that you will experience being in the presence of God in this fixed position in place, time and state as you rest in Christ Jesus. Rest in perfect love. Simply exist. Be.

At the end of your contemplation, inhale deeply and hold it for a second, aware that you exist in God's abounding grace. Only in God's abounding grace do you exist. In God's abounding grace you are you, the real you.

*2 Cor 9:8 - And **God is able** to make all grace abound to you, so that having all sufficiency in all things at all times, **you may** abound in every good work.*

Exhale slowly and deeply, anticipating that God's abounding grace, in which you exist and are, will flow around you and through you to enlighten and empower you to love as you have been loved so that you may abound in every good work this day.

4 – Make Me Know

Pray: Ask God to prepare your heart and mind and soul to receive his words, to receive truth that will set you free, which will heal and perfect your understanding and knowledge of who God is and who you are.

Ps 119:25-32 - I'm feeling terrible — I couldn't feel worse! Get me on my feet again. You promised, remember? When I told my story, you responded; train me well in your deep wisdom. Help me understand these things inside and out so I can ponder your miracle-wonders. My sad life's dilapidated, a falling-down barn; build me up again by your Word. Barricade the road that goes Nowhere; grace me with your clear revelation. I choose the true road to Somewhere, I post your road signs at every curve and corner. I grasp and cling to whatever you tell me; God, don't let me down! I'll run the course you lay out for me if you'll just show me how. (MSG)

[Murmur and mumble the words. Phrase by phrase. Word by word. Syllable by syllable. Pause. Breathe. Inhale and exhale. Reflect. Listen.]

Journal:

Note how this prayer stirs you today and what you hear God saying to you.

Job 13:23 - How many are my iniquities and my sins? Make me know my transgression and my sin.

How many, God?

Make me ***know***.

Make me know.

Make me know my ***transgression*** and my ***sin***.

Make ***me know*** my transgression and my sin, God!

My transgression.

..."to transgress, rebel." The basic sense... is "to rebel." There are

two stages of rebellion. First, the whole process of rebellion has independence in view… Second, the final result of the rebellion is the state of independence… A more radical meaning is the state of rebellion in which there is no end of the rebellion in view. The process is no longer goal-oriented. …It is best translated as an absolute, radical act "to break away from". …The most common translations are: "to act unpiously"; [having or showing no religious devotion] "to go away, withdraw"; "lawless"; and "sin".[1]

Make me know my transgression and my sin.

[Murmur and mumble the words. Phrase by phrase. Word by word. Syllable by syllable. Take pleasure in making the sounds of the words, getting the feel of the meaning. Experience pleasurable anticipation of taking in what will make you more yourself, the self that God made in his own image and likeness. The self that God made for intimate communion with him. The self that God created for good works, that you should walk in them. Eat God's words. Let God's words become a joy and the delight of your heart.]

Journal:

Pray. Ask God to help you see as he sees:

"Make me know how I have rebelled, God. What stage am I in? Am I desiring independence? Am I in a state of independence? Have I completely broken away from you? Am I lawless? Is there no end of my rebellion in view?"

"Make me know how I've withdrawn from you, God. Make me know how I've broken away."

Are you rebelling against God? Are you wanting to be independent of him? Why or why not?

Do you feel like you're separated from God even if you don't want to be?

Job 13:23 - How many are my iniquities and my sins? Make me know my transgression and my sin.

[Pause. Breathe. Inhale and exhale. Reflect. Listen.]

Give me life according to your word, God!

Journal:

What do you hear God saying to you in these Scripture texts? What do they reveal about God and about you? Converse with God about what you're hearing him say. Verbalize and describe your thoughts, memories that come to mind, questions and emotions, concerns, desires.

Is there a particular word or phrase that disturbs or soothes you?

Do the Scripture texts create a picture or an impression that draws you to linger in exploring and experiencing it?

Choose a word or a phrase from your meditation to write on a slip of paper to carry with you today. Refer to it often throughout the day to remind you of your conversation with God and to continue the conversation all day long. Throughout the day pause to become aware of your thoughts and feelings and will. Ask yourself, "What drives me in this moment? Life according to God's word? Or life according to someone else's word?"

Anticipate that God's words stirred your heart for a reason. He's conversing with you through them. Anticipate that God will bring his word to life in you, to bear fruit in your heart and mind and soul and body. Anticipate that God will reveal the secrets of your heart, for anything that is visible is light. And anticipate that God will cause his words to become a joy and the delight of your heart.

CONTEMPLATE

God is spirit, and those who worship him must worship in spirit and truth. Seek him. Feel your way to him. Reach out. Find him.

Take in a deep breath and hold it for a second, aware that this breath, this moment, this place is a precious gift from God. Then exhale, aware that you are giving God's breath, this moment, this place back to him.

Again inhale deeply, aware that God *is* in your hidden parts, that it is *his* breath that makes you understand his word. Then deeply and completely exhale, aware that you are completely emptying yourself while trusting that God will fill you with his breath and with himself once again.

Be still. Be silent. Simply be. Simply know. In this moment, in this state, you are giving God the gift that he most desires from you, your exposed and surrendered heart, mind, soul, spirit, and body, your whole self, both outer and inner.

Each time you find that your outer self has pulled your attention away, quietly and gently say the word or phrase you chose and then dive back down deep to the hidden person of your heart to return to the Lord. He is not far from you. Feel your way toward him in your spirit, your consciousness, your intuition. Your own thoughts can't help you find him. In him, you live and move and have your being (in him you are, in him you exist). Bask in him.

Be still. Be silent. Wait. Listen. Anticipate with pleasure that you will experience being in the presence of God in this fixed position in place, time and state as you rest in Christ Jesus. Rest in perfect love. Simply exist. Be.

At the end of your contemplation, inhale deeply and hold it for a second, aware that you exist in God's abounding grace. Only in God's abounding grace do you exist. In God's abounding grace you are you, the real you.

*2 Cor 9:8 - And **God is able** to make all grace abound to you, so that having all sufficiency in all things at all times, **you may** abound in every good work.*

Exhale slowly and deeply, anticipating that God's abounding grace, in which you exist and are, will flow around you and through you to enlighten and empower you to love as you have been loved so that you may abound in every good work this day.

Resources:

[1]Transgress: pasha± OT:6586, "to transgress, rebel." The basic sense of pasha± is "to rebel." There are two stages of rebellion. First, the whole process of rebellion has independence in view... Second, the final result of the rebellion is the state of independence... A more radical meaning is the state of rebellion in which there is no end of the rebellion in view. The process is no longer goal-oriented. ...It is best translated as an absolute, radical act ("to break away from").

...The Septuagint translators are not consistent in the translation of pasha±. The most common translations are: asebeo ("to act unpiously"); aphistemi ("to go away, withdraw"); anomos ("lawless"); and hamartia ("sin"). (from Vine's Expository Dictionary of Biblical Words, Copyright © 1985, Thomas Nelson Publishers.)

5 – Whoever Trusts in His Own Mind is a Fool

Pray: Ask God to prepare your heart and mind and soul to receive his words, to receive truth that will set you free, which will heal and perfect your understanding and knowledge of who God is and who you are.

Ps 119:25-32 - My soul clings to the dust; give me life according to your word! When I told of my ways, you answered me; teach me your statutes! Make me understand the way of your precepts, and I will meditate on your wondrous works. My soul melts away for sorrow; strengthen me according to your word! Put false ways far from me and graciously teach me your law! I have chosen the way of faithfulness; I set your rules before me. I cling to your testimonies, O Lord; let me not be put to shame! I will run in the way of your commandments when you enlarge my heart! (ESV)

[Murmur and mumble the words. Phrase by phrase. Word by word. Syllable by syllable. Pause. Breathe. Inhale and exhale. Reflect. Listen.]

Journal:

Note how this prayer stirs you today and what you hear God saying to you.

Job 13:23 - How many are my iniquities and my sins? Make me know my transgression and my sin.

Prov 28:26 - Whoever trusts in his own mind is a fool, but he who walks in wisdom will be delivered.

Whoever ***trusts***...

Whoever trusts in his ***own mind***...

Whoever <u>takes refuge</u> in his own mind...

Whoever <u>is confident</u> in his own mind...

Whoever ***trusts*** in his own mind...

...***is*** a fool.

...is silly. ...is stupid.

Whoever trusts in his own mind is ***a fool***...

[Murmur and mumble the words. Phrase by phrase. Word by word. Syllable by syllable. Take pleasure in making the sounds of the words, getting the feel of the meaning. Experience pleasurable anticipation of taking in what will make you more yourself, the self that God made in his own image and likeness. The self that God made for intimate communion with him. The self that God created for good works, that you should walk in them. Eat God's words. Let God's words become a joy and the delight of your heart.]

Ask God to help you see as he sees. Ask God to bring the secrets of your heart into the light.

"Make me know, God! Do I trust in my own mind? Do I define truth through my own perceptions and reasoning and judgments?"

Journal:

Seek the one who has searched you and known you. Seek the one who knows the secrets of your heart. Ask him to help you see and know as he sees and knows. Ask God to help you discover answers to the following questions:

Are the conclusions I've made about who you are and what you're like accurate, God?

God, are the conclusions I've made about who I am accurate?

Are the conclusions I've made about what is right and what is wrong accurate, God?

Are the conclusions I've made about how to get what I need and want accurate, God?

God, are the conclusions I've made about how to define what is real and true accurate?

Are the conclusions I've made about how to make sense out of the disappointments and suffering in life accurate, God?

God, are the conclusions I've made about how to improve myself and my world accurate?

Do I trust in my own mind, God?

Consider the following questions. Next to them write down what you base your answers on. Do you base your answers on your own mind? Or do you base your answers on what God himself has revealed about himself to you?

Do I believe that God exists? Am I absolutely convinced that God does or does not exist? Why have I reached that conclusion?

Who is God?

What is God like?

What is God doing?

How does God feel about human beings in general?

How does God feel about me, in particular?

What does God want from me?

What does God do to those who don't give God what he wants from them?

Who am I? What is my meaning?

Is there something specific I should do or become while I have the breath of life in me and the ability to think and feel and act?

Do I trust in my own mind to find answers to these questions, God?

Job 13:23 - How many are my iniquities and my sins? Make me know my transgression and my sin.

Prov 28:26 - Whoever trusts in his own mind is a fool, but he who walks in wisdom will be delivered.

[Pause. Breathe. Inhale and exhale. Reflect. Listen.]

Give me life according to your word, God!

Journal:

What do you hear God saying to you in these Scripture texts? What do they reveal about God and about you? Converse with God about what you're hearing him say. Verbalize and describe your thoughts, memories that come to mind, questions and emotions, concerns, desires.

Is there a particular word or phrase that disturbs or soothes you?

Do the Scripture texts create a picture or an impression that draws you to linger in exploring and experiencing it?

Choose a word or a phrase from your meditation to write on a slip of paper to carry with you today. Refer to it often throughout the day to remind you of your conversation with God and to continue the conversation all day long. Throughout the day pause to become aware of your thoughts and feelings and will. Ask yourself, "What drives me in this moment? Life according to God's word? Or life according to someone else's word?"

Anticipate that God's words stirred your heart for a reason. He's conversing with you through them. Anticipate that God will bring his word to life in you, to bear fruit in your heart and mind and soul and body. Anticipate that God will reveal the secrets of your heart, for anything that is visible is light. And anticipate that God will cause his words to become a joy and the delight of your heart.

CONTEMPLATE

God is spirit, and those who worship him must worship in spirit and truth. Seek him. Feel your way to him. Reach out. Find him.

Take in a deep breath and hold it for a second, aware that this breath, this moment, this place is a precious gift from God. Then exhale, aware that you are giving God's breath, this moment, this place back to him.

Again inhale deeply, aware that God *is* in your hidden parts, that it is *his* breath that makes you understand his word. Then deeply and completely exhale, aware that you are completely emptying yourself while trusting that God will fill you with his breath and with himself once again.

Be still. Be silent. Simply be. Simply know. In this moment, in this state, you are giving God the gift that he most desires from you, your exposed and surrendered heart, mind, soul, spirit, and body, your whole self, both outer and inner.

Each time you find that your outer self has pulled your attention away, quietly and gently say the word or phrase you chose and then dive back down deep to the hidden person of your heart to return to the Lord. He is not far from you. Feel your way toward him in your spirit, your consciousness, your intuition. Your own thoughts can't help you find him. In him, you live and move and have your being (in him you are, in him you exist). Bask in him.

Be still. Be silent. Wait. Listen. Anticipate with pleasure that you will experience being in the presence of God in this fixed position in place, time and state as you rest in Christ Jesus. Rest in perfect love. Simply exist. Be.

At the end of your contemplation, inhale deeply and hold it for a second, aware that you exist in God's abounding grace. Only in God's abounding grace do you exist. In God's abounding grace you are you, the real you.

*2 Cor 9:8 - And **God is able** to make all grace abound to you, so that having all sufficiency in all things at all times, **you may** abound in every good work.*

Exhale slowly and deeply, anticipating that God's abounding grace, in which you exist and are, will flow around you and through you to enlighten and empower you to love as you have been loved so that you may abound in every good work this day.

6 – He Who Walks In Wisdom Will Be Delivered

Pray: Ask God to prepare your heart and mind and soul to receive his words, to receive truth that will set you free, which will heal and perfect your understanding and knowledge of who God is and who you are.

Ps 119:25-32 - I'm feeling terrible — I couldn't feel worse! Get me on my feet again. You promised, remember? When I told my story, you responded; train me well in your deep wisdom. Help me understand these things inside and out so I can ponder your miracle-wonders. My sad life's dilapidated, a falling-down barn; build me up again by your Word. Barricade the road that goes Nowhere; grace me with your clear revelation. I choose the true road to Somewhere, I post your road signs at every curve and corner. I grasp and cling to whatever you tell me; God, don't let me down! I'll run the course you lay out for me if you'll just show me how. (MSG)

[Murmur and mumble the words. Phrase by phrase. Word by word. Syllable by syllable. Pause. Breathe. Inhale and exhale. Reflect. Listen.]

Journal:

Note how this prayer stirs you today and what you hear God saying to you.

Prov 28:26 - Whoever trusts in his own mind is a fool, but he who walks in wisdom will be delivered.

Wisdom: a primitive root, to be wise [in mind, word or act[1]]

Wisdom. To be wise in mind, word or act. Having or showing good judgment. Enlightenment.

He who walks in ***wisdom***…

He who walks in wisdom ***will be*** delivered.

He who walks in wisdom will be ***delivered***.

[Murmur and mumble the words. Phrase by phrase. Word by word.

Syllable by syllable. Take pleasure in making the sounds of the words, getting the feel of the meaning. Experience pleasurable anticipation of taking in what will make you more yourself, the self that God made in his own image and likeness. The self that God made for intimate communion with him. The self that God created for good works, that you should walk in them. Eat God's words. Let God's words become a joy and the delight of your heart.]

Journal:

What would you like to be delivered from?

Do you think that what you want to be delivered from aligns with what God wants to deliver you from?

Might the deliverance that God has in mind, first and foremost, be related to your transgression and sin? Might it be related to your withdrawal and rebellion, your desire for and/or state of independence from him? Might it be related to delivering you from foreign gods? Might it be delivering you from trusting in your own mind?

Prov 28:26 - Whoever trusts in his own mind is a fool, but he who walks in wisdom will be delivered.

[Pause. Breathe. Inhale and exhale. Reflect. Listen.]

Give me life according to your word, God!

Journal:

What do you hear God saying to you in these Scripture texts? What do they reveal about God and about you? Converse with God about what you're hearing him say. Verbalize and describe your thoughts, memories that come to mind, questions and emotions, concerns, desires.

Is there a particular word or phrase that disturbs or soothes you?

Do the Scripture texts create a picture or an impression that draws you to linger in exploring and experiencing it?

Choose a word or a phrase from your meditation to write on a slip of paper to carry with you today. Refer to it often throughout the day to remind you of your conversation with God and to continue the conversation all day long. Throughout the day pause to become aware of your thoughts and feelings and will. Ask yourself, “What drives me in this moment? Life according to God’s word? Or life according to someone else’s word?”

Anticipate that God’s words stirred your heart for a reason. He’s conversing with you through them. Anticipate that God will bring his word to life in you, to bear fruit in your heart and mind and soul and body. Anticipate that God will reveal the secrets of your heart, for anything that is visible is light. And anticipate that God will cause his words to become a joy and the delight of your heart.

CONTEMPLATE

God is spirit, and those who worship him must worship in spirit and truth. Seek him. Feel your way to him. Reach out. Find him.

Take in a deep breath and hold it for a second, aware that this breath, this moment, this place is a precious gift from God. Then exhale, aware that you are giving God’s breath, this moment, this place back to him.

Again inhale deeply, aware that God *is* in your hidden parts, that it is *his* breath that makes you understand his word. Then deeply and completely exhale, aware that you are completely emptying yourself while trusting that God will fill you with his breath and with himself once again.

Be still. Be silent. Simply be. Simply know. In this moment, in this state, you are giving God the gift that he most desires from you, your exposed and surrendered heart, mind, soul, spirit, and body, your whole self, both outer and inner.

Each time you find that your outer self has pulled your attention away, quietly and gently say the word or phrase you chose and then dive back down deep to the hidden person of your heart to return to the Lord. He is not far from you. Feel your way toward him in your spirit, your consciousness, your intuition. Your own thoughts can't help you find him. In him, you live and move and have your being (in him you are, in him you exist). Bask in him.

Be still. Be silent. Wait. Listen. Anticipate with pleasure that you will experience being in the presence of God in this fixed position in place, time and state as you rest in Christ Jesus. Rest in perfect love. Simply exist. Be.

At the end of your contemplation, inhale deeply and hold it for a second, aware that you exist in God's abounding grace. Only in God's abounding grace do you exist. In God's abounding grace you are you, the real you.

2 Cor 9:8 - And ***God is able*** *to make all grace abound to you, so that having all sufficiency in all things at all times,* ***you may*** *abound in every good work.*

Exhale slowly and deeply, anticipating that God's abounding grace, in which you exist and are, will flow around you and through you to enlighten and empower you to love as you have been loved so that you may abound in every good work this day.

Resources:

[1]Wisdom: OT:2449 <START HEBREW><k^j*<END HEBREW> chakam (khaw-kam'); a primitive root, to be wise (in mind, word or act): (Biblesoft's New Exhaustive Strong's Numbers and Concordance with Expanded Greek-Hebrew Dictionary. Copyright © 1994, 2003, 2006, 2010 Biblesoft, Inc. and International Bible Translators, Inc.)

7 – Do Not Lean on Your Own Understanding

Pray: Ask God to prepare your heart and mind and soul to receive his words, to receive truth that will set you free, which will heal and perfect your understanding and knowledge of who God is and who you are.

Ps 119:25-32 - My soul clings to the dust; give me life according to your word! When I told of my ways, you answered me; teach me your statutes! Make me understand the way of your precepts, and I will meditate on your wondrous works. My soul melts away for sorrow; strengthen me according to your word! Put false ways far from me and graciously teach me your law! I have chosen the way of faithfulness; I set your rules before me. I cling to your testimonies, O Lord; let me not be put to shame! I will run in the way of your commandments when you enlarge my heart! (ESV)

[Murmur and mumble the words. Phrase by phrase. Word by word. Syllable by syllable. Pause. Breathe. Inhale and exhale. Reflect. Listen.]

Journal:

Note how this prayer stirs you today and what you hear God saying to you.

Prov 3:5 - Trust in the Lord with all your heart, and do not lean on your own understanding.

Do not ***lean*** on your own understanding.

Do not bend or incline your body and mind and heart and soul so as to rest or depend on your own understanding for encouragement or aid.

Whoever trusts in his ***own mind*** is a fool.

[Murmur and mumble the words. Phrase by phrase. Word by word. Syllable by syllable. Take pleasure in making the sounds of the words, getting the feel of the meaning. Experience pleasurable anticipation of taking in what will make you more yourself, the self that God made in his own image and likeness. The self that God made

for intimate communion with him. The self that God created for good works, that you should walk in them. Eat God's words. Let God's words become a joy and the delight of your heart.]

Pray: Ask God to help you see as he sees. "God, please reveal to me any areas in which I am leaning on my own understanding. And deliver me."

Exposing and acknowledging our hurts and failings and longings and doubts is the first step toward healing. List whatever the Lord reveals.

Journal:

Trust ***in the Lord*** with all your heart.

Trust.

Confident. Sure. Secure. Strive or hurry for refuge. Anticipation. Reliance. Expectation.

Trust.

Pray: Ask God to help you see as he sees as you and he together probe your heart. "God, would you look deep into the very center of me and reveal what you see? What are the secrets of my heart, God?"

What do I expect of myself? Should I have such expectations of myself?

What do I expect of you, God? Should I have such expectations of you?

What do I anticipate from you, God?

Does what I expect and anticipate from God nurture and produce trust in him?

What do I know about God's character?

Does what I expect and anticipate from myself produce trust within me? Do I trust myself more than I trust God?

What do I know about my character and abilities to meet my expectations?

Prov 3:5 - Trust in the Lord with all your heart, and do not lean on your own understanding.

[Murmur and mumble the words. Phrase by phrase. Word by word. Syllable by syllable. Take pleasure in making the sounds of the words, getting the feel of the meaning. Experience pleasurable anticipation of taking in what will make you more yourself, the self that God made in his own image and likeness. The self that God made for intimate communion with him. The self that God created for good works, that you should walk in them. Eat God's words. Let God's words become a joy and the delight of your heart.]

Journal:

Is your whole heart engaged in confident anticipation and hope in the words and character of God? Or are there parts and pieces that you hold back from God? Why?

Do you feel like God has let you down at times? Do you doubt that you can trust God's words and character? Why?

Prov 28:26 - Whoever trusts in his own mind is a fool, but he who walks in wisdom will be delivered.

Prov 3:5 - Trust in the Lord with all your heart, and do not lean on your own understanding.

[Pause. Breathe. Inhale and exhale. Reflect. Listen.]

Give me life according to your word, God!

Journal:

What do you hear God saying to you in these Scripture texts? What do they reveal about God and about you? Converse with God about what you're hearing him say. Verbalize and describe your thoughts, memories that come to mind, questions and emotions, concerns, desires.

Is there a particular word or phrase that disturbs or soothes you?

Do the Scripture texts create a picture or an impression that draws you to linger in exploring and experiencing it?

Choose a word or a phrase from your meditation to write on a slip of paper to carry with you today. Refer to it often throughout the day to remind you of your conversation with God and to continue the conversation all day long. Throughout the day pause to become aware of your thoughts and feelings and will. Ask yourself, "What drives me in this moment? Life according to God's word? Or life according to someone else's word?"

Anticipate that God's words stirred your heart for a reason. He's conversing with you through them. Anticipate that God will bring his word to life in you, to bear fruit in your heart and mind and soul and body. Anticipate that God will reveal the secrets of your heart, for anything that is visible is light. And anticipate that God will cause his words to become a joy and the delight of your heart.

CONTEMPLATE

God is spirit, and those who worship him must worship in spirit and truth. Seek him. Feel your way to him. Reach out. Find him.

Take in a deep breath and hold it for a second, aware that this breath, this moment, this place is a precious gift from God. Then exhale, aware that you are giving God's breath, this moment, this place back to him.

Again inhale deeply, aware that God *is* in your hidden parts, that it is *his* breath that makes you understand his word. Then deeply and completely exhale, aware that you are completely emptying yourself while trusting that God will fill you with his breath and with himself once again.

Be still. Be silent. Simply be. Simply know. In this moment, in this state, you are giving God the gift that he most desires from you, your exposed and surrendered heart, mind, soul, spirit, and body, your whole self, both outer and inner.

Each time you find that your outer self has pulled your attention away, quietly and gently say the word or phrase you chose and then dive back down deep to the hidden person of your heart to return to the Lord. He is not far from you. Feel your way toward him in your spirit, your consciousness, your intuition. Your own thoughts can't help you find him. In him, you live and move and have your being (in him you are, in him you exist). Bask in him.

Be still. Be silent. Wait. Listen. Anticipate with pleasure that you will experience being in the presence of God in this fixed position in place, time and state as you rest in Christ Jesus. Rest in perfect love. Simply exist. Be.

At the end of your contemplation, inhale deeply and hold it for a second, aware that you exist in God's abounding grace. Only in God's abounding grace do you exist. In God's abounding grace you are you, the real you.

2 Cor 9:8 - And ***God is able*** *to make all grace abound to you, so that having all sufficiency in all things at all times,* ***you may*** *abound in every good work.*

Exhale slowly and deeply, anticipating that God's abounding grace, in which you exist and are, will flow around you and through you to enlighten and empower you to love as you have been loved so that you may abound in every good work this day.

8 – Trust in the Lord with All Your Heart

Pray: Ask God to prepare your heart and mind and soul to receive his words, to receive truth that will set you free, which will heal and perfect your understanding and knowledge of who God is and who you are.

Ps 119:25-32 - I'm feeling terrible — I couldn't feel worse! Get me on my feet again. You promised, remember? When I told my story, you responded; train me well in your deep wisdom. Help me understand these things inside and out so I can ponder your miracle-wonders. My sad life's dilapidated, a falling-down barn; build me up again by your Word. Barricade the road that goes Nowhere; grace me with your clear revelation. I choose the true road to Somewhere, I post your road signs at every curve and corner. I grasp and cling to whatever you tell me; God, don't let me down! I'll run the course you lay out for me if you'll just show me how. (MSG)

[Murmur and mumble the words. Phrase by phrase. Word by word. Syllable by syllable. Pause. Breathe. Inhale and exhale. Reflect. Listen.]

Journal:

Note how this prayer stirs you today and what you hear God saying to you.

Prov 3:5 - Trust in the Lord with all your heart, and do not lean on your own understanding.

Trust.

Trust in the ***Lord***. Have confident anticipation in the Lord. Hope in the words and character of the Lord.

Trust in the Lord with ***all***

Trust in the Lord with all ***your heart***. With all your feelings. With all your will. With all your intellect. With the very center of yourself. ***Trust*** in the Lord.

Trust ***in*** the Lord

And

Trust in the Lord, ***thereupon*** do not lean on your own understanding.

Trust in the Lord, ***then*** do not lean on your own understanding.

Trust in the Lord, ***next*** do not lean on your own understanding.

Trust in the Lord

And do not

Do not lean on your ***own*** understanding.

Is God saying we can either trust the Lord, or we can lean on our own understanding, but we can't do both at the same time? Is he saying that we cannot stop leaning on our own understanding *unless/until* we trust in him?

[Murmur and mumble the words. Phrase by phrase. Word by word. Syllable by syllable. Take pleasure in making the sounds of the words, getting the feel of the meaning. Experience pleasurable anticipation of taking in what will make you more yourself, the self that God made in his own image and likeness. The self that God made for intimate communion with him. The self that God created for good works, that you should walk in them. Eat God's words. Let God's words become a joy and the delight of your heart.]

Journal:

Where is your heart leaning today? Do you trust in God in some things but not in others? Why?

Prov 3:5 - Trust in the Lord with all your heart, and do not lean on your own understanding.

[Pause. Breathe. Inhale and exhale. Reflect. Listen.]

Give me life according to your word, God!

Journal:

What do you hear God saying to you in these Scripture texts? What do they reveal about God and about you? Converse with God about what you're hearing him say. Verbalize and describe your thoughts, memories that come to mind, questions and emotions, concerns, desires.

Is there a particular word or phrase that disturbs or soothes you?

Do the Scripture texts create a picture or an impression that draws you to linger in exploring and experiencing it?

Choose a word or a phrase from your meditation to write on a slip of paper to carry with you today. Refer to it often throughout the day to remind you of your conversation with God and to continue the conversation all day long. Throughout the day pause to become aware of your thoughts and feelings and will. Ask yourself, "What drives me in this moment? Life according to God's word? Or life according to someone else's word?"

Anticipate that God's words stirred your heart for a reason. He's conversing with you through them. Anticipate that God will bring his word to life in you, to bear fruit in your heart and mind and soul and body. Anticipate that God will reveal the secrets of your heart, for anything that is visible is light. And anticipate that God will cause his words to become a joy and the delight of your heart.

CONTEMPLATE

God is spirit, and those who worship him must worship in spirit and truth. Seek him. Feel your way to him. Reach out. Find him.

Take in a deep breath and hold it for a second, aware that this breath, this moment, this place is a precious gift from God. Then exhale, aware that you are giving God's breath, this moment, this place back to him.

Again inhale deeply, aware that God *is* in your hidden parts, that it is *his* breath that makes you understand his word. Then deeply and completely exhale, aware that you are completely emptying yourself while trusting that God will fill you with his breath and with himself once again.

Be still. Be silent. Simply be. Simply know. In this moment, in this state, you are giving God the gift that he most desires from you, your exposed and surrendered heart, mind, soul, spirit, and body, your whole self, both outer and inner.

Each time you find that your outer self has pulled your attention away, quietly and gently say the word or phrase you chose and then dive back down deep to the hidden person of your heart to return to the Lord. He is not far from you. Feel your way toward him in your spirit, your consciousness, your intuition. Your own thoughts can't help you find him. In him, you live and move and have your being (in him you are, in him you exist). Bask in him.

Be still. Be silent. Wait. Listen. Anticipate with pleasure that you will experience being in the presence of God in this fixed position in place, time and state as you rest in Christ Jesus. Rest in perfect love. Simply exist. Be.

At the end of your contemplation, inhale deeply and hold it for a second, aware that you exist in God's abounding grace. Only in God's abounding grace do you exist. In God's abounding grace you are you, the real you.

2 Cor 9:8 - And ***God is able*** *to make all grace abound to you, so that having all sufficiency in all things at all times,* ***you may*** *abound in every good work.*

Exhale slowly and deeply, anticipating that God's abounding grace, in which you exist and are, will flow around you and through you to enlighten and empower you to love as you have been loved so that you may abound in every good work this day.

9 – In the Abundance of Your Steadfast Love

Pray: Ask God to prepare your heart and mind and soul to receive his words, to receive truth that will set you free, which will heal and perfect your understanding and knowledge of who God is and who you are.

Ps 119:25-32 - My soul clings to the dust; give me life according to your word! When I told of my ways, you answered me; teach me your statutes! Make me understand the way of your precepts, and I will meditate on your wondrous works. My soul melts away for sorrow; strengthen me according to your word! Put false ways far from me and graciously teach me your law! I have chosen the way of faithfulness; I set your rules before me. I cling to your testimonies, O Lord; let me not be put to shame! I will run in the way of your commandments when you enlarge my heart! (ESV)

[Murmur and mumble the words. Phrase by phrase. Word by word. Syllable by syllable. Pause. Breathe. Inhale and exhale. Reflect. Listen.]

Journal:

Note how this prayer stirs you today and what you hear God saying to you.

Prov 3:5 - Trust in the Lord with all your heart, and do not lean on your own understanding.

Ps 69:13 - But as for me, my prayer is to you, O Lord. At an acceptable time, O God, in the abundance of your steadfast love answer me in your saving faithfulness.

Might your struggle to trust God be that your timing and his timing are not aligned? Might your struggle to trust God be that you are ignorant of God's abundance of steadfast love? Might your struggle to trust God be that your understanding of being saved does not align with God's?

As for ***me***

My prayer

My prayer ***is to you***, O Lord.

My prayer is to you, ***O Lord***.

At an ***acceptable*** time, O God

Acceptable [to be pleased with, delight]

At a time that you are <u>pleased with</u>, O Lord

At a time when you <u>delight</u>, O Lord

At an acceptable ***time***, O God

At an acceptable time, O God, ***in the abundance***

At an acceptable time, O God, in the abundance ***of your steadfast love***

In the abundance of your steadfast love ***answer me***

Answer me in your saving ***faithfulness***.

Answer me in your ***saving*** faithfulness

At an ***acceptable*** time, O God

[Murmur and mumble the words. Phrase by phrase. Word by word. Syllable by syllable. Take pleasure in making the sounds of the words, getting the feel of the meaning. Experience pleasurable anticipation of taking in what will make you more yourself, the self that God made in his own image and likeness. The self that God made for intimate communion with him. The self that God created for good works, that you should walk in them. Eat God's words. Let God's words become a joy and the delight of your heart.]

Journal:

What does this Scripture text tell you about the intimacy of relationship that the psalmist, David, had with God? What does it tell you about his trust in God and trust in himself?

How are your prayers similar and/or different from this prayer that David prayed?

Prov 3:5 - Trust in the Lord with all your heart, and do not lean on your own understanding.

Ps 69:13 - But as for me, my prayer is to you, O Lord. At an acceptable time, O God, in the abundance of your steadfast love answer me in your saving faithfulness.

[Pause. Breathe. Inhale and exhale. Reflect. Listen.]

Give me life according to your word, God!

Journal:

What do you hear God saying to you in these Scripture texts? What do they reveal about God and about you? Converse with God about what you're hearing him say. Verbalize and describe your thoughts, memories that come to mind, questions and emotions, concerns, desires.

Is there a particular word or phrase that disturbs or soothes you?

Do the Scripture texts create a picture or an impression that draws you to linger in exploring and experiencing it?

Choose a word or a phrase from your meditation to write on a slip of paper to carry with you today. Refer to it often throughout the day to remind you of your conversation with God and to continue the conversation all day long. Throughout the day pause to become aware of your thoughts and feelings and will. Ask yourself, "What drives me in this moment? Life according to God's word? Or life according to someone else's word?"

Anticipate that God's words stirred your heart for a reason. He's conversing with you through them. Anticipate that God will bring his word to life in you, to bear fruit in your heart and mind and soul and body. Anticipate that God will reveal the secrets of your heart, for anything that is visible is light. And anticipate that God will cause his words to become a joy and the delight of your heart.

CONTEMPLATE

God is spirit, and those who worship him must worship in spirit and truth. Seek him. Feel your way to him. Reach out. Find him.

Take in a deep breath and hold it for a second, aware that this breath, this moment, this place is a precious gift from God. Then exhale, aware that you are giving God's breath, this moment, this place back to him.

Again inhale deeply, aware that God *is* in your hidden parts, that it is *his* breath that makes you understand his word. Then deeply and completely exhale, aware that you are completely emptying yourself while trusting that God will fill you with his breath and with himself once again.

Be still. Be silent. Simply be. Simply know. In this moment, in this state, you are giving God the gift that he most desires from you, your exposed and surrendered heart, mind, soul, spirit, and body, your whole self, both outer and inner.

Each time you find that your outer self has pulled your attention away, quietly and gently say the word or phrase you chose and then dive back down deep to the hidden person of your heart to return to the Lord. He is not far from you. Feel your way toward him in your spirit, your consciousness, your intuition. Your own thoughts can't help you find him. In him, you live and move and have your being (in him you are, in him you exist). Bask in him.

Be still. Be silent. Wait. Listen. Anticipate with pleasure that you will experience being in the presence of God in this fixed position in place, time and state as you rest in Christ Jesus. Rest in perfect love. Simply exist. Be.

At the end of your contemplation, inhale deeply and hold it for a second, aware that you exist in God's abounding grace. Only in God's abounding grace do you exist. In God's abounding grace you are you, the real you.

2 Cor 9:8 - And ***God is able*** *to make all grace abound to you, so that having all sufficiency in all things at all times,* ***you may*** *abound in every good work.*

Exhale slowly and deeply, anticipating that God's abounding grace, in which you exist and are, will flow around you and through you to enlighten and empower you to love as you have been loved so that you may abound in every good work this day.

10 – See if There Be Any Grievous Way in Me

Prov 3:5 - Trust in the Lord with all your heart, and do not lean on your own understanding.

I used to have a long list of evidence from personal experience and observation that, to my warped thinking and deceitful heart, seemed to prove that God's character and his actions did not align with his words.

I discovered that I couldn't make my heart trust God, no matter what I told myself or what I did. To deny or ignore or discount my doubts didn't make me develop confidence in him. I learned that I can create a façade and work hard to give the illusion that I trust God through the things I say and do. I could get approval from people that way. I became very good at stuffing and denying and ignoring my doubts along with the frustration and bitterness and anger that blossomed in my heart as a result. But I couldn't change my heart. And I was well on my way in the process of withdrawing from God, from others and from myself.

Jer 17:9 - The heart is deceitful above all things, and desperately sick; who can understand it?

Pray: Ask God to prepare your heart and mind and soul to receive his words, to receive truth that will set you free, which will heal and perfect your understanding and knowledge of who God is and who you are.

Ps 119:25-32 - I'm feeling terrible — I couldn't feel worse! Get me on my feet again. You promised, remember? When I told my story, you responded; train me well in your deep wisdom. Help me understand these things inside and out so I can ponder your miracle-wonders. My sad life's dilapidated, a falling-down barn; build me up again by your Word. Barricade the road that goes Nowhere; grace me with your clear revelation. I choose the true road to Somewhere, I post your road signs at every curve and corner. I grasp and cling to whatever you tell me; God, don't let me down! I'll run the course you lay out for me if you'll just show me how. (MSG)

[Murmur and mumble the words. Phrase by phrase. Word by word. Syllable by syllable. Pause. Breathe. Inhale and exhale. Reflect. Listen.]

Journal:

Note how this prayer stirs you today and what you hear God saying to you.

Ps 139:23-24 - Search me, O God, and know my heart! Try me and know my thoughts! And see if there be any grievous way in me [an idol as fashioned; also bodily or mental pain], and lead me in the way everlasting!

Search me, O God.

Know

Know ***my heart***, God!

Try me, God.

Know

Know ***my thoughts***, God!

And ***see***, God.

See if there be any ***grievous*** way in me, God.

See if there be an ***idol fashioned*** in me.

See if there be any bodily or mental ***pain*** in me.

And lead me.

Lead me, God.

Lead me in ***the way*** everlasting!

[Murmur and mumble the words. Phrase by phrase. Word by word. Syllable by syllable. Take pleasure in making the sounds of the words, getting the feel of the meaning. Experience pleasurable anticipation of taking in what will make you more yourself, the self that God made in his own image and likeness. The self that God made for intimate communion with him. The self that God created for good works, that you should walk in them. Eat God's words. Let God's words become a joy and the delight of your heart.]

Journal:

Ask God to bring the secrets of your heart into the light. Is there any pain in you that causes you to doubt and withdraw from God? Is there any pain in you that causes you to hide who you are?

Are you willing to join the psalmist in praying this prayer? Why or why not?

Are you aware of any grievous way in you? Any idol that has been fashioned in you? Any bodily or mental pain?

Ps 139:23-24 - Search me, O God, and know my heart! Try me and know my thoughts! And see if there be any grievous way in me [an idol as fashioned; also bodily or mental pain], and lead me in the way everlasting!

[Pause. Breathe. Inhale and exhale. Reflect. Listen.]

Give me life according to your word, God!

Journal:

What do you hear God saying to you in these Scripture texts? What do they reveal about God and about you? Converse with God about what you're hearing him say. Verbalize and describe your thoughts, memories that come to mind, questions and emotions, concerns, desires.

Is there a particular word or phrase that disturbs or soothes you?

Do the Scripture texts create a picture or an impression that draws you to linger in exploring and experiencing it?

Choose a word or a phrase from your meditation to write on a slip of paper to carry with you today. Refer to it often throughout the day to remind you of your conversation with God and to continue the conversation all day long. Throughout the day pause to become aware of your thoughts and feelings and will. Ask yourself, "What drives me in this moment? Life according to God's word? Or life according to someone else's word?"

Anticipate that God's words stirred your heart for a reason. He's conversing with you through them. Anticipate that God will bring his word to life in you, to bear fruit in your heart and mind and soul and body. Anticipate that God will reveal the secrets of your heart, for anything that is visible is light. And anticipate that God will cause his words to become a joy and the delight of your heart.

CONTEMPLATE

God is spirit, and those who worship him must worship in spirit and truth. Seek him. Feel your way to him. Reach out. Find him.

Take in a deep breath and hold it for a second, aware that this breath, this moment, this place is a precious gift from God. Then exhale, aware that you are giving God's breath, this moment, this place back to him.

Again inhale deeply, aware that God *is* in your hidden parts, that it is *his* breath that makes you understand his word. Then deeply and completely exhale, aware that you are completely emptying yourself while trusting that God will fill you with his breath and with himself once again.

Be still. Be silent. Simply be. Simply know. In this moment, in this state, you are giving God the gift that he most desires from you, your exposed and surrendered heart, mind, soul, spirit, and body, your whole self, both outer and inner.

Each time you find that your outer self has pulled your attention away, quietly and gently say the word or phrase you chose and then dive back down deep to the hidden person of your heart to return to the Lord. He is not far from you. Feel your way toward him in your spirit, your consciousness, your intuition. Your own thoughts can't help you find him. In him, you live and move and have your being (in him you are, in him you exist). Bask in him.

Be still. Be silent. Wait. Listen. Anticipate with pleasure that you will experience being in the presence of God in this fixed position in place, time and state as you rest in Christ Jesus. Rest in perfect love. Simply exist. Be.

At the end of your contemplation, inhale deeply and hold it for a second, aware that you exist in God's abounding grace. Only in God's abounding grace do you exist. In God's abounding grace you are you, the real you.

2 Cor 9:8 - And ***God is able*** *to make all grace abound to you, so that having all sufficiency in all things at all times,* ***you may*** *abound in every good work.*

Exhale slowly and deeply, anticipating that God's abounding grace, in which you exist and are, will flow around you and through you to enlighten and empower you to love as you have been loved so that you may abound in every good work this day.

11 – This God - His Way Is Perfect

Pray: Ask God to prepare your heart and mind and soul to receive his words, to receive truth that will set you free, which will heal and perfect your understanding and knowledge of who God is and who you are.

Ps 119:25-32 - My soul clings to the dust; give me life according to your word! When I told of my ways, you answered me; teach me your statutes! Make me understand the way of your precepts, and I will meditate on your wondrous works. My soul melts away for sorrow; strengthen me according to your word! Put false ways far from me and graciously teach me your law! I have chosen the way of faithfulness; I set your rules before me. I cling to your testimonies, O Lord; let me not be put to shame! I will run in the way of your commandments when you enlarge my heart! (ESV)

[Murmur and mumble the words. Phrase by phrase. Word by word. Syllable by syllable. Pause. Breathe. Inhale and exhale. Reflect. Listen.]

Journal:

Note how this prayer stirs you today and what you hear God saying to you.

Ps 139:23-24 - Search me, O God, and know my heart! Try me and know my thoughts! And see if there be any grievous way in me [an idol as fashioned; also bodily or mental pain], and lead me in the way everlasting!

Search

Search ***me***.

Know

Know ***my heart***.

Know ***my thoughts***.

See

See ***me***.

Try me. ***Test*** me.

[Murmur and mumble the words. Phrase by phrase. Word by word. Syllable by syllable. Take pleasure in making the sounds of the words, getting the feel of the meaning. Experience pleasurable anticipation of taking in what will make you more yourself, the self that God made in his own image and likeness. The self that God made for intimate communion with him. The self that God created for good works, that you should walk in them. Eat God's words. Let God's words become a joy and the delight of your heart.]

Test: "to refine, try, smelt, test." Tsarap is also used metaphorically with the sense "to refine by means of suffering."[1]

Try me. Test me. Refine me. Smelt me. Melt me or fuse me [as in smelting ore] so as to separate impurities from pure metal. Refine me by suffering.

Journal:

What are you agreeing to participate in with God when you pray this prayer?

Are you willing to pray this prayer? Why or why not?

How does God test you? How does he refine you and smelt you?

Prov 30:5 - Every word of God proves true; he is a shield to those who take refuge in him.

Ps 18:30 - This God—his way is perfect; the word of the Lord proves true; he is a shield for all those who take refuge in him.

Every

Every ***word***

Every word ***of God***

Every word of God ***proves***

Every word of God proves ***true***

Journal:

Are you willing to allow God to make every one of his words prove true in you? If not, are you rejecting your protector (shield) and perfecter?

Are you willing to be fused or joined to God by taking refuge [shelter, protection, help, comfort] in him? What, if anything, causes you to hesitate?

In order to take refuge in God, what areas of withdrawal and independence will you have to give up?

This God

This God-***his way***

This God-his way ***is perfect***.

[Murmur and mumble the words. Phrase by phrase. Word by word. Syllable by syllable. Take pleasure in making the sounds of the words, getting the feel of the meaning. Experience pleasurable anticipation of taking in what will make you more yourself, the self that God made in his own image and likeness. The self that God made for intimate communion with him. The self that God created for good works, that you should walk in them. Eat God's words. Let God's words become a joy and the delight of your heart.]

Journal:

Is there anything in your life experience, in your understanding that causes you to question this statement? *This God-his way is perfect.*

Ps 139:23-24 - Search me, O God, and know my heart! Try me and know my thoughts! And see if there be any grievous way in me [an idol as fashioned; also bodily or mental pain], and lead me in the way everlasting!

Prov 30:5 - Every word of God proves true; he is a shield to those who take refuge in him.

Ps 18:30 - This God—his way is perfect; the word of the Lord proves true; he is a shield for all those who take refuge in him.

[Pause. Breathe. Inhale and exhale. Reflect. Listen.]

Give me life according to your word, God!

Journal:

What do you hear God saying to you in these Scripture texts? What do they reveal about God and about you? Converse with God about what you're hearing him say. Verbalize and describe your thoughts, memories that come to mind, questions and emotions, concerns, desires.

Is there a particular word or phrase that disturbs or soothes you?

Do the Scripture texts create a picture or an impression that draws you to linger in exploring and experiencing it?

Choose a word or a phrase from your meditation to write on a slip of paper to carry with you today. Refer to it often throughout the day to remind you of your conversation with God and to continue the conversation all day long. Throughout the day pause to become aware of your thoughts and feelings and will. Ask yourself, "What drives me in this moment? Life according to God's word? Or life according to someone else's word?"

Anticipate that God's words stirred your heart for a reason. He's conversing with you through them. Anticipate that God will bring his word to life in you, to bear fruit in your heart and mind and soul and body. Anticipate that God will reveal the secrets of your heart, for anything that is visible is light. And anticipate that God will cause his words to become a joy and the delight of your heart.

CONTEMPLATE

God is spirit, and those who worship him must worship in spirit and truth. Seek him. Feel your way to him. Reach out. Find him.

Inhale deeply, aware that God *is* in your hidden parts, that it is *his* breath that makes you understand his word. Exhale. Give God the gift that he most desires from you, your exposed and surrendered heart, mind, soul, spirit, and body, your whole self, both outer and inner.

Each time you find that your outer self has pulled your attention away, quietly and gently say the word or phrase you chose and then dive back down deep to the hidden person of your heart to return to the Lord. Bask in him. Rest in perfect love.

At the end of your contemplation, inhale deeply and hold it for a second, aware that you exist in God's abounding grace. Only in God's abounding grace do you exist. In God's abounding grace you are you, the real you, able to worship God in spirit and truth.

2 Cor 9:8 - And ***God is able*** *to make all grace abound to you, so that having all sufficiency in all things at all times,* ***you may*** *abound in every good work.*

Exhale slowly and deeply, anticipating that God's abounding grace, in which you exist and are, will flow around you and through you to enlighten and empower you to love as you have been loved so that you may abound in every good work this day.

Resources:

[1]Test: tsarap OT:6884, "to refine, try, smelt, test." Tsarap is also used metaphorically with the sense "to refine by means of suffering." (from Vine's Expository Dictionary of Biblical Words, Copyright © 1985, Thomas Nelson Publishers.)

12 – A Place of Abundance

Pray: Ask God to prepare your heart and mind and soul to receive his words, to receive truth that will set you free, which will heal and perfect your understanding and knowledge of who God is and who you are.

Ps 119:25-32 - I'm feeling terrible — I couldn't feel worse! Get me on my feet again. You promised, remember? When I told my story, you responded; train me well in your deep wisdom. Help me understand these things inside and out so I can ponder your miracle-wonders. My sad life's dilapidated, a falling-down barn; build me up again by your Word. Barricade the road that goes Nowhere; grace me with your clear revelation. I choose the true road to Somewhere, I post your road signs at every curve and corner. I grasp and cling to whatever you tell me; God, don't let me down! I'll run the course you lay out for me if you'll just show me how. (MSG)

[Murmur and mumble the words. Phrase by phrase. Word by word. Syllable by syllable. Pause. Breathe. Inhale and exhale. Reflect. Listen.]

Journal:

Note how this prayer stirs you today and what you hear God saying to you.

Ps 139:23-24 - Search me, O God, and know my heart! Try me and know my thoughts! And see if there be any grievous way in me [an idol as fashioned; also bodily or mental pain], and lead me in the way everlasting!

David and his people worshiped God, expressing their experience and approval of God's ways.

Ps 66:10, 12 - For you, O God, have tested us; you have tried us as silver is tried. ...we went through fire and through water; yet you have brought us out to a place of abundance.

For you, O God, have ***tested us***

You have ***tried us***

We went through fire and water, O God

Yet

Yet ***you have brought us out***

Yet you have brought us out ***to a place of abundance***.

A place of ***abundance***.

This God

This God-***his way*** is perfect.

[Murmur and mumble the words. Phrase by phrase. Word by word. Syllable by syllable. Take pleasure in making the sounds of the words, getting the feel of the meaning. Experience pleasurable anticipation of taking in what will make you more yourself, the self that God made in his own image and likeness. The self that God made for intimate communion with him. The self that God created for good works, that you should walk in them. Eat God's words. Let God's words become a joy and the delight of your heart.]

Journal:

Might the purpose of the fire and water be to enlighten us regarding the ways in which we've rebelled and withdrawn from God as we seek independence? Might they be God's acts of mercy to draw us back to himself?

Might coming back home to God, to take refuge in him, to be in complete dependence upon him be the place of abundance?

Are you willing to go through fire and water with God?

Are you willing to trust that he will also bring you out of the fire and water to a place of abundance?

Isa 35:4-8 - Say to those who have an anxious heart, "Be strong; fear not! Behold, your God <u>will come</u> with vengeance, with the *recompense of God. He will come and save you." Then the eyes of the blind shall be opened, and the ears of the deaf unstopped; then shall the lame man leap like a deer, and the tongue of the mute sing for joy. For waters break forth in the wilderness, and streams in the desert; the burning sand shall become a pool, and the thirsty ground springs of water; in the haunt of jackals, where they lie down, the grass shall become reeds and rushes. And a highway shall be there, and it shall be called the Way of Holiness; the unclean shall not pass over it. It shall belong to those who walk on the way; even if they are fools, they shall not go astray.*

Be strong

Fear not

Behold

Your God ***will come*** with vengeance

He will come ***and save you***

Mal 3:1-3 - "Behold, I send my messenger and he will prepare the way before me. And the Lord whom you seek will suddenly come to his temple; and the messenger of the covenant in whom you delight, behold, he is coming, says the Lord of hosts. But who can endure the day of his coming, and who can stand when he appears? For he is like a refiner's fire and like fullers' soap. He will sit as a refiner and purifier of silver, and he will purify the sons of Levi and refine them like gold and silver, and they will bring offerings in righteousness to the Lord.

The Lord whom you seek ***will suddenly come*** to his temple

He will purify

And they will bring offerings

They will bring offerings ***in righteousness*** to the Lord

Rom 15:15-16 - But on some points I have written to you very boldly by way of reminder, because of the grace given me by God to be a minister of Christ Jesus to the Gentiles in the priestly service of the gospel of God, so that the offering of the Gentiles may be acceptable, sanctified by the Holy Spirit.

John 4:22-24 - You worship what you do not know; we worship what we know, for salvation is from the Jews. But the hour is coming, and is now here, when the true worshipers will worship the Father in spirit and truth, for the Father is seeking such people to worship him. God is spirit, and those who worship him must worship in spirit and truth."

They will bring ***offerings*** in righteousness to the Lord

The ***offering***

Maybe be ***acceptable***

Sanctified

Sanctified ***by the Holy Spirit***

The true worshipers will worship the Father ***in spirit and truth***

[Murmur and mumble the words. Phrase by phrase. Word by word. Syllable by syllable. Take pleasure in making the sounds of the words, getting the feel of the meaning. Experience pleasurable anticipation of taking in what will make you more yourself, the self that God made in his own image and likeness. The self that God made for intimate communion with him. The self that God created for good works, that you should walk in them. Eat God's words. Let God's words become a joy and the delight of your heart.]

Journal:

Do you have an anxious heart where God's testing and trying is concerned?

What is the purpose of God's vengeance?

What is God's purpose in testing and trying you?

Prov 3:5 - Trust in the Lord with all your heart, and do not lean on your own understanding.

Jer 17:9 - The heart is deceitful above all things, and desperately sick; who can understand it?

Ps 139:23-24 - Search me, O God, and know my heart! Try me and know my thoughts! And see if there be any grievous way in me, and lead me in the way everlasting!

Prov 30:5 - Every word of God proves true; he is a shield to those who take refuge in him.

Ps 18:30 - This God—his way is perfect; the word of the Lord proves true; he is a shield for all those who take refuge in him.

Ps 66:10, 12 - For you, O God, have tested us; you have tried us as silver is tried. ...we went through fire and through water; yet you have brought us out to a place of abundance.

Rom 15:16b - ...so that the offering of the Gentiles may be acceptable, sanctified by the Holy Spirit.

John 4:24 - God is spirit, and those who worship him must worship in spirit and truth."

[Pause. Breathe. Inhale and exhale. Reflect. Listen.]

Give me life according to your word, God!

Journal:

What do you hear God saying to you in these Scripture texts? What do they reveal about God and about you? Converse with God about what you're hearing him say. Verbalize and describe your thoughts, memories that come to mind, questions and emotions, concerns, desires.

Is there a particular word or phrase that disturbs or soothes you?

Do the Scripture texts create a picture or an impression that draws you to linger in exploring and experiencing it?

Choose a word or a phrase from your meditation to write on a slip of paper to carry with you today. Refer to it often throughout the day to remind you of your conversation with God and to continue the conversation all day long. Throughout the day pause to become aware of your thoughts and feelings and will. Ask yourself, "What drives me

in this moment? Life according to God's word? Or life according to someone else's word?"

Anticipate that God's words stirred your heart for a reason. He's conversing with you through them. Anticipate that God will bring his word to life in you, to bear fruit in your heart and mind and soul and body. Anticipate that God will reveal the secrets of your heart, for anything that is visible is light. And anticipate that God will cause his words to become a joy and the delight of your heart.

CONTEMPLATE

God is spirit, and those who worship him must worship in spirit and truth. Seek him. Feel your way to him. Reach out. Find him.

Inhale deeply, aware that God *is* in your hidden parts, that it is *his* breath that makes you understand his word. Exhale. Give God the gift that he most desires from you, your exposed and surrendered heart, mind, soul, spirit, and body, your whole self, both outer and inner.

Each time you find that your outer self has pulled your attention away, quietly and gently say the word or phrase you chose and then dive back down deep to the hidden person of your heart to return to the Lord. Bask in him. Rest in perfect love.

At the end of your contemplation, inhale deeply and hold it for a second, aware that you exist in God's abounding grace. Only in God's abounding grace do you exist. In God's abounding grace you are you, the real you, able to worship God in spirit and truth.

2 Cor 9:8 - And ***God is able*** *to make all grace abound to you, so that having all sufficiency in all things at all times,* ***you may*** *abound in every good work.*

Exhale slowly and deeply, anticipating that God's abounding grace, in which you exist and are, will flow around you and through you to enlighten and empower you to love as you have been loved so that you may abound in every good work this day.

13 – Know the Name of the Lord

Pray: Ask God to prepare your heart and mind and soul to receive his words, to receive truth that will set you free, which will heal and perfect your understanding and knowledge of who God is and who you are.

Ps 119:25-32 - My soul clings to the dust; give me life according to your word! When I told of my ways, you answered me; teach me your statutes! Make me understand the way of your precepts, and I will meditate on your wondrous works. My soul melts away for sorrow; strengthen me according to your word! Put false ways far from me and graciously teach me your law! I have chosen the way of faithfulness; I set your rules before me. I cling to your testimonies, O Lord; let me not be put to shame! I will run in the way of your commandments when you enlarge my heart! (ESV)

[Murmur and mumble the words. Phrase by phrase. Word by word. Syllable by syllable. Pause. Breathe. Inhale and exhale. Reflect. Listen.]

Journal:

Note how this prayer stirs you today and what you hear God saying to you.

Ps 9:10 - And those who know your name put their trust in you, for you, O Lord, have not forsaken those who seek you.

Those who **know**…

Who know: a primitive root; to know [properly, to ascertain by seeing]; used in a great variety of senses… including observation, care, recognition; and causatively, instruction, designation, punishment, etc.[1]

Those who ***know***

Know. To ascertain by seeing.

Observation

Care

Recognition

Instruction

Designation. To point out.

Punishment

Know

[Murmur and mumble the words. Phrase by phrase. Word by word. Syllable by syllable. Take pleasure in making the sounds of the words, getting the feel of the meaning. Experience pleasurable anticipation of taking in what will make you more yourself, the self that God made in his own image and likeness. The self that God made for intimate communion with him. The self that God created for good works, that you should walk in them. Eat God's words. Let God's words become a joy and the delight of your heart.]

Journal:

What have you found out with certainty about God by seeing?

What knowledge and awareness have you received about God through your eyes?

Are you aware of eyes and seeing other than your physical sense of sight? What have you seen through mental impressions?

What have you seen through personal experience?

What have you seen through perception or intuition?

What have you seen by keeping company with God?

What have you seen through instruction or punishment?

Ps 145:8-9 - The Lord is gracious and merciful, slow to anger and abounding in steadfast love. The Lord is good to all, and his mercy is over all that he has made.

The Lord

The Lord ***is***

The Lord is ***gracious*** [to bend or stoop in kindness to an inferior; to favor, to implore i.e. move to favor by petition[2]]

The Lord is ***merciful*** [full of compassion]

The Lord is ***slow to anger***

The Lord is abounding in steadfast ***love***

The Lord is abounding in ***steadfast*** love

The Lord is ***abounding*** in steadfast love

The Lord is ***good***

The Lord is good ***to all***

The Lord's ***mercy***

The Lord's mercy is ***over all***

The Lord's mercy is over all ***that he has made***

Those who ***know*** your name, O Lord…

Those who know ***your name***…

Those who know your name **put their trust in you**…

[Murmur and mumble the words. Phrase by phrase. Word by word.

Syllable by syllable. Take pleasure in making the sounds of the words, getting the feel of the meaning. Experience pleasurable anticipation of taking in what will make you more yourself, the self that God made in his own image and likeness. The self that God made for intimate communion with him. The self that God created for good works, that you should walk in them. Eat God's words. Let God's words become a joy and the delight of your heart.]

Journal:

As you look around you, at nature and at humankind, do you see examples of these attributes of God everywhere?

Is there one or a few personal experiences that call these attributes of God into question so you can't see beyond your experience in order to know that indeed God's mercy *is* over all that he has made, including you?

Is your questioning of God's grace, mercy, goodness, abounding steadfast love simply due to your not getting your own way?

Do you know from experience that God loves you? That his love is steadfast? That his love is abounding? Describe.

Do you know God's name?

Have you put your trust in God? Is there anything in your understanding or experience that stands in your way of trusting God?

Ps 9:10 - And those who know your name put their trust in you, for you, O Lord, have not forsaken those who seek you.

Ps 145:8-9 - The Lord is gracious and merciful, slow to anger and abounding in steadfast love. The Lord is good to all, and his mercy is over all that he has made.

[Pause. Breathe. Inhale and exhale. Reflect. Listen.]

Give me life according to your word, God!

Journal:

What do you hear God saying to you in these Scripture texts? What do they reveal about God and about you? Converse with God about what you're hearing him say. Verbalize and describe your thoughts, memories that come to mind, questions and emotions, concerns, desires.

Is there a particular word or phrase that disturbs or soothes you?

Do the Scripture texts create a picture or an impression that draws you to linger in exploring and experiencing it?

Choose a word or a phrase from your meditation to write on a slip of paper to carry with you today. Refer to it often throughout the day to remind you of your conversation with God and to continue the conversation all day long. Throughout the day pause to become aware of your thoughts and feelings and will. Ask yourself, "What drives me

in this moment? Life according to God's word? Or life according to someone else's word?"

Anticipate that God's words stirred your heart for a reason. He's conversing with you through them. Anticipate that God will bring his word to life in you, to bear fruit in your heart and mind and soul and body. Anticipate that God will reveal the secrets of your heart, for anything that is visible is light. And anticipate that God will cause his words to become a joy and the delight of your heart.

CONTEMPLATE

God is spirit, and those who worship him must worship in spirit and truth. Seek him. Feel your way to him. Reach out. Find him.

Inhale deeply, aware that God *is* in your hidden parts, that it is *his* breath that makes you understand his word. Exhale. Give God the gift that he most desires from you, your exposed and surrendered heart, mind, soul, spirit, and body, your whole self, both outer and inner.

Each time you find that your outer self has pulled your attention away, quietly and gently say the word or phrase you chose and then dive back down deep to the hidden person of your heart to return to the Lord. Bask in him. Rest in perfect love.

At the end of your contemplation, inhale deeply and hold it for a second, aware that you exist in God's abounding grace. Only in God's abounding grace do you exist. In God's abounding grace you are you, the real you, able to worship God in spirit and truth.

2 Cor 9:8 - And ***God is able*** *to make all grace abound to you, so that having all sufficiency in all things at all times,* ***you may*** *abound in every good work.*

Exhale slowly and deeply, anticipating that God's abounding grace, in which you exist and are, will flow around you and through you to enlighten and empower you to love as you have been loved so that you may abound in every good work this day.

Resources:

[1]Who know: OT:3045 <START HEBREW>ud^y*<END HEBREW> yada` (yaw-dah'); a primitive root; to know (properly, to ascertain by seeing); used in a great variety of senses, figuratively, literally, euphemistically and inferentially (including observation, care, recognition; and causatively, instruction, designation, punishment, etc.) (Biblesoft's New Exhaustive Strong's Numbers and Concordance with Expanded Greek-Hebrew Dictionary. Copyright © 1994, 2003, 2006 Biblesoft, Inc. and International Bible Translators, Inc.)

[2]Gracious: OT:2603 <START HEBREW>/n^j*<END HEBREW> chanan (khaw-nan'); a primitive root [compare OT:2583]; properly, to bend or stoop in kindness to an inferior; to favor, bestow; causatively to implore (i.e. move to favor by petition): (Biblesoft's New Exhaustive Strong's Numbers and Concordance with Expanded Greek-Hebrew Dictionary. Copyright © 1994, 2003, 2006, 2010 Biblesoft, Inc. and International Bible Translators, Inc.)

14 – Those Who Know

Pray: Ask God to prepare your heart and mind and soul to receive his words, to receive truth that will set you free, which will heal and perfect your understanding and knowledge of who God is and who you are.

Ps 119:25-32 - I'm feeling terrible — I couldn't feel worse! Get me on my feet again. You promised, remember? When I told my story, you responded; train me well in your deep wisdom. Help me understand these things inside and out so I can ponder your miracle-wonders. My sad life's dilapidated, a falling-down barn; build me up again by your Word. Barricade the road that goes Nowhere; grace me with your clear revelation. I choose the true road to Somewhere, I post your road signs at every curve and corner. I grasp and cling to whatever you tell me; God, don't let me down! I'll run the course you lay out for me if you'll just show me how. (MSG)

[Murmur and mumble the words. Phrase by phrase. Word by word. Syllable by syllable. Pause. Breathe. Inhale and exhale. Reflect. Listen.]

Journal:

Note how this prayer stirs you today and what you hear God saying to you.

Ps 9:10 - And those who know your name put their trust in you, for you, O Lord, have not forsaken those who seek you.

Do you know God's name? How can we know God's name?

Journal:

You, O Lord, have not forsaken those who seek you.

You, O Lord, ***have <u>not</u> forsaken***...

Have not forsaken ***those who seek you***.

Seek

Seek ***you***

O Lord

You, O Lord, ***have not forsaken*** those who seek you.

Seek: a primitive root; properly, to tread or frequent; usually to follow [for pursuit or search]; by implication, to seek or ask; specifically to worship[1]

Seek. To tread or frequent. Follow for pursuit or search. Seek. Ask. Worship.

You, O Lord, have not forsaken those who seek you. You have not forsaken those who follow you for pursuit or search. You have not forsaken those who ask. You have not forsaken those who worship.

Those who ***know***

Those who know ***your name***

Those who know your name ***put their trust in you***.

Seek

Follow

Ask

Worship

[Murmur and mumble the words. Phrase by phrase. Word by word. Syllable by syllable. Take pleasure in making the sounds of the words, getting the feel of the meaning. Experience pleasurable anticipation of taking in what will make you more yourself, the self that God made in his own image and likeness. The self that God made for intimate communion with him. The self that God created for good works, that you should walk in them. Eat God's words. Let God's words become a joy and the delight of your heart.]

Journal:

Must we know God's name in order to seek him? Must we seek him in order to know his name?

Do you know God's name? Do you seek him? How?

When I first admitted that I did not know God's name, I had no idea how to answer these questions.

How do I seek God?

How or where do I tread or frequent in order to seek and know God's name?

How do I follow God for pursuit or search?

How do I ask and how do I listen for responses in order to get answers to the questions I ask?

How do I worship?

I've since discovered that I begin by learning to not lean on my own understanding!

I began to simply ask God to reveal *his* answers to my questions. I found the answers I sought through Scripture, through the words and experiences of other people who interacted with God and knew God's name. I hope that sharing what I've discovered about seeking God will encourage you to keep seeking him, too.

Ps 62:1 - For God alone my soul waits in silence; from him comes my ***salvation****.*

Lam 3:25-26 - The Lord is good to those who wait for him, to the soul who seeks him. It is good that one should wait quietly for the ***salvation*** *of the Lord.*

Matt 1:21 - She will bear a son, and you shall call ***his name*** *Jesus, for* ***he will save*** *his people from their sins."*

I discovered that seeking God entails, at least in part, waiting for him. Waiting in silence. Waiting quietly. And God's name has everything to do with salvation. Delivering me from leaning on my own understanding. Delivering me from trusting in my own mind. Delivering me from my withdrawal and independence from him. Delivering me from foreign gods. Delivering me from not believing his words and actions.

My soul ***waits***. Wait. To stay in a place or remain in readiness or in anticipation.

Journal:

Do you regularly stay in a place, remaining in readiness and anticipation, waiting for God? Describe.

Ps 9:10 - And those who know your name put their trust in you, for you, O Lord, have not forsaken those who seek you.

Ps 62:1 - For God alone my soul waits in silence; from him comes my salvation.

Lam 3:25-26 - The Lord is good to those who wait for him, to the soul who seeks him. It is good that one should wait quietly for the salvation of the Lord.

Matt 1:21 - She will bear a son, and you shall call his name Jesus, for he will save his people from their sins."

[Pause. Breathe. Inhale and exhale. Reflect. Listen.]

Give me life according to your word, God!

Journal:

What do you hear God saying to you in these Scripture texts? What do they reveal about God and about you? Converse with God about what you're hearing him say. Verbalize and describe your thoughts, memories that come to mind, questions and emotions, concerns, desires.

Is there a particular word or phrase that disturbs or soothes you?

Do the Scripture texts create a picture or an impression that draws you to linger in exploring and experiencing it?

Choose a word or a phrase from your meditation to write on a slip of paper to carry with you today. Refer to it often throughout the day to remind you of your conversation with God and to continue the conversation all day long. Throughout the day pause to become aware of your thoughts and feelings and will. Ask yourself, "What drives me in this moment? Life according to God's word? Or life according to someone else's word?"

Anticipate that God's words stirred your heart for a reason. He's conversing with you through them. Anticipate that God will bring his word to life in you, to bear fruit in your heart and mind and soul and body. Anticipate that God will reveal the secrets of your heart, for anything that is visible is light. And anticipate that God will cause his words to become a joy and the delight of your heart.

CONTEMPLATE

God is spirit, and those who worship him must worship in spirit and truth. Seek him. Feel your way to him. Reach out. Find him.

Inhale deeply, aware that God *is* in your hidden parts, that it is *his* breath that makes you understand his word. Exhale. Give God the gift that he most desires from you, your exposed and surrendered heart, mind, soul, spirit, and body, your whole self, both outer and inner.

Each time you find that your outer self has pulled your attention away, quietly and gently say the word or phrase you chose and then dive back down deep to the hidden person of your heart to return to the Lord. Bask in him. Rest in perfect love.

At the end of your contemplation, inhale deeply and hold it for a second, aware that you exist in God's abounding grace. Only in God's abounding grace do you exist. In God's abounding grace you are you, the real you, able to worship God in spirit and truth.

*2 Cor 9:8 - And **God is able** to make all grace abound to you, so that having all sufficiency in all things at all times, **you may** abound in every good work.*

Exhale slowly and deeply, anticipating that God's abounding grace, in which you exist and are, will flow around you and through you to enlighten and empower you to love as you have been loved so that you may abound in every good work this day.

Resources:

[1]Seek: OT:1875 <START HEBREW>vr^D*<END HEBREW> darash (daw-rash'); a primitive root; properly, to tread or frequent; usually to follow (for pursuit or search); by implication, to seek or ask; specifically to worship: (Biblesoft's New Exhaustive Strong's Numbers and Concordance with Expanded Greek-Hebrew Dictionary. Copyright © 1994, 2003, 2006 Biblesoft, Inc. and International Bible Translators, Inc.)

15 – For God Alone My Soul Waits in Silence

Pray: Ask God to prepare your heart and mind and soul to receive his words, to receive truth that will set you free, which will heal and perfect your understanding and knowledge of who God is and who you are.

Ps 119:25-32 - My soul clings to the dust; give me life according to your word! When I told of my ways, you answered me; teach me your statutes! Make me understand the way of your precepts, and I will meditate on your wondrous works. My soul melts away for sorrow; strengthen me according to your word! Put false ways far from me and graciously teach me your law! I have chosen the way of faithfulness; I set your rules before me. I cling to your testimonies, O Lord; let me not be put to shame! I will run in the way of your commandments when you enlarge my heart! (ESV)

[Murmur and mumble the words. Phrase by phrase. Word by word. Syllable by syllable. Pause. Breathe. Inhale and exhale. Reflect. Listen.]

Journal:

Note how this prayer stirs you today and what you hear God saying to you.

Ps 9:10 - And those who know your name put their trust in you, for you, O Lord, have not forsaken those who seek you.

Ps 62:1 - For God alone my soul waits in silence; from him comes my salvation.

Lam 3:25-26 - The Lord is good to those who wait for him, to the soul who seeks him. It is good that one should wait quietly for the salvation of the Lord.

Matt 1:21 - She will bear a son, and you shall call his name Jesus, for he will save his people from their sins."

For ***God alone***

My ***soul***

My soul ***waits*** in silence

The Lord is good…to ***the soul who seeks him***

My ***soul***

Soul: properly, a breathing creature, i.e. animal of (abstractly) vitality; used very widely in a literal, accommodated or figurative sense (bodily or mental):

…a primitive root; to breathe; passively, to be breathed upon, i.e. (figuratively) refreshed (as if by a current of air):[1]

My soul. A breathing creature. Animal of vitality. Bodily or mental vigor, energy. To breathe. To be breathed upon. Refreshed as if by a current of air.

For ***God***…

For God ***alone***…

My ***soul***…

My soul ***waits***… in readiness and in anticipation…

My soul waits ***in silence***… stillness, quietness, refraining from speech…

For ***God alone*** my soul waits in silence…

From him…

From **God**…

From God comes my ***salvation***… [deliverance]

The Lord is good to those ***who wait***…

The Lord is good to those who wait ***for him***

The Lord is good to the soul who ***seeks him***

It is good that one should wait ***quietly***…

To breathe.

To be breathed upon.

To be refreshed as if by a current of air.

It is good that one should wait quietly for the ***salvation*** of the Lord

...***He*** will save his people...

He ***will***

He ***will save***...

...From their sins. From their rebellion. From their independence. From their withdrawal from God. From their withdrawal from themselves. From their withdrawal from each other. From their unbelief. From leaning on their own understanding. He will save.

Those who know your ***name***...

Your name... ***Salvation***...

Those who know your name ***put their trust in you***.

[Murmur and mumble the words. Phrase by phrase. Word by word. Syllable by syllable. Take pleasure in making the sounds of the words, getting the feel of the meaning. Experience pleasurable anticipation of taking in what will make you more yourself, the self that God made in his own image and likeness. The self that God made for intimate communion with him. The self that God created for good works, that you should walk in them. Eat God's words. Let God's words become a joy and the delight of your heart.]

Journal:

What is your soul?

Do you provide time and space for your soul to wait for God?

Ps 9:10 - And those who know your name put their trust in you, for you, O Lord, have not forsaken those who seek you.

Ps 62:1 - For God alone my soul waits in silence; from him comes my salvation.

Lam 3:25-26 - The Lord is good to those who wait for him, to the soul who seeks him. It is good that one should wait quietly for the salvation of the Lord.

Matt 1:21 - She will bear a son, and you shall call his name Jesus, for he will save his people from their sins."

[Pause. Breathe. Inhale and exhale. Reflect. Listen.]

Give me life according to your word, God!

Journal:

What do you hear God saying to you in these Scripture texts? What do they reveal about God and about you? Converse with God about what you're hearing him say. Verbalize and describe your thoughts, memories that come to mind, questions and emotions, concerns, desires.

Is there a particular word or phrase that disturbs or soothes you?

Do the Scripture texts create a picture or an impression that draws you to linger in exploring and experiencing it?

Choose a word or a phrase from your meditation to write on a slip of paper to carry with you today. Refer to it often throughout the day to remind you of your conversation with God and to continue the conversation all day long. Throughout the day pause to become aware of your thoughts and feelings and will. Ask yourself, "What drives me in this moment? Life according to God's word? Or life according to someone else's word?"

Anticipate that God's words stirred your heart for a reason. He's conversing with you through them. Anticipate that God will bring his word to life in you, to bear fruit in your heart and mind and soul and body. Anticipate that God will reveal the secrets of your heart, for anything that is visible is light. And anticipate that God will cause his words to

become a joy and the delight of your heart.

CONTEMPLATE

God is spirit, and those who worship him must worship in spirit and truth. Seek him. Feel your way to him. Reach out. Find him.

Inhale deeply, aware that God *is* in your hidden parts, that it is *his* breath that makes you understand his word. Exhale. Give God the gift that he most desires from you, your exposed and surrendered heart, mind, soul, spirit, and body, your whole self, both outer and inner.

Each time you find that your outer self has pulled your attention away, quietly and gently say the word or phrase you chose and then dive back down deep to the hidden person of your heart to return to the Lord. Bask in him. Rest in perfect love.

At the end of your contemplation, inhale deeply and hold it for a second, aware that you exist in God's abounding grace. Only in God's abounding grace do you exist. In God's abounding grace you are you, the real you, able to worship God in spirit and truth.

2 Cor 9:8 - And ***God is able*** *to make all grace abound to you, so that having all sufficiency in all things at all times,* ***you may*** *abound in every good work.*

Exhale slowly and deeply, anticipating that God's abounding grace, in which you exist and are, will flow around you and through you to enlighten and empower you to love as you have been loved so that you may abound in every good work this day.

Resources:

[1]Soul: OT:5315 <START HEBREW>vp#n#<END HEBREW> nephesh (neh'-fesh); from OT:5314; properly, a breathing creature, i.e. animal of (abstractly) vitality; used very widely in a literal, accommodated or figurative sense (bodily or mental):

OT:5314 <START HEBREW>vp^n*<END HEBREW> naphash (naw-fash'); a primitive root; to breathe; passively, to be breathed upon, i.e. (figuratively) refreshed (as if by a current of air): (Biblesoft's New Exhaustive Strong's Numbers and Concordance with Expanded Greek-Hebrew Dictionary. Copyright © 1994, 2003, 2006 Biblesoft, Inc. and International Bible Translators, Inc.)

16 – One Thing Have I Asked of the Lord

Pray: Ask God to prepare your heart and mind and soul to receive his words, to receive truth that will set you free, which will heal and perfect your understanding and knowledge of who God is and who you are.

Ps 119:25-32 - I'm feeling terrible — I couldn't feel worse! Get me on my feet again. You promised, remember? When I told my story, you responded; train me well in your deep wisdom. Help me understand these things inside and out so I can ponder your miracle-wonders. My sad life's dilapidated, a falling-down barn; build me up again by your Word. Barricade the road that goes Nowhere; grace me with your clear revelation. I choose the true road to Somewhere, I post your road signs at every curve and corner. I grasp and cling to whatever you tell me; God, don't let me down! I'll run the course you lay out for me if you'll just show me how. (MSG)

[Murmur and mumble the words. Phrase by phrase. Word by word. Syllable by syllable. Pause. Breathe. Inhale and exhale. Reflect. Listen.]

Journal:

Note how this prayer stirs you today and what you hear God saying to you.

Ps 27:4 - One thing have I asked of the Lord, that will I seek after: that I may dwell in the house of the Lord all the days of my life, to gaze upon the beauty of the Lord and to inquire in his temple.

One thing

One thing have ***I asked***

One thing have I asked ***of the Lord***

That one thing

That ***will I seek after***

One thing

That will I seek after…

That I may ***dwell*** in the house of the Lord all the days of my life

One thing

That will I seek after…

To ***gaze***

To gaze upon the ***beauty of the Lord***

And

And to ***inquire in his temple***.

[Murmur and mumble the words. Phrase by phrase. Word by word. Syllable by syllable. Take pleasure in making the sounds of the words, getting the feel of the meaning. Experience pleasurable anticipation of taking in what will make you more yourself, the self that God made in his own image and likeness. The self that God made for intimate communion with him. The self that God created for good works, that you should walk in them. Eat God's words. Let God's words become a joy and the delight of your heart.]

Inquire: a primitive root; properly, to plough, or (generally) break forth, i.e. (figuratively) to inspect, admire, care for, consider[1]

Inquire. Plow. Cut a way through. To inspect, admire, care for, consider.

To gaze upon the beauty of the Lord and to <u>inquire</u> in his temple.

Journal:

What is the psalmist revealing about his heart in this Scripture text?

How many things do you ask of the Lord? Is this *one* thing that David asked of the Lord also on your list? Do you seek after the same things that David sought after? Why or why not?

Do you plow, plod, advance laboriously, and work vigorously to enter God's presence to look upon the beauty of the Lord? Or is your laborious and vigorous work directed toward some other goal, some other beauty?

Ps 105:4 - Seek the Lord and his strength [force, security, majesty, praise[2]]; seek his presence [face] continually!

Seek

Tread or frequent

Follow for pursuit or search

Ask

Worship

Seek ***the Lord***

And ***his strength***

Seek ***his presence***

Seek his face

Seek the Lord ***continually***.

[Murmur and mumble the words. Phrase by phrase. Word by word. Syllable by syllable. Take pleasure in making the sounds of the words, getting the feel of the meaning. Experience pleasurable anticipation of taking in what will make you more yourself, the self that God made in his own image and likeness. The self that God made for intimate communion with him. The self that God created for good works, that you should walk in them. Eat God's words. Let God's words become a joy and the delight of your heart.]

Journal:

What is God saying to you in this Scripture text? How will you seek him? Where will you seek him? When will you seek him? Why will you seek him?

Ps 27:4 - One thing have I asked of the Lord, that will I seek after: that I may dwell in the house of the Lord all the days of my life, to gaze upon the beauty of the Lord and to inquire in his temple.

Ps 105:4 - Seek the Lord and his strength; seek his presence continually!

[Pause. Breathe. Inhale and exhale. Reflect. Listen.]

Give me life according to your word, God!

Journal:

What do you hear God saying to you in these Scripture texts? What do they reveal about God and about you? Converse with God about what you're hearing him say. Verbalize and describe your thoughts, memories that come to mind, questions and emotions, concerns, desires.

Is there a particular word or phrase that disturbs or soothes you?

Do the Scripture texts create a picture or an impression that draws you to linger in exploring and experiencing it?

Choose a word or a phrase from your meditation to write on a slip of paper to carry with you today. Refer to it often throughout the day to remind you of your conversation with God and to continue the conversation all day long. Throughout the day pause to become aware of your thoughts and feelings and will. Ask yourself, "What drives me in this moment? Life according to God's word? Or life according to someone else's word?"

Anticipate that God's words stirred your heart for a reason. He's conversing with you through them. Anticipate that God will bring his word to life in you, to bear fruit in your heart and mind and soul and body. Anticipate that God will reveal the secrets of your heart, for anything that is visible is light. And anticipate that God will cause his words to become a joy and the delight of your heart.

CONTEMPLATE

God is spirit, and those who worship him must worship in spirit and truth. Seek him. Feel your way to him. Reach out. Find him.

Inhale deeply, aware that God *is* in your hidden parts, that it is *his* breath that makes you understand his word. Exhale. Give God the gift that he most desires from you, your exposed and surrendered heart, mind, soul, spirit, and body, your whole self, both outer and inner.

Each time you find that your outer self has pulled your attention away, quietly and gently say the word or phrase you chose and then dive back down deep to the hidden person of your heart to return to the Lord. Bask in him. Rest in perfect love.

At the end of your contemplation, inhale deeply and hold it for a second, aware that you exist in God's abounding grace. Only in God's abounding grace do you exist. In God's abounding grace you are you, the real you, able to worship God in spirit and truth.

2 Cor 9:8 - And ***God is able*** *to make all grace abound to you, so that having all sufficiency in all things at all times,* ***you may*** *abound in every good work.*

Exhale slowly and deeply, anticipating that God's abounding grace, in which you exist and are, will flow around you and through you to enlighten and empower you to love as you have been loved so that you may abound in every good work this day.

Resources:

[1]Inquire: OT:1239 <START HEBREW>rq^B*<END HEBREW> baqar (baw-kar); a primitive root; properly, to plough, or (generally) break forth, i.e. (figuratively) to inspect, admire, care for, consider: (Biblesoft's New Exhaustive Strong's Numbers and Concordance with Expanded Greek-Hebrew Dictionary. Copyright © 1994, 2003, 2006, 2010 Biblesoft, Inc. and International Bible Translators, Inc.)

[2]Strength: OT:5797 <START HEBREW>zu)<END HEBREW> `oz (oze); or (fully) `owz (oze); from OT:5810; strength in various applica-

tions (force, security, majesty, praise):

OT:5810 <START HEBREW>zz^u*<END HEBREW> `azaz (aw-zaz'); a primitive root; to be stout (literally or figuratively): (Biblesoft's New Exhaustive Strong's Numbers and Concordance with Expanded Greek-Hebrew Dictionary. Copyright © 1994, 2003, 2006, 2010 Biblesoft, Inc. and International Bible Translators, Inc.)

17 – Earnestly Seek God

Pray: Ask God to prepare your heart and mind and soul to receive his words, to receive truth that will set you free, which will heal and perfect your understanding and knowledge of who God is and who you are.

Ps 119:25-32 - My soul clings to the dust; give me life according to your word! When I told of my ways, you answered me; teach me your statutes! Make me understand the way of your precepts, and I will meditate on your wondrous works. My soul melts away for sorrow; strengthen me according to your word! Put false ways far from me and graciously teach me your law! I have chosen the way of faithfulness; I set your rules before me. I cling to your testimonies, O Lord; let me not be put to shame! I will run in the way of your commandments when you enlarge my heart! (ESV)

[Murmur and mumble the words. Phrase by phrase. Word by word. Syllable by syllable. Pause. Breathe. Inhale and exhale. Reflect. Listen.]

Journal:

Note how this prayer stirs you today and what you hear God saying to you.

Ps 63:1-3 - O God, you are my God; earnestly I seek you; my soul thirsts for you; my flesh faints for you, as in a dry and weary land where there is no water. So I have looked upon you in the sanctuary, beholding your power and glory. Because your steadfast love is better than life, my lips will praise you.

O God,

You are my God

You ***are*** my God

You are ***my*** God

Earnestly

I seek

I seek ***you***

Earnestly I seek you

My ***soul***

My soul ***thirsts for you***

My ***flesh***

My flesh ***faints for you***, as in a dry and weary land where there is no water.

So

So ***I have looked***

So I have looked ***upon you***

So I have looked upon you ***in the sanctuary*** [a sacred place, a holy place]

Beholding

Beholding ***your power and glory***

Because ***your steadfast love*** is better than life

Your steadfast love ***is better***

Because your steadfast love is better ***than life***

My lips will ***praise you***.

[Murmur and mumble the words. Phrase by phrase. Word by word. Syllable by syllable. Take pleasure in making the sounds of the words, getting the feel of the meaning. Experience pleasurable anticipation of taking in what will make you more yourself, the self that God made in his own image and likeness. The self that God made for intimate communion with him. The self that God created for good works, that you should walk in them. Eat God's words. Let God's words become a joy and the delight of your heart.]

Journal:

Do you know the steadfast love of the Lord that is better than life?

Have you experienced the thirst for God deep in your soul that the psalmist David describes? Have you experienced your flesh fainting for God? Describe.

If not, can you make your heart thirst and your flesh faint for God?

Might any longing and dissatisfaction and restlessness you experience actually be this thirst for God that David describes, but your deceitful heart has convinced you that you thirst and faint for something or someone else?

Where is the sanctuary where you can go to look upon God and behold his power and glory and steadfast love?

Isa 57:15 - For thus says the One who is high and lifted up, who inhabits eternity, whose name is Holy: "I dwell in the high and holy place, and also with him who is of a contrite and lowly spirit, to revive the spirit of the lowly, and to revive the heart of the contrite.

For thus ***says***

For thus says the ***One*** who is high and lifted up

Who inhabits ***eternity***...

Dwells in the ***high and holy place***

Also dwells ***with***

Also dwells with him who is ***of a contrite and lowly spirit***

Journal:

Might the above Scripture text be saying that God is everywhere, and everywhere that God is, is holy? Even the sanctuary in your own soul? Even the sanctuary in your neighbor's soul?

Will you speak with God about your fears and shortcomings and doubts and troubles and longings? Will you ask him to deliver you from all these and revive your spirit and heart so you can trust the abundance of his steadfast love, so you can anticipate that he will hear and will answer you at an acceptable time in his saving faithfulness?

Ps 63:1-3 - O God, you are my God; earnestly I seek you; my soul thirsts for you; my flesh faints for you, as in a dry and weary land where there is no water. So I have looked upon you in the sanctuary, beholding your power and glory. Because your steadfast love is better than life, my lips will praise you.

Isa 57:15 - For thus says the One who is high and lifted up, who inhabits eternity, whose name is Holy: "I dwell in the high and holy place, and also with him who is of a contrite and lowly spirit, to revive the spirit of the lowly, and to revive the heart of the contrite.

Ps 69:13 - But as for me, my prayer is to you, O Lord. At an acceptable time, O God, in the abundance of your steadfast love answer me in your saving faithfulness.

[Pause. Breathe. Inhale and exhale. Reflect. Listen.]

Give me life according to your word, God!

Journal:

What do you hear God saying to you in these Scripture texts? What do they reveal about God and about you? Converse with God about what you're hearing him say. Verbalize and describe your thoughts, memories that come to mind, questions and emotions, concerns, desires.

Is there a particular word or phrase that disturbs or soothes you?

Do the Scripture texts create a picture or an impression that draws you to linger in exploring and experiencing it?

Choose a word or a phrase from your meditation to write on a slip of paper to carry with you today. Refer to it often throughout the day to remind you of your conversation with God and to continue the conversation all day long. Throughout the day pause to become aware of your thoughts and feelings and will. Ask yourself, “What drives me in this moment? Life according to God’s word? Or life according to someone else’s word?”

Anticipate that God’s words stirred your heart for a reason. He’s conversing with you through them. Anticipate that God will bring his word to life in you, to bear fruit in your heart and mind and soul and body. Anticipate that God will reveal the secrets of your heart, for anything that is visible is light. And anticipate that God will cause his words to become a joy and the delight of your heart.

CONTEMPLATE

God is spirit, and those who worship him must worship in spirit and truth. Seek him. Feel your way to him. Reach out. Find him.

Inhale deeply, aware that God *is* in your hidden parts, that it is *his* breath that makes you understand his word. Exhale. Give God the gift that he most desires from you, your exposed and surrendered heart, mind, soul, spirit, and body, your whole self, both outer and inner.

Each time you find that your outer self has pulled your attention away, quietly and gently say the word or phrase you chose and then dive back down deep to the hidden person of your heart to return to the Lord. Bask in him. Rest in perfect love.

At the end of your contemplation, inhale deeply and hold it for a second, aware that you exist in God’s abounding grace. Only in God’s abounding grace do you exist. In God’s abounding grace you are you, the real you, able to worship God in spirit and truth.

2 Cor 9:8 - And ***God is able*** *to make all grace abound to you, so that having all sufficiency in all things at all times,* ***you may*** *abound in every good work.*

Exhale slowly and deeply, anticipating that God's abounding grace, in which you exist and are, will flow around you and through you to enlighten and empower you to love as you have been loved so that you may abound in every good work this day.

18 - Delight Yourself in the Lord

Pray: Ask God to prepare your heart and mind and soul to receive his words, to receive truth that will set you free, which will heal and perfect your understanding and knowledge of who God is and who you are.

Ps 119:25-32 - I'm feeling terrible — I couldn't feel worse! Get me on my feet again. You promised, remember? When I told my story, you responded; train me well in your deep wisdom. Help me understand these things inside and out so I can ponder your miracle-wonders. My sad life's dilapidated, a falling-down barn; build me up again by your Word. Barricade the road that goes Nowhere; grace me with your clear revelation. I choose the true road to Somewhere, I post your road signs at every curve and corner. I grasp and cling to whatever you tell me; God, don't let me down! I'll run the course you lay out for me if you'll just show me how. (MSG)

[Murmur and mumble the words. Phrase by phrase. Word by word. Syllable by syllable. Pause. Breathe. Inhale and exhale. Reflect. Listen.]

Journal:

Note how this prayer stirs you today and what you hear God saying to you.

Prov 3:5 - Trust in the Lord with all your heart, and do not lean on your own understanding.

Trust.

Confident. Sure. Secure. Striving or hurry for refuge. Anticipation. Reliance. Expectation.

Trust ***in the Lord***. Sure in the Lord. Secure in the Lord. Urgency, eagerness for refuge in the Lord.

Expectation

Anticipation

Confident expectation, anticipation, and hope in the words and character of God.

Expectation. Anticipation.

[Murmur and mumble the words. Phrase by phrase. Word by word. Syllable by syllable. Take pleasure in making the sounds of the words, getting the feel of the meaning. Experience pleasurable anticipation of taking in what will make you more yourself, the self that God made in his own image and likeness. The self that God made for intimate communion with him. The self that God created for good works, that you should walk in them. Eat God's words. Let God's words become a joy and the delight of your heart.]

Journal:

Do these words describe how you feel about God? Do they describe your interaction and relationship with him? Why or why not?

Pray: Ask God to help you see as he sees. "What do I expect of you, God? What do I anticipate from you?"

"Is there a difference between what I expect and what I anticipate?"

"Does what I expect and anticipate from you, God, nurture and produce trust in you? Does what I expect and anticipate from you stir an urgency and eagerness within me to seek refuge in you, God?

Do I look to God, or elsewhere, for refuge and security?

[Pause. Breathe. Inhale and exhale. Reflect. Listen.]

Ask God to bring the secrets of your heart into the light.

Ps 37:4-6 - Delight yourself in the Lord, and he will give you the desires of your heart. Commit your way to the Lord; trust in him, and he will act. He will bring forth your righteousness as the light, and your justice as the noonday.

Delight [be soft or pliable[1]]

Delight ***yourself***

Delight yourself ***in the Lord***

And

He will give you the desires [requests[2]] of your heart.

Commit [roll, be carried in a flow; trust] your way

Commit your way [course of life[3]] ***to the Lord***

Trust [hurry or hasten for refuge[4]] in him

And

And he ***will*** act.

He will

He will ***bring forth***

He will bring forth ***your righteousness as the light***

He will bring forth ***your justice as the noonday***.

[Murmur and mumble the words. Phrase by phrase. Word by word. Syllable by syllable. Take pleasure in making the sounds of the words, getting the feel of the meaning. Experience pleasurable anticipation of taking in what will make you more yourself, the self that God made in his own image and likeness. The self that God made for intimate communion with him. The self that God created for good works, that you should walk in them. Eat God's words. Let God's words become a joy and the delight of your heart.]

Journal:

What do you hear God saying to you in this Scripture text?

Do you delight yourself in the Lord? Do you make yourself soft and pliable toward him?

Have you committed your way to the Lord? Have you agreed to be carried along in his flow? Have you given yourself into his charge for safekeeping?

Do you always hurry to him for refuge?

Do you see God acting on your behalf? Are you aware that he is bringing forth your righteousness and justice as the light? What does that mean?

What are the desires of your heart? Are the desires of your heart aligned with the desires of God's heart? Do they flow as one course? Are the desires of your heart for God to bring forth your righteousness and justice as the light?

Prov 3:5 - Trust in the Lord with all your heart, and do not lean on your own understanding.

Ps 37:4-6 - Delight yourself in the Lord, and he will give you the desires of your heart. Commit your way to the Lord; trust in him, and he will act. He will bring forth your righteousness as the light, and your justice as the noonday.

[Pause. Breathe. Inhale and exhale. Reflect. Listen.]

Give me life according to your word, God!

Journal:

What do you hear God saying to you in these Scripture texts? What do they reveal about God and about you? Converse with God about what you're hearing him say. Verbalize and describe your thoughts, memories that come to mind, questions and emotions, concerns, desires.

Is there a particular word or phrase that disturbs or soothes you?

Do the Scripture texts create a picture or an impression that draws you to linger in exploring and experiencing it?

Choose a word or a phrase from your meditation to write on a slip of paper to carry with you today. Refer to it often throughout the day to remind you of your conversation with God and to continue the conversation all day long. Throughout the day pause to become aware of your thoughts and feelings and will. Ask yourself, "What drives me in this moment? Life according to God's word? Or life according to someone else's word?"

Anticipate that God's words stirred your heart for a reason. He's conversing with you through them. Anticipate that God will bring his word to life in you, to bear fruit in your heart and mind and soul and body. Anticipate that God will reveal the secrets of your heart, for anything that is visible is light. And anticipate that God will cause his words to

become a joy and the delight of your heart.

CONTEMPLATE

God is spirit, and those who worship him must worship in spirit and truth. Seek him. Feel your way to him. Reach out. Find him.

Inhale deeply, aware that God *is* in your hidden parts, that it is *his* breath that makes you understand his word. Exhale. Give God the gift that he most desires from you, your exposed and surrendered heart, mind, soul, spirit, and body, your whole self, both outer and inner.

Each time you find that your outer self has pulled your attention away, quietly and gently say the word or phrase you chose and then dive back down deep to the hidden person of your heart to return to the Lord. Bask in him. Rest in perfect love.

At the end of your contemplation, inhale deeply and hold it for a second, aware that you exist in God's abounding grace. Only in God's abounding grace do you exist. In God's abounding grace you are you, the real you, able to worship God in spirit and truth.

2 Cor 9:8 - And ***God is able*** *to make all grace abound to you, so that having all sufficiency in all things at all times,* ***you may*** *abound in every good work.*

Exhale slowly and deeply, anticipating that God's abounding grace, in which you exist and are, will flow around you and through you to enlighten and empower you to love as you have been loved so that you may abound in every good work this day.

Resources:

[1]Delight yourself: OT:6026 <START HEBREW>gn^u*<END HEBREW> `anag (aw-nag'); a primitive root; to be soft or pliable, i.e. (figuratively) effeminate or luxurious: (Biblesoft's New Exhaustive Strong's Numbers and Concordance with Expanded Greek-Hebrew Dictionary. Copyright © 1994, 2003, 2006, 2010 Biblesoft, Inc. and International Bible Translators, Inc.)

[2]The desires of: OT:4862 <START HEBREW>hl*a*v=m!<END HEBREW> mish'alah (mish-aw-law'); from OT:7592; a request: (Biblesoft's New Exhaustive Strong's Numbers and Concordance with Expanded Greek-Hebrew Dictionary. Copyright © 1994, 2003, 2006, 2010 Biblesoft, Inc. and International Bible Translators, Inc.)

[3]Your way: OT:1870 <START HEBREW>Er#D#<END HEBREW> derek (deh'-rek); from OT:1869; a road (as trodden); figuratively, a course of life or mode of action, often adverb: (Biblesoft's New Exhaustive Strong's Numbers and Concordance with Expanded Greek-Hebrew Dictionary. Copyright © 1994, 2003, 2006, 2010 Biblesoft, Inc. and International Bible Translators, Inc.)

[4]Trust: OT:982 <START HEBREW>jf^B*<END HEBREW> batach (baw-takh'); a primitive root; properly, to hie for refuge [but not so precipitately as OT:2620]; figuratively, to trust, be confident or sure:

OT:2620 <START HEBREW>hs*j*<END HEBREW> chacah (khaw-saw'); a primitive root; to flee for protection [compare OT:982]; figuratively, to confide in: (Biblesoft's New Exhaustive Strong's Numbers and Concordance with Expanded Greek-Hebrew Dictionary. Copyright © 1994, 2003, 2006, 2010 Biblesoft, Inc. and International Bible Translators, Inc.)

19 - The Hope of the Righteous Brings Joy

Pray: Ask God to prepare your heart and mind and soul to receive his words, to receive truth that will set you free, which will heal and perfect your understanding and knowledge of who God is and who you are.

Ps 119:25-32 - My soul clings to the dust; give me life according to your word! When I told of my ways, you answered me; teach me your statutes! Make me understand the way of your precepts, and I will meditate on your wondrous works. My soul melts away for sorrow; strengthen me according to your word! Put false ways far from me and graciously teach me your law! I have chosen the way of faithfulness; I set your rules before me. I cling to your testimonies, O Lord; let me not be put to shame! I will run in the way of your commandments when you enlarge my heart! (ESV)

[Murmur and mumble the words. Phrase by phrase. Word by word. Syllable by syllable. Pause. Breathe. Inhale and exhale. Reflect. Listen.]

Journal:

Note how this prayer stirs you today and what you hear God saying to you.

Prov 3:5 - Trust in the Lord with all your heart, and do not lean on your own understanding.

Trust[1]

Confident. Sure. Secure. Striving or hurry for refuge. Anticipation. Reliance. Expectation.

Trust ***in the Lord***. Sure in the Lord. Secure in the Lord. Urgency, eagerness for refuge in the Lord.

Anticipation

Expectation

To ***wait for***. Look forward to. Anticipate. To look for as due, proper or necessary. To presume.

[Murmur and mumble the words. Phrase by phrase. Word by word. Syllable by syllable. Take pleasure in making the sounds of the words, getting the feel of the meaning. Experience pleasurable anticipation of taking in what will make you more yourself, the self that God made in his own image and likeness. The self that God made for intimate communion with him. The self that God created for good works, that you should walk in them. Eat God's words. Let God's words become a joy and the delight of your heart.]

Journal:

What do you look to God in anticipation as due, proper or necessary for you?

Is it possible for our anticipation and expectation to turn sour and bitter, becoming a detriment to our trusting God and knowing his name? Is it possible that waiting for, looking forward to, anticipating, expecting can deteriorate into a demand, an entitlement, or a requirement?

Perhaps the fruit of our anticipation or expectation depends upon whose understanding we lean as we look for what we presume is due, proper and necessary for us.

Prov 10:28 - The hope of the righteous [those who hurry to take refuge in God[2]] brings joy, but the expectation of the wicked [those who have transgressed, rebelled, withdrawn] will perish. (ESV)

Prov 10:28 - The hope of righteous people leads to joy, but the eager waiting of wicked people comes to nothing. (God's Word)

Hope: a primitive root; to wait; by implication, to be patient, hope[3]

Expectation: literally, a cord (as an attachment); figuratively, expectancy. ...a primitive root; to bind together (perhaps by twisting), i.e. collect; (figuratively) to expect. ...a (measuring) cord (as if for binding)[4]

Hope. To wait. To be patient. Hope. Those who take refuge in God.

Expectation. A cord. Expectancy. To bind together, perhaps by twisting. Collect. To expect. Those who have withdrawn from God.

Ps 139:1 - O Lord, you have searched me and known me!

[Murmur and mumble the words. Phrase by phrase. Word by word. Syllable by syllable. Take pleasure in making the sounds of the words, getting the feel of the meaning. Experience pleasurable anticipation of taking in what will make you more yourself, the self that God made in his own image and likeness. The self that God made for intimate communion with him. The self that God created for good works, that you should walk in them. Eat God's words. Let God's words become a joy and the delight of your heart.]

Journal:

Pray: Ask God to help you see as he sees. "God, whose understanding do I rely on to define what is due, proper and necessary for me? Are my expectations of you a help or hindrance in my coming to trust and know you so that I will take refuge in you?"

"What is my method of going after, and pursuing what I think is due, proper and necessary for me?"

"Upon whose power and resources and understanding do I rely in order to receive what is due, proper and necessary for me, God? Do I wait? Do I hope? Am I patient? Do I look forward to? Do I anticipate? Do I trust in you, God, to provide what you define as due, proper and necessary for me?"

"Or do I assume that you need my help, God? Do I take it upon myself to plan and work and scheme to get what I presume is due, proper and necessary for me?"

Jer 17:9 - The heart is deceitful above all things, and desperately sick; who can understand it?

Do you perceive a difference in the experience, in the feeling, in the outcome of pursing what is due, proper and necessary by hope versus expectation? Do the words hope, wait, patient give the idea of *mutual* freedom? Does the idea of cord and binding together perhaps feel like antagonism or compulsion?

Ps 69:13 - But as for me, my prayer is to you, O Lord. At an acceptable time, O God, in the abundance of your steadfast love answer me in your saving faithfulness.

My prayer is to **you**, O Lord.

At ***an acceptable time***, O God

In the ***abundance***

In the abundance of ***your steadfast love***

Answer me in ***your saving faithfulness***.

[Murmur and mumble the words. Phrase by phrase. Word by word. Syllable by syllable. Take pleasure in making the sounds of the words, getting the feel of the meaning. Experience pleasurable anticipation of taking in what will make you more yourself, the self that God made in his own image and likeness. The self that God made for intimate communion with him. The self that God created for good works, that you should walk in them. Eat God's words. Let God's words become a joy and the delight of your heart.]

Journal:

When you have waited on God, anticipating that he would provide what was due, proper and necessary for you, and your expectations remained unmet, what did you do? Did you continue to wait? Did you continue to look forward to? Did you continue to anticipate? Did you continue to trust in God? Record a circumstance that comes to mind.

When you have waited on God, anticipating that he would provide what was due, proper and necessary for you, and your expectations remained unmet did you become discouraged? Did you doubt? Did you become angry? Did you blame? Did you give up? Did you separate yourself from God? Did you take upon yourself without permission or authority to get what you wanted? Record a circumstance that comes to mind.

[Pause. Breathe. Inhale and exhale. Reflect. Listen.]

Ask God to bring the secrets of your heart into the light.

Hope. Freedom.

Expectation. Bondage.

Prov 3:5 - Trust in the Lord with all your heart, and do not lean on your own understanding.

Prov 10:28 - The hope of the righteous brings joy, but the expectation of the wicked will perish. (ESV)

Ps 139:1 - O Lord, you have searched me and known me!

Jer 17:9 - The heart is deceitful above all things, and desperately sick; who can understand it?

Ps 69:13 - But as for me, my prayer is to you, O Lord. At an acceptable time, O God, in the abundance of your steadfast love answer me in your saving faithfulness.

[Pause. Breathe. Inhale and exhale. Reflect. Listen.]

Give me life according to your word, God!

Journal:

What do you hear God saying to you in these Scripture texts? What do they reveal about God and about you? Converse with God about what you're hearing him say. Verbalize and describe your thoughts, memories that come to mind, questions and emotions, concerns, desires.

Is there a particular word or phrase that disturbs or soothes you?

Do the Scripture texts create a picture or an impression that draws you to linger in exploring and experiencing it?

Choose a word or a phrase from your meditation to write on a slip of paper to carry with you today. Refer to it often throughout the day to remind you of your conversation with God and to continue the conversation all day long. Throughout the day pause to become aware of your thoughts and feelings and will. Ask yourself, "What drives me in this moment? Life according to God's word? Or life according to someone else's word?"

Anticipate that God's words stirred your heart for a reason. He's conversing with you through them. Anticipate that God will bring his word to life in you, to bear fruit in your heart and mind and soul and body. Anticipate that God will reveal the secrets of your heart, for anything that is visible is light. And anticipate that God will cause his words to become a joy and the delight of your heart.

CONTEMPLATE

God is spirit, and those who worship him must worship in spirit and truth. Seek him. Feel your way to him. Reach out. Find him.

Inhale deeply, aware that God *is* in your hidden parts, that it is *his* breath that makes you understand his word. Exhale. Give God the gift that he most desires from you, your exposed and surrendered heart, mind, soul, spirit, and body, your whole self, both outer and inner.

Each time you find that your outer self has pulled your attention away, quietly and gently say the word or phrase you chose and then dive back down deep to the hidden person of your heart to return to the Lord. Bask in him. Rest in perfect love.

At the end of your contemplation, inhale deeply and hold it for a second, aware that you exist in God's abounding grace. Only in God's abounding grace do you exist. In God's abounding grace you are you, the real you, able to worship God in spirit and truth.

2 Cor 9:8 - And ***God is able*** *to make all grace abound to you, so that having all sufficiency in all things at all times,* ***you may*** *abound in every good work.*

Exhale slowly and deeply, anticipating that God's abounding grace, in which you exist and are, will flow around you and through you to enlighten and empower you to love as you have been loved so that you may abound in every good work this day.

Resources:

[1]Trust: OT:982 <START HEBREW>jf^B*<END HEBREW> batach (baw-takh'); a primitive root; properly, to hie for refuge [but not so precipitately as OT:2620]; figuratively, to trust, be confident or sure:

OT:2620 <START HEBREW>hs*j*<END HEBREW> chacah (khaw-saw'); a primitive root; to flee for protection [compare OT:982]; figuratively, to confide in: (Biblesoft's New Exhaustive Strong's Numbers and Concordance with Expanded Greek-Hebrew Dictionary. Copyright © 1994, 2003, 2006, 2010 Biblesoft, Inc. and International Bible Translators, Inc.)

Also Webster's Dictionary.

[2]Righteous: tsadaq OT:6663, "to be righteous, be in the right, be justified, be just." ...The basic meaning of tsadaq is "to be righteous." It is a legal term which involves the whole process of justice. God "is righteous" in all of His relations, and in comparison with Him man is not righteous: "Shall mortal man be more just [righteous] than God?" Job 4:17. In a derived sense, the case presented may be characterized as a just cause in that all facts indicate that the person is to be

cleared of all charges. (from Vine's Expository Dictionary of Biblical Words, Copyright © 1985, Thomas Nelson Publishers.)

[3]Hope: OT:8431 <START HEBREW>tl#j#oT<END HEBREW> tow-cheleth (to-kheh'-leth); from OT:3176; expectation:

OT:3176 <START HEBREW>lj^y*<END HEBREW> yachal (yaw-chal'); a primitive root; to wait; by implication, to be patient, hope: (Biblesoft's New Exhaustive Strong's Numbers and Concordance with Expanded Greek-Hebrew Dictionary. Copyright © 1994, 2003, 2006 Biblesoft, Inc. and International Bible Translators, Inc.)

[4]Expectation: OT:8615 <START HEBREW>hw*q=T!<END HEBREW> tiqvah (tik-vaw'); from OT:6960; literally, a cord (as an attachment [compare OT:6961]); figuratively, expectancy:

OT:6960 <START HEBREW>hw*q*<END HEBREW> qavah (kaw-vaw'); a primitive root; to bind together (perhaps by twisting), i.e. collect; (figuratively) to expect:

OT:6961 <START HEBREW>hw#q*<END HEBREW> qaveh (kaw-veh'); from OT:6960; a (measuring) cord (as if for binding): (Biblesoft's New Exhaustive Strong's Numbers and Concordance with Expanded Greek-Hebrew Dictionary. Copyright © 1994, 2003, 2006 Biblesoft, Inc. and International Bible Translators, Inc.)

20 – A Man's Life is not His Own

Pray: Ask God to prepare your heart and mind and soul to receive his words, to receive truth that will set you free, which will heal and perfect your understanding and knowledge of who God is and who you are.

Ps 119:25-32 - I'm feeling terrible — I couldn't feel worse! Get me on my feet again. You promised, remember? When I told my story, you responded; train me well in your deep wisdom. Help me understand these things inside and out so I can ponder your miracle-wonders. My sad life's dilapidated, a falling-down barn; build me up again by your Word. Barricade the road that goes Nowhere; grace me with your clear revelation. I choose the true road to Somewhere, I post your road signs at every curve and corner. I grasp and cling to whatever you tell me; God, don't let me down! I'll run the course you lay out for me if you'll just show me how. (MSG)

[Murmur and mumble the words. Phrase by phrase. Word by word. Syllable by syllable. Pause. Breathe. Inhale and exhale. Reflect. Listen.]

Journal:

Note how this prayer stirs you today and what you hear God saying to you.

Prov 10:28 - The hope of the righteous brings joy, but the expectation of the wicked will perish.

What does God say about our plans and efforts to determine our life course; to get what we presume is due, proper and necessary for us?

Jer 10:23 - I know, O Lord, that the way of man is not in himself, that it is not in man who walks to direct his steps. (ESV)

Jer 10:23 - I know, O Lord, that a man's life is not his own; it is not for man to direct his steps. (NIV)

Jer 10:23 - I know, God, that mere mortals can't run their own lives, That men and women don't have what it takes to take charge of life.

(MSG)

Prov 19:21 - Many are the plans in the mind of a man, but it is the purpose of the Lord that will stand.

Prov 21:30 - There is no wisdom, understanding, or advice that can succeed against the Lord. (NCV)

I know

I know, ***O Lord***

The ***way of man***

The way of man ***is not*** in himself

A man's life ***is not his own***

Mere mortals ***can't run*** their own lives

It is not in man who walks to direct his steps

It is not for man ***to direct his steps***

Men and women ***don't have what it takes*** to take charge of life

Men and women don't have what it takes ***to take charge of life***

Many are ***the plans***

In the mind of a man

But

But it is ***the purpose*** of the Lord

The purpose ***of the Lord that will stand***

There is ***no wisdom***

There is ***no understanding***

There is ***no advice***

There is no wisdom, understanding, or advice ***that can succeed against the Lord***.

[Murmur and mumble the words. Phrase by phrase. Word by word. Syllable by syllable. Take pleasure in making the sounds of the words, getting the feel of the meaning. Experience pleasurable anticipation of taking in what will make you more yourself, the self that God made in his own image and likeness. The self that God made for intimate communion with him. The self that God created for good works, that you should walk in them. Eat God's words. Let God's words become a joy and the delight of your heart.]

Journal:

What do you hear God saying to you? What does he want from you?

How do you respond to these statements declared by prophet and wisdom? Do you respond with resentment and resistance? With relief? With distrust and suspicion? With confidence and anticipation?

What questions do these statements raise in your mind?

At those times when we think and speak and act as if we are independent or when we long for freedom to have things our own way, is that evidence of just how deceitful and desperately sick our hearts are?

Jer 17:9 - The heart is deceitful above all things, and desperately sick; who can understand it?

Why can't we run our own lives?

Prov 16:2 - All the ways of a man are pure in his own eyes, but the Lord weighs the spirit.

Prov 21:2 - Every way of a man is right in his own eyes, but the Lord weighs the heart.

Prov 16:25 - There is a way that seems right to a man, but its end is the way to death.

Ps 36:1-2 - Transgression speaks to the wicked deep in his heart; there is no fear of God before his eyes. For he flatters himself in his own eyes that his iniquity cannot be found out and hated.

All the ways

Every way

Of a man are pure and right

In his own eyes

But ***the Lord***

But the Lord ***weighs the spirit*** [test, ponder, tell]

The Lord ***weighs the heart***

There is a way that ***seems*** right to a man

But ***its end***

But its end is the ***way to death***

Transgression speaks to the wicked ***deep in his heart***

There is ***no fear of God*** before his eyes

For he ***flatters himself***

He flatters himself ***in his own eyes***

That his iniquity cannot be ***found out***

That his iniquity cannot be found out ***and hated***

I know, O Lord, that a man's ***life*** is not his own

I know, O Lord, that the ***way of man*** is not in himself

I know, God, that mere mortals can't run their ***own lives***, That men and women don't have what it takes to take charge of ***life***.

[Murmur and mumble the words. Phrase by phrase. Word by word. Syllable by syllable. Take pleasure in making the sounds of the words, getting the feel of the meaning. Experience pleasurable anticipation of taking in what will make you more yourself, the self that God made in his own image and likeness. The self that God made for intimate communion with him. The self that God created for good works, that you should walk in them. Eat God's words. Let God's words become a joy and the delight of your heart.]

Ask God to bring the secrets of your heart into the light.

Journal:

Recall a time when you were certain you were correct in your actions or analysis of a situation and later realized you were wrong.

Were there painful consequences? Were relationships damaged?

What do you learn about God and about yourself in these Scripture texts?

Prov 10:28 - The hope of the righteous brings joy, but the expectation of the wicked will perish.

Jer 10:23 - I know, O Lord, that the way of man is not in himself, that it is not in man who walks to direct his steps.

Prov 19:21 - Many are the plans in the mind of a man, but it is the purpose of the Lord that will stand.

Prov 21:30 - There is no wisdom, understanding, or advice that can succeed against the Lord. (NCV)

Prov 16:2 - All the ways of a man are pure in his own eyes, but the Lord weighs the spirit.

Prov 21:2 - Every way of a man is right in his own eyes, but the Lord weighs the heart.

Prov 16:25 - There is a way that seems right to a man, but its end is the way to death.

Ps 36:1-2 - Transgression speaks to the wicked deep in his heart; there is no fear of God before his eyes. For he flatters himself in his own eyes that his iniquity cannot be found out and hated.

[Pause. Breathe. Inhale and exhale. Reflect. Listen.]

Give me life according to your word, God!

Journal:

What do you hear God saying to you in these Scripture texts? What do they reveal about God and about you? Converse with God about what you're hearing him say. Verbalize and describe your thoughts, memories that come to mind, questions and emotions, concerns, desires.

Is there a particular word or phrase that disturbs or soothes you?

Do the Scripture texts create a picture or an impression that draws you to linger in exploring and experiencing it?

Choose a word or a phrase from your meditation to write on a slip of paper to carry with you today. Refer to it often throughout the day to remind you of your conversation with God and to continue the conversation all day long. Throughout the day pause to become aware of your thoughts and feelings and will. Ask yourself, "What drives me in this moment? Life according to God's word? Or life according to someone else's word?"

Anticipate that God's words stirred your heart for a reason. He's conversing with you through them. Anticipate that God will bring his word to life in you, to bear fruit in your heart and mind and soul and body. Anticipate that God will reveal the secrets of your heart, for anything that is visible is light. And anticipate that God will cause his words to become a joy and the delight of your heart.

CONTEMPLATE

God is spirit, and those who worship him must worship in spirit and truth. Seek him. Feel your way to him. Reach out. Find him.

Inhale deeply, aware that God *is* in your hidden parts, that it is *his* breath that makes you understand his word. Exhale. Give God the gift that he most desires from you, your exposed and surrendered heart, mind, soul, spirit, and body, your whole self, both outer and inner.

Each time you find that your outer self has pulled your attention away, quietly and gently say the word or phrase you chose and then dive back down deep to the hidden person of your heart to return to the Lord. Bask in him. Rest in perfect love.

At the end of your contemplation, inhale deeply and hold it for a second, aware that you exist in God's abounding grace. Only in God's abounding grace do you exist. In God's abounding grace you are you, the real you, able to worship God in spirit and truth.

2 Cor 9:8 - And ***God is able*** *to make all grace abound to you, so that having all sufficiency in all things at all times,* ***you may*** *abound in every good work.*

Exhale slowly and deeply, anticipating that God's abounding grace, in which you exist and are, will flow around you and through you to enlighten and empower you to love as you have been loved so that you may abound in every good work this day.

21 – By the Power of the Holy Spirit

Pray: Ask God to prepare your heart and mind and soul to receive his words, to receive truth that will set you free, which will heal and perfect your understanding and knowledge of who God is and who you are.

Ps 119:25-32 - My soul clings to the dust; give me life according to your word! When I told of my ways, you answered me; teach me your statutes! Make me understand the way of your precepts, and I will meditate on your wondrous works. My soul melts away for sorrow; strengthen me according to your word! Put false ways far from me and graciously teach me your law! I have chosen the way of faithfulness; I set your rules before me. I cling to your testimonies, O Lord; let me not be put to shame! I will run in the way of your commandments when you enlarge my heart! (ESV)

[Murmur and mumble the words. Phrase by phrase. Word by word. Syllable by syllable. Pause. Breathe. Inhale and exhale. Reflect. Listen.]

Journal:

Note how this prayer stirs you today and what you hear God saying to you.

Jer 10:23 - I know, O Lord, that a man's life is not his own; it is not for man to direct his steps. (NIV)

If our life is not our own, and we cannot direct our steps and take charge of our life, what then should occupy our time and attention and efforts?

Prov 30:12 - There are those who are clean [pure] in their own eyes but are not washed of their filth [excrement, dirt, pollution[1]].

Ps 7:9 - Oh, let the evil of the wicked come to an end, and may you establish the righteous—you who test the minds and hearts, O righteous God!

There are those who are clean ***in their own eyes***

But ***are not washed*** of their filth

Oh, let the ***evil*** [to spoil by breaking to pieces, to be good for nothing, bad physically, socially or morally[2]]

Let the evil of the ***wicked*** [morally wrong]

Come to an ***end***

And may ***you***

May you ***establish*** the righteous

Establish: to be erect i.e. stand perpendicular; to set up, render sure, proper or prosperous[3]

And may you establish the ***righteous***

You who ***test***

You who test the ***minds and hearts***

O ***righteous*** God

[Murmur and mumble the words. Phrase by phrase. Word by word. Syllable by syllable. Take pleasure in making the sounds of the words, getting the feel of the meaning. Experience pleasurable anticipation of taking in what will make you more yourself, the self that God made in his own image and likeness. The self that God made for intimate communion with him. The self that God created for good works, that you should walk in them. Eat God's words. Let God's words become a joy and the delight of your heart.]

Journal:

What do you discover about yourself and about God in these Scripture texts?

If our life is not our own, and we cannot direct our steps and take charge of our life, what then should occupy our time and attention and efforts? What is the purpose and pleasure of the Lord?

Rom 15:8-13 - For I tell you that Christ became a servant to the circumcised to show God's truthfulness, in order to confirm the promises given to the patriarchs, and in order that the Gentiles might glorify God for his mercy. As it is written, "Therefore I will praise you among the Gentiles, and sing to your name."

And again it is said, "Rejoice, O Gentiles, with his people." And again, "Praise the Lord, all you Gentiles, and let all the peoples extol him." And again Isaiah says, "The root of Jesse will come, even he who arises to rule the Gentiles; in him will the Gentiles hope."

May the God of hope fill you with all joy and peace in believing, so that by the power of the Holy Spirit you may abound in hope.

Christ

Christ became ***a servant***

To show

To show God's truthfulness to the circumcised [Israel]

In order to ***confirm***

To confirm the promises given to the patriarchs [Abraham, Isaac, Jacob]

In order

In order that the Gentiles

In order that the Gentiles ***might glorify God for his mercy***

Rejoice, O Gentiles, ***with*** his people

Praise the Lord, all you Gentiles, and ***let all the peoples*** extol him

The root of Jesse [Christ Jesus] ***will come***

Even he who arises ***to rule*** [to be first]

Even he who arises to rule the Gentiles; ***in him will the Gentiles hope*** [trust; anticipate, usually with pleasure; confidence]

May the ***God of hope***

May the God of hope ***fill you...***

May the God of hope fill you ***with all joy***

May the God of hope fill you with all joy ***and peace***

Fill you with all joy and peace ***in believing*** [in entrusting your soul to Christ[4]]

So that

So that ***by the power of the Holy Spirit***

So that by the power of the Holy Spirit ***you may abound in hope***

Abound in hope. Trust. Anticipate with pleasure and confidence. To wait. To be patient. Those who take refuge in God.

[Murmur and mumble the words. Phrase by phrase. Word by word. Syllable by syllable. Take pleasure in making the sounds of the words, getting the feel of the meaning. Experience pleasurable anticipation of taking in what will make you more yourself, the self that God made in his own image and likeness. The self that God made for intimate communion with him. The self that God created for good works, that you should walk in them. Eat God's words. Let God's words become a joy and the delight of your heart.]

Journal:

In your own words record what you hear God saying to you in these Scripture texts about your life not being your own, your inability to direct your steps, and Christ's role in accomplishing God's promises and purposes for you.

Jer 10:23 - I know, O Lord, that the way of man is not in himself, that it is not in man who walks to direct his steps. (ESV)

Prov 30:12 - There are those who are clean in their own eyes but are not washed of their filth.

Ps 7:9 - Oh, let the evil of the wicked come to an end, and may you establish the righteous—you who test the minds and hearts, O righteous God!

Jer 17:9 - The heart is deceitful above all things, and desperately sick; who can understand it?

Rom 15:8-13 - For I tell you that Christ became a servant to the circumcised to show God's truthfulness, in order to confirm the promises given to the patriarchs, and in order that the Gentiles might glorify God for his mercy. As it is written, "Therefore I will praise you among the Gentiles, and sing to your name."

And again it is said, "Rejoice, O Gentiles, with his people." And again, "Praise the Lord, all you Gentiles, and let all the peoples extol him." And again Isaiah says, "The root of Jesse will come, even he who arises to rule the Gentiles; in him will the Gentiles hope."

May the God of hope fill you with all joy and peace in believing, so that by the power of the Holy Spirit you may abound in hope.

[Pause. Breathe. Inhale and exhale. Reflect. Listen.]

Give me life according to your word, God!

Journal:

What do you hear God saying to you in these Scripture texts? What do they reveal about God and about you? Converse with God about what you're hearing him say. Verbalize and describe your thoughts, memories that come to mind, questions and emotions, concerns, desires.

Is there a particular word or phrase that disturbs or soothes you?

Do the Scripture texts create a picture or an impression that draws you to linger in exploring and experiencing it?

Choose a word or a phrase from your meditation to write on a slip of paper to carry with you today. Refer to it often throughout the day to remind you of your conversation with God and to continue the conversation all day long. Throughout the day pause to become aware of your thoughts and feelings and will. Ask yourself, "What drives me in this moment? Life according to God's word? Or life according to someone else's word?"

Anticipate that God's words stirred your heart for a reason. He's conversing with you through them. Anticipate that God will bring his word to life in you, to bear fruit in your heart and mind and soul and body. Anticipate that God will reveal the secrets of your heart, for anything that is visible is light. And anticipate that God will cause his words to become a joy and the delight of your heart.

CONTEMPLATE

God is spirit, and those who worship him must worship in spirit and truth. Seek him. Feel your way to him. Reach out. Find him.

Inhale deeply, aware that God *is* in your hidden parts, that it is *his* breath that makes you understand his word. Exhale. Give God the gift that he most desires from you, your exposed and surrendered heart, mind, soul, spirit, and body, your whole self, both outer and inner.

Each time you find that your outer self has pulled your attention away, quietly and gently say the word or phrase you chose and then dive back down deep to the hidden person of your heart to return to the Lord. Bask in him. Rest in perfect love.

At the end of your contemplation, inhale deeply and hold it for a second, aware that you exist in God's abounding grace. Only in God's abounding grace do you exist. In God's abounding grace you are you, the real you, able to worship God in spirit and truth.

*2 Cor 9:8 - And **God is able** to make all grace abound to you, so that having all sufficiency in all things at all times, **you may** abound in every good work.*

Exhale slowly and deeply, anticipating that God's abounding grace, in which you exist and are, will flow around you and through you to enlighten and empower you to love as you have been loved so that you may abound in every good work this day.

Resources:

[1]Filth: OT:6675 <START HEBREW>ha*ox<END HEBREW> tsow'ah (tso-aw'); or tso'ah (tso-aw'): feminine of OT:6674; excrement; generally, dirt; figuratively, pollution: (Biblesoft's New Exhaustive Strong's Numbers and Concordance with Expanded Greek-Hebrew Dictionary. Copyright © 1994, 2003, 2006, 2010 Biblesoft, Inc. and International Bible Translators, Inc.)

[2]Evil: OT:7489 <START HEBREW>uu^r*<END HEBREW> ra`a` (raw-ah'); a primitive root; properly, to spoil (literally, by breaking to pieces); figuratively, to make (or be) good for nothing, i.e. bad (physically, socially or morally): (Biblesoft's New Exhaustive Strong's Numbers and Concordance with Expanded Greek-Hebrew Dictionary. Copyright © 1994, 2003, 2006, 2010 Biblesoft, Inc. and International Bible Translators, Inc.)

[3]Establish: OT:3559 <START HEBREW>/WK<END HEBREW> kuwn (koon); a primitive root; properly, to be erect (i.e. stand perpendicular); hence (causatively) to set up, in a great variety of applications,

whether literal (establish, fix, prepare, apply), or figurative (appoint, render sure, proper or prosperous): (Biblesoft's New Exhaustive Strong's Numbers and Concordance with Expanded Greek-Hebrew Dictionary. Copyright © 1994, 2003, 2006, 2010 Biblesoft, Inc. and International Bible Translators, Inc.)

[4]Believing: NT:4100<START GREEK>pisteu/w<END GREEK> pisteuo (pist-yoo'-o); from NT:4102; to have faith (in, upon, or with respect to, a person or thing), i.e. credit; by implication, to entrust (especially one's spiritual well-being to Christ):

NT:4102<START GREEK>pi/sti$<END GREEK> pistis (pis'-tis); from NT:3982; persuasion, i.e. credence; moral conviction (of religious truth, or the truthfulness of God or a religious teacher), especially reliance upon Christ for salvation; abstractly, constancy in such profession; by extension, the system of religious (Gospel) truth itself:

NT:3982<START GREEK>pei/qw<END GREEK> peitho (pi'-tho); a primary verb; to convince (by argument, true or false); by analogy, to pacify or conciliate (by other fair means); reflexively or passively, to assent (to evidence or authority), to rely (by inward certainty): (Biblesoft's New Exhaustive Strong's Numbers and Concordance with Expanded Greek-Hebrew Dictionary. Copyright © 1994, 2003, 2006, 2010 Biblesoft, Inc. and International Bible Translators, Inc.)

22 - The Lord Will Fulfill His Purpose for Me

Pray: Ask God to prepare your heart and mind and soul to receive his words, to receive truth that will set you free, which will heal and perfect your understanding and knowledge of who God is and who you are.

Ps 119:25-32 - I'm feeling terrible — I couldn't feel worse! Get me on my feet again. You promised, remember? When I told my story, you responded; train me well in your deep wisdom. Help me understand these things inside and out so I can ponder your miracle-wonders. My sad life's dilapidated, a falling-down barn; build me up again by your Word. Barricade the road that goes Nowhere; grace me with your clear revelation. I choose the true road to Somewhere, I post your road signs at every curve and corner. I grasp and cling to whatever you tell me; God, don't let me down! I'll run the course you lay out for me if you'll just show me how. (MSG)

[Murmur and mumble the words. Phrase by phrase. Word by word. Syllable by syllable. Pause. Breathe. Inhale and exhale. Reflect. Listen.]

Journal:

Note how this prayer stirs you today and what you hear God saying to you.

Ps 138:8 - The Lord will fulfill his purpose for me; your steadfast love, O Lord, endures forever. Do not forsake the work of your hands. (ESV)

Ps 138:8 - The Lord will perfect that which concerns me; Your mercy, O Lord, endures forever; Do not forsake the works of Your hands. (NKJV)

Ps 138:8 - Jehovah doth perfect for me, O Jehovah, Thy kindness [is] to the age, The works of Thy hands let not fall! (YLT)

The Lord ***will*** fulfill. The Lord ***will*** perfect. The Lord ***will*** complete

The Lord will fulfill ***his purpose*** for me

The Lord will perfect ***that which concerns me***

Your steadfast ***love***, O Lord

Your ***mercy***, O Lord. Your kindness. Your favor.

Your ***steadfast*** love, O Lord, is to the age. Your steadfast ***love***, O Lord, endures forever.

Do not forsake. Do not slacken. Do not cease. Do not fail. Do not let alone the works of your hands.

Do not forsake the actions, the transactions, the product, the property of your hands.

Do not forsake ***me***, the work of your hands, O Lord.

[Murmur and mumble the words. Phrase by phrase. Word by word. Syllable by syllable. Take pleasure in making the sounds of the words, getting the feel of the meaning. Experience pleasurable anticipation of taking in what will make you more yourself, the self that God made in his own image and likeness. The self that God made for intimate communion with him. The self that God created for good works, that you should walk in them. Eat God's words. Let God's words become a joy and the delight of your heart.]

Journal:

Describe the confidence that David expressed in God in this Scripture text.

Yet he asks God not to forsake the work of his hands. Are you ever concerned that God might forsake you?

Ps 7:9 - Oh, let the evil of the wicked come to an end, and may you establish the righteous—you who test the minds and hearts, O righteous God!

Oh, let the ***evil*** of the wicked

Let what is spoiled ***in me***, what is broken, what is good for nothing, what is bad physically, socially and morally ***come to an end***.

May you ***establish*** the righteous

May you cause ***me*** to stand among the righteous. Cause ***me*** to become sure, proper, right.

You who ***test*** the minds and hearts

O God test ***my*** mind and heart

O ***righteous*** God

Fill ***me*** with all joy and peace in believing, in entrusting my soul to Christ Jesus

So that ***by the power*** of the Holy Spirit

I, ***even I***, may abound in hope.

By the power ***of the Holy Spirit***

The Lord ***will*** fulfill. The Lord ***will*** perfect. The Lord ***will*** complete.

The Lord will fulfill ***his purpose***

The Lord will fulfill his purpose ***for me***.

The Lord will perfect ***that which concerns me***.

Your steadfast love, O Lord, ***endures forever***.

Your steadfast love ***for me***, O Lord, endures forever.

Do not forsake the work of your hands.

[Murmur and mumble the words. Phrase by phrase. Word by word. Syllable by syllable. Take pleasure in making the sounds of the words, getting the feel of the meaning. Experience pleasurable anticipation of taking in what will make you more yourself, the self that God made in his own image and likeness. The self that God made for intimate communion with him. The self that God created for good works, that you should walk in them. Eat God's words. Let God's words become a joy and the delight of your heart.]

Journal:

Was it himself that David referred to when he asked God to let the evil of the wicked come to an end?

Was it himself that David referred to when he asked God to establish the righteous?

Is bringing the evil of the wicked to an end and establishing the righteous the goal and end result of the righteous God testing the hearts and minds of all of humankind?

Do you recognize yourself as being both the wicked and the righteous? Do you regularly invite and welcome the righteous God to test your heart and mind?

Record your response to David's prayer and his confidence in God.

Ps 138:8 - The Lord will fulfill his purpose for me; your steadfast love, O Lord, endures forever. Do not forsake the work of your hands. (ESV)

Ps 7:9 - Oh, let the evil of the wicked come to an end, and may you establish the righteous—you who test the minds and hearts, O righteous God!

[Pause. Breathe. Inhale and exhale. Reflect. Listen.]

Give me life according to your word, God!

Journal:

What do you hear God saying to you in these Scripture texts? What do they reveal about God and about you? Converse with God about what you're hearing him say. Verbalize and describe your thoughts, memories that come to mind, questions and emotions, concerns, desires.

Is there a particular word or phrase that disturbs or soothes you?

Do the Scripture texts create a picture or an impression that draws you to linger in exploring and experiencing it?

Choose a word or a phrase from your meditation to write on a slip of paper to carry with you today. Refer to it often throughout the day to remind you of your conversation with God and to continue the conversation all day long. Throughout the day pause to become aware of your thoughts and feelings and will. Ask yourself, "What drives me in this moment? Life according to God's word? Or life according to someone else's word?"

Anticipate that God's words stirred your heart for a reason. He's conversing with you through them. Anticipate that God will bring his word to life in you, to bear fruit in your heart and mind and soul and body. Anticipate that God will reveal the secrets of your heart, for anything that is visible is light. And anticipate that God will cause his words to become a joy and the delight of your heart.

CONTEMPLATE

God is spirit, and those who worship him must worship in spirit and truth. Seek him. Feel your way to him. Reach out. Find him.

Inhale deeply, aware that God *is* in your hidden parts, that it is *his* breath that makes you understand his word. Exhale. Give God the gift that he most desires from you, your exposed and surrendered heart, mind, soul, spirit, and body, your whole self, both outer and inner.

Each time you find that your outer self has pulled your attention away, quietly and gently say the word or phrase you chose and then dive back down deep to the hidden person of your heart to return to the Lord. Bask in him. Rest in perfect love.

At the end of your contemplation, inhale deeply and hold it for a second, aware that you exist in God's abounding grace. Only in God's abounding grace do you exist. In God's abounding grace you are you, the real you, able to worship God in spirit and truth.

*2 Cor 9:8 - And **God is able** to make all grace abound to you, so that having all sufficiency in all things at all times, **you may** abound in every good work.*

Exhale slowly and deeply, anticipating that God's abounding grace, in which you exist and are, will flow around you and through you to enlighten and empower you to love as you have been loved so that you may abound in every good work this day.

23 – Reconciled to God While We Were Enemies

Pray: Ask God to prepare your heart and mind and soul to receive his words, to receive truth that will set you free, which will heal and perfect your understanding and knowledge of who God is and who you are.

Ps 119:25-32 - My soul clings to the dust; give me life according to your word! When I told of my ways, you answered me; teach me your statutes! Make me understand the way of your precepts, and I will meditate on your wondrous works. My soul melts away for sorrow; strengthen me according to your word! Put false ways far from me and graciously teach me your law! I have chosen the way of faithfulness; I set your rules before me. I cling to your testimonies, O Lord; let me not be put to shame! I will run in the way of your commandments when you enlarge my heart! (ESV)

[Murmur and mumble the words. Phrase by phrase. Word by word. Syllable by syllable. Pause. Breathe. Inhale and exhale. Reflect. Listen.]

Journal:

Note how this prayer stirs you today and what you hear God saying to you.

Rom 5:10-11 - For if while we were enemies we were reconciled to God by the death of his Son, much more, now that we are reconciled, shall we be saved by his life. More than that, we also rejoice in God through our Lord Jesus Christ, through whom we have now received reconciliation.

For if ***while***

While ***we were*** enemies

For if while we were ***enemies***

We ***were reconciled*** to God

While we were enemies

We were reconciled to God by the ***death*** of ***his Son***

By the death of his Son

We ***were reconciled***

While we were enemies

Much more

Now

Now that ***we are***

Now that we ***are reconciled***

Much more, now that we are reconciled, shall we be ***saved***

Much more, now that we are reconciled, shall we be saved ***by his life.***

Reconciled [to change mutually[1]]

Mutually. A sharing jointly. Done, felt, etc. by each for or toward the other.

Reconciled to God ***by the death*** of his Son

While we were enemies

Saved

Saved [delivered, protected[2]] ***by the life*** of his Son.

More than that

We also rejoice ***in God***

Rejoice

Through our Lord Jesus Christ

Through whom ***we have now received*** reconciliation

While we were enemies ***we were*** reconciled to God by the death of his Son

Through our Lord Jesus Christ

Through. By means of. As a result of. Extending from one place to another.

Through our Lord Jesus Christ ***we have now received*** [to take, to get hold of]

Reconciliation

Through ***our Lord*** Jesus Christ

[Murmur and mumble the words. Phrase by phrase. Word by word. Syllable by syllable. Take pleasure in making the sounds of the words, getting the feel of the meaning. Experience pleasurable anticipation of taking in what will make you more yourself, the self that God made in his own image and likeness. The self that God made for intimate communion with him. The self that God created for good works, that you should walk in them. Eat God's words. Let God's words become a joy and the delight of your heart.]

Journal:

What does it mean to be God's enemy? Are/were you God's enemy? Explain.

What did God do for all of us while we were his enemies? How did he accomplish that for us?

What does it mean to be reconciled? Are you reconciled to God?

..."to change, exchange" (especially of money); hence, of persons, "to change from enmity to friendship, to reconcile." With regard to the relationship between God and man, the use of this and connected words shows that primarily <u>"reconciliation" is what God accomplishes, exercising His grace towards sinful man</u> on the ground of the death of Christ in propitiatory sacrifice under the judgment due to sin... By reason of this men in their sinful condition and alienation from God are invited to be "reconciled" to Him; that is to say, to change their attitude, and accept the provision God has made, whereby their sins can be remitted and they themselves be justified in His sight in Christ.

Rom 5:10 expresses this in another way: "For if, while we were enemies, we were reconciled to God through the death of His Son..."; that we were "enemies" not only <u>expresses man's hostile attitude to</u>

God but signifies that until this change of attitude takes place men are under condemnation, exposed to God's wrath. The death of His Son is the means of the removal of this, and thus we "receive the reconciliation,"[3]

Take time to ponder and meditate on God's gift of reconciliation.

Humankind is under condemnation, exposed to God's wrath until their hostile attitude to God changes. Reconciliation. To be changed mutually. Done, felt, etc. by each for or toward the other. Reconciliation is what God accomplishes, exercising his grace towards sinful man on the ground of the death of Christ Jesus. The death of Christ Jesus is the means of the removal of man's hostile attitude to God, and thus the removal of condemnation.

Rom 5:10-11 - For if while we were enemies we were reconciled to God by the death of his Son, much more, now that we are reconciled, shall we be saved by his life. More than that, we also rejoice in God through our Lord Jesus Christ, through whom we have now received reconciliation.

Are you aware of the gift that God has given you through his Son?

What does God want from you in response?

Rom 5:10-11 - For if while we were enemies we were reconciled to God by the death of his Son, much more, now that we are reconciled, shall we be saved by his life. More than that, we also rejoice in God through our Lord Jesus Christ, through whom we have now received reconciliation.

[Pause. Breathe. Inhale and exhale. Reflect. Listen.]

Give me life according to your word, God!

Journal:

What do you hear God saying to you in these Scripture texts? What do they reveal about God and about you? Converse with God about what you're hearing him say. Verbalize and describe your thoughts, memories that come to mind, questions and emotions, concerns, desires.

Is there a particular word or phrase that disturbs or soothes you?

Do the Scripture texts create a picture or an impression that draws you to linger in exploring and experiencing it?

Choose a word or a phrase from your meditation to write on a slip of paper to carry with you today. Refer to it often throughout the day to remind you of your conversation with God and to continue the conversation all day long. Throughout the day pause to become aware of your thoughts and feelings and will. Ask yourself, "What drives me in this moment? Life according to God's word? Or life according to someone else's word?"

Anticipate that God's words stirred your heart for a reason. He's conversing with you through them. Anticipate that God will bring his word to life in you, to bear fruit in your heart and mind and soul and body. Anticipate that God will reveal the secrets of your heart, for anything that is visible is light. And anticipate that God will cause his words to become a joy and the delight of your heart.

CONTEMPLATE

God is spirit, and those who worship him must worship in spirit and truth. Seek him. Feel your way to him. Reach out. Find him.

Inhale deeply, aware that God *is* in your hidden parts, that it is *his* breath that makes you understand his word. Exhale. Give God the gift that he most desires from you, your exposed and surrendered heart, mind, soul, spirit, and body, your whole self, both outer and inner.

Each time you find that your outer self has pulled your attention away, quietly and gently say the word or phrase you chose and then dive back down deep to the hidden person of your heart to return to the Lord. Bask in him. Rest in perfect love.

At the end of your contemplation, inhale deeply and hold it for a second, aware that you exist in God's abounding grace. Only in God's abounding grace do you exist. In God's abounding grace you are you, the real you, able to worship God in spirit and truth.

2 Cor 9:8 - And ***God is able*** *to make all grace abound to you, so that having all sufficiency in all things at all times,* ***you may*** *abound in every good work.*

Exhale slowly and deeply, anticipating that God's abounding grace, in which you exist and are, will flow around you and through you to enlighten and empower you to love as you have been loved so that you may abound in every good work this day.

Resources:

[1]Reconciled: NT:2644<START GREEK>katalla/ssw<END GREEK> katallasso (kat-al-las'-so); from NT:2596 and NT:236; to change mutually, i.e. (figuratively) to compound a difference:

NT:236<START GREEK>a)lla/ssw<END GREEK> allasso (al-las'-so); from NT:243; to make different: (Biblesoft's New Exhaustive Strong's Numbers and Concordance with Expanded Greek-Hebrew Dictionary. Copyright © 1994, 2003, 2006, 2010 Biblesoft, Inc. and International Bible Translators, Inc.)

[2]We shall be saved: NT:4982<START GREEK>sw/zw<END GREEK> sozo (sode'-zo); from a primary sos (contraction for obsolete saoz, "safe"); to save, i.e. deliver or protect (literally or figuratively): (Biblesoft's New Exhaustive Strong's Numbers and Concordance with Expanded Greek-Hebrew Dictionary. Copyright © 1994, 2003, 2006, 2010 Biblesoft, Inc. and International Bible Translators, Inc.)

[3]Reconciled: Katallasso (<START GREEK>katalla/ssw<END GREEK>, NT:2644) properly denotes "to change, exchange" (especially of money); hence, of persons, "to change from enmity to

friendship, to reconcile." With regard to the relationship between God and man, the use of this and connected words shows that primarily "reconciliation" is what God accomplishes, exercising His grace towards sinful man on the ground of the death of Christ in propitiatory sacrifice under the judgment due to sin, 2 Cor 5:19, where both the verb and the noun are used (cf. No. 2, in Col 1:21). By reason of this men in their sinful condition and alienation from God are invited to be "reconciled" to Him; that is to say, to change their attitude, and accept the provision God has made, whereby their sins can be remitted and they themselves be justified in His sight in Christ.

Rom 5:10 expresses this in another way: "For if, while we were enemies, we were reconciled to God through the death of His Son..."; that we were "enemies" not only expresses man's hostile attitude to God but signifies that until this change of attitude takes place men are under condemnation, exposed to God's wrath. The death of His Son is the means of the removal of this, and thus we "receive the reconciliation," (from Vine's Expository Dictionary of Biblical Words, Copyright © 1985, Thomas Nelson Publishers.)

24 – Come Now, Let Us Reason Together

Pray: Ask God to prepare your heart and mind and soul to receive his words, to receive truth that will set you free, which will heal and perfect your understanding and knowledge of who God is and who you are.

Ps 119:25-32 - I'm feeling terrible — I couldn't feel worse! Get me on my feet again. You promised, remember? When I told my story, you responded; train me well in your deep wisdom. Help me understand these things inside and out so I can ponder your miracle-wonders. My sad life's dilapidated, a falling-down barn; build me up again by your Word. Barricade the road that goes Nowhere; grace me with your clear revelation. I choose the true road to Somewhere, I post your road signs at every curve and corner. I grasp and cling to whatever you tell me; God, don't let me down! I'll run the course you lay out for me if you'll just show me how. (MSG)

[Murmur and mumble the words. Phrase by phrase. Word by word. Syllable by syllable. Pause. Breathe. Inhale and exhale. Reflect. Listen.]

Journal:

Note how this prayer stirs you today and what you hear God saying to you.

Rom 5:10-11 - For if while we were enemies we were reconciled to God by the death of his Son, much more, now that we are reconciled, shall we be saved by his life. More than that, we also rejoice in God through our Lord Jesus Christ, through whom we have now received reconciliation.

Are you aware of the gift that God has given you through his Son?

What does God want from you in response?

Jer 2:5 - Thus says the Lord: "What wrong did your fathers find in me that they went far from me, and went after worthlessness, and became worthless?

2 Cor 5:20b-21 - ...We implore you on behalf of Christ, be reconciled to God. For our sake he [God] made him [Christ] to be sin who knew no sin, so that in him we might become the righteousness of God.

Job 22:21 - "Agree with God, and be at peace; thereby good will come to you.

Isa 1:18 - "Come now, let us reason together, says the Lord: though your sins are like scarlet, they shall be as white as snow; though they are red like crimson, they shall become like wool.

Rom 8:32 - He who did not spare his own Son but gave him up for us all, how will he not also with him graciously give us all things?

What wrong did your fathers find in me?

What wrong did you ***find in me***?

They ***went***

They went ***far from me***

They went ***after worthlessness***

They ***became worthless***

We ***implore*** you [beseech; to call near, i.e. invite; ask or beg earnestly; urge, encourage, incite; solace[1]]

We implore you ***on behalf of Christ***

Be reconciled to God

For ***our sake***

For our sake ***he [God] made him***

For our sake he made him [Christ] to ***be sin*** who knew no sin

So that ***in him***

So that in him ***we might become*** the righteousness of God

Agree with God

And ***be at peace***

"Come now, ***let us reason together***," says the Lord.

Let us reason together. To be right i.e. correct; reciprocal, to argue; causatively, to decide, justify or convict: appoint, argue, chasten, convince, dispute, judge, maintain, plead, rebuke, reprove.[2]

Though your sins ***are like*** scarlet

They ***shall be*** as white as snow

Though they ***are*** red like crimson

They ***shall become*** like wool

He who did not spare ***his own Son***

He who did not spare his own Son but ***gave him up for us all***

How will he not ***also with him***...?

How will he not also with him ***graciously give us all things***?

[Murmur and mumble the words. Phrase by phrase. Word by word. Syllable by syllable. Take pleasure in making the sounds of the words, getting the feel of the meaning. Experience pleasurable anticipation of taking in what will make you more yourself, the self that God made in his own image and likeness. The self that God made for intimate communion with him. The self that God created for good works, that you should walk in them. Eat God's words. Let God's words become a joy and the delight of your heart.]

Journal:

Can you identify with Abraham's descendants? Have you gone far from God? Have you gone after worthlessness? Describe.

What does it mean to become worthless?

How has God responded to those who have gone far from him, going after worthless things, and becoming worthless?

Are you willing to reason together with God about your desire and/or state of independence from him so your sin shall be as white as snow and shall become like wool? Clean. Pure. Forgiven. One with Christ Jesus and with God.

Why would anyone not want to receive reconciliation with God?

Do you have confidence that he who loves you as he loves his own Son, and did not spare his own Son but gave him up for you, will also with him graciously give you whatever you need so can and will receive his gift, so you will take or get hold of reconciliation?

Much more, now that we are reconciled, shall we be saved by the life of his Son! What does it mean to be saved by the life of Christ Jesus? Are you saved by the life of Christ Jesus?

Rom 5:10-11 - For if while we were enemies we were reconciled to God by the death of his Son, much more, now that we are reconciled, shall we be saved by his life. More than that, we also rejoice in God through our Lord Jesus Christ, through whom we have now received reconciliation.

Jer 2:5 - Thus says the Lord: "What wrong did your fathers find in me that they went far from me, and went after worthlessness, and became worthless?

2 Cor 5:20b-21 - …We implore you on behalf of Christ, be reconciled to God. For our sake he made him to be sin who knew no sin, so that in him we might become the righteousness of God.

Job 22:21 - "Agree with God, and be at peace; thereby good will come to you.

Isa 1:18 - "Come now, let us reason together, says the Lord: though your sins are like scarlet, they shall be as white as snow; though they are red like crimson, they shall become like wool.

Rom 8:32 - He who did not spare his own Son but gave him up for us all, how will he not also with him graciously give us all things?

[Pause. Breathe. Inhale and exhale. Reflect. Listen.]

Give me life according to your word, God!

Journal:

What do you hear God saying to you in these Scripture texts? What do they reveal about God and about you? Converse with God about what you're hearing him say. Verbalize and describe your thoughts, memories that come to mind, questions and emotions, concerns, desires.

Is there a particular word or phrase that disturbs or soothes you?

Do the Scripture texts create a picture or an impression that draws you to linger in exploring and experiencing it?

Choose a word or a phrase from your meditation to write on a slip of paper to carry with you today. Refer to it often throughout the day to remind you of your conversation with God and to continue the conversation all day long. Throughout the day pause to become aware of your thoughts and feelings and will. Ask yourself, "What drives me in this moment? Life according to God's word? Or life according to someone else's word?"

Anticipate that God's words stirred your heart for a reason. He's conversing with you through them. Anticipate that God will bring his word to life in you, to bear fruit in your heart and mind and soul and body. Anticipate that God will reveal the secrets of your heart, for anything that is visible is light. And anticipate that God will cause his words to become a joy and the delight of your heart.

CONTEMPLATE

God is spirit, and those who worship him must worship in spirit and truth. Seek him. Feel your way to him. Reach out. Find him.

Inhale deeply, aware that God *is* in your hidden parts, that it is *his* breath that makes you understand his word. Exhale. Give God the gift that he most desires from you, your exposed and surrendered heart, mind, soul, spirit, and body, your whole self, both outer and inner.

Each time you find that your outer self has pulled your attention away, quietly and gently say the word or phrase you chose and then dive back down deep to the hidden person of your heart to return to the Lord. Bask in him. Rest in perfect love.

At the end of your contemplation, inhale deeply and hold it for a second, aware that you exist in God's abounding grace. Only in God's abounding grace do you exist. In God's abounding grace you are you, the real you, able to worship God in spirit and truth.

*2 Cor 9:8 - And **God is able** to make all grace abound to you, so that having all sufficiency in all things at all times, **you may** abound in every good work.*

Exhale slowly and deeply, anticipating that God's abounding grace, in which you exist and are, will flow around you and through you to enlighten and empower you to love as you have been loved so that you may abound in every good work this day.

Resources:

[1]Implore/beseech: NT:3870 <START GREEK>parakale/w<END GREEK> parakaleo (par-ak-al-eh'-o); from NT:3844 and NT:2564; to call near, i.e. invite, invoke (by imploration, hortation or consolation):

(Biblesoft's New Exhaustive Strong's Numbers and Concordance with Expanded Greek-Hebrew Dictionary. Copyright © 1994, 2003, 2006, 2010 Biblesoft, Inc. and International Bible Translators, Inc.). Also Webster's Dictionary.

[2]Let us reason together: OT:3198 <START HEBREW>jk^y*<END HEBREW> yakach (yaw-kahh'); a primitive root; to be right (i.e. correct); reciprocal, to argue; causatively, to decide, justify or convict: -appoint, argue, chasten, convince, correct (-ion), daysman, dispute, judge, maintain, plead, reason (together), rebuke, reprove (-r), surely, in any wise. (Biblesoft's New Exhaustive Strong's Numbers and Concordance with Expanded Greek-Hebrew Dictionary. Copyright © 1994, 2003, 2006, 2010 Biblesoft, Inc. and International Bible Translators, Inc.)

25 – The Lord Takes Pleasure

Pray: Ask God to prepare your heart and mind and soul to receive his words, to receive truth that will set you free, which will heal and perfect your understanding and knowledge of who God is and who you are.

Ps 119:25-32 - My soul clings to the dust; give me life according to your word! When I told of my ways, you answered me; teach me your statutes! Make me understand the way of your precepts, and I will meditate on your wondrous works. My soul melts away for sorrow; strengthen me according to your word! Put false ways far from me and graciously teach me your law! I have chosen the way of faithfulness; I set your rules before me. I cling to your testimonies, O Lord; let me not be put to shame! I will run in the way of your commandments when you enlarge my heart! (ESV)

[Murmur and mumble the words. Phrase by phrase. Word by word. Syllable by syllable. Pause. Breathe. Inhale and exhale. Reflect. Listen.]

Journal:

Note how this prayer stirs you today and what you hear God saying to you.

Rom 5:10-11 - For if while we were enemies we were reconciled to God by the death of his Son, much more, now that we are reconciled, shall we be saved by his life. More than that, we also rejoice in God through our Lord Jesus Christ, through whom we have now received reconciliation.

For if while we were enemies we ***were reconciled*** to God <u>by the death of his Son</u>

Much more, now that we ***are reconciled***, shall we be ***saved*** by <u>his life</u>!

How are we saved by Christ Jesus' life?

Heb 7:23-25 - The former priests were many in number, because they were prevented by death from continuing in office, but he [Christ

Jesus] holds his priesthood permanently, because he continues forever. Consequently, he is able to save to the uttermost those who draw near to God through him [Christ Jesus], since he always lives to make intercession for them.

Priesthood

Christ Jesus holds his priesthood ***permanently***

He continues ***forever***

Consequently, ***he is able to save to the uttermost*** *[full ended, entire]*

Consequently, he is able to save to the uttermost ***those who draw near to God*** [approach, come near, worship, assent to]

Those who draw near to God ***through Christ Jesus***, he is able to save to the uttermost

Through Christ Jesus [the channel of an act]

Since Christ Jesus always lives to make ***intercession*** for them [to chance upon, i.e. by implication confer with; by extension to entreat in favor or against[1]]

[Murmur and mumble the words. Phrase by phrase. Word by word. Syllable by syllable. Take pleasure in making the sounds of the words, getting the feel of the meaning. Experience pleasurable anticipation of taking in what will make you more yourself, the self that God made in his own image and likeness. The self that God made for intimate communion with him. The self that God created for good works, that you should walk in them. Eat God's words. Let God's words become a joy and the delight of your heart.]

Journal:

What does it mean to approach, come near, worship God *though* Christ Jesus?

Christ Jesus is the channel that enables you to draw near to God. What effort or activity is required from you to receive reconciliation through Christ's death and to be delivered and protected by his life?

Ps 37:23-24 - The steps of a man are established by the Lord, when he delights in his way; though he fall, he shall not be cast headlong, for the Lord upholds his hand.

Ps 37:23-24 - From Jehovah [are] the steps of a man, They have been prepared, And his way he desireth. When he falleth, he is not cast down, For Jehovah is sustaining his hand. (YLT)

Ps 37:23-24 - Stalwart walks in step with God; his path blazed by God, he's happy. If he stumbles, he's not down for long; God has a grip on his hand. (MSG)

The ***steps*** of a man

The steps of a man are established (prepared) ***by the Lord***

When he delights in God's way

Murmur and mumble the words. Phrase by phrase. Word by word. Syllable by syllable. Take pleasure in making the sounds of the words, getting the feel of the meaning. Experience pleasurable anticipation of taking in what will make you more yourself, the self that God made in his own image and likeness. The self that God made for intimate communion with him. The self that God created for good works, that you should walk in them. Eat God's words. Let God's words become a joy and the delight of your heart.]

Journal:

Do you delight in God's way? Do you desire God's way? Do you walk in step with God? Describe.

Ps 73:28 - But for me it is good to be near God; I have made the Lord God my refuge, that I may tell of all your works.

But for ***me***

For me ***it is good***

For me it is good ***to be near God***

I have made

I have made the Lord God ***my refuge*** [shelter, trust]

That I may tell of all your works

Murmur and mumble the words. Phrase by phrase. Word by word. Syllable by syllable. Take pleasure in making the sounds of the words, getting the feel of the meaning. Experience pleasurable anticipation of taking in what will make you more yourself, the self that God made in his own image and likeness. The self that God made for intimate communion with him. The self that God created for good works, that you should walk in them. Eat God's words. Let God's words become a joy and the delight of your heart.]

Journal:

Have you made God your refuge, your shelter, your trust? Describe.

Ps 147:10-11 - His delight is not in the strength of the horse, nor his pleasure in the legs of a man, but the Lord takes pleasure in those who fear him, in those who hope in his steadfast love.

His delight ***is not*** in the strength of the horse

His pleasure ***is not*** in the legs of a man

But the Lord takes pleasure in those who ***fear*** [revere] him

The Lord takes pleasure in those who ***hope*** [to wait; to be patient] in his steadfast love

Murmur and mumble the words. Phrase by phrase. Word by word. Syllable by syllable. Take pleasure in making the sounds of the words, getting the feel of the meaning. Experience pleasurable anticipation of taking in what will make you more yourself, the self that God made in his own image and likeness. The self that God made for intimate communion with him. The self that God created for good works, that you should walk in them. Eat God's words. Let God's words become a joy and the delight of your heart.]

Journal:

Do you fear the Lord? Do you hope in his steadfast love? Describe.

Prov 11:20 - Those of crooked [distorted, false] heart are an abomination [disgusting] to the Lord, but those of blameless ways [com-

plete, entire integrity, truth] *are his delight*.

Those of ***crooked heart*** [distorted, false] are an abomination [disgusting] to the Lord

But those of ***blameless ways*** [complete, entire integrity, truth]

Are ***his delight***

Murmur and mumble the words. Phrase by phrase. Word by word. Syllable by syllable. Take pleasure in making the sounds of the words, getting the feel of the meaning. Experience pleasurable anticipation of taking in what will make you more yourself, the self that God made in his own image and likeness. The self that God made for intimate communion with him. The self that God created for good works, that you should walk in them. Eat God's words. Let God's words become a joy and the delight of your heart.]

Journal:

Are your heart and ways crooked or blameless? Describe.

How do we exchange our crooked heart and ways for a heart and ways that are blameless?

The root of Jesse [Christ Jesus] ***will come***

The root of Jesse will come ***to rule***

May the God of hope fill you with all joy and peace ***in believing****, so that by the power of the Holy Spirit you may abound in hope (Rom 15:13).*

May ***the God of hope***

May the God of hope ***fill you*** with all joy and peace in believing…

So that

So that by the power of ***the Holy Spirit***

You may ***abound in hope***

[Murmur and mumble the words. Phrase by phrase. Word by word. Syllable by syllable. Take pleasure in making the sounds of the words, getting the feel of the meaning. Experience pleasurable anticipation of taking in what will make you more yourself, the self that God made in his own image and likeness. The self that God made

for intimate communion with him. The self that God created for good works, that you should walk in them. Eat God's words. Let God's words become a joy and the delight of your heart.]

Journal:

What has God, whose steadfast love is better than life, done for you and for all of humankind?

What does God, whose steadfast love is better than life, want from you?

Rom 5:10-11 - For if while we were enemies we were reconciled to God by the death of his Son, much more, now that we are reconciled, shall we be saved by his life. More than that, we also rejoice in God through our Lord Jesus Christ, through whom we have now received reconciliation.

Heb 7:23-25 - The former priests were many in number, because they were prevented by death from continuing in office, but he [Christ Jesus] holds his priesthood permanently, because he continues forever. Consequently, he is able to save to the uttermost those who draw near to God through him [Christ Jesus], since he always lives to make intercession for them.

Ps 147:10-11 - His delight is not in the strength of the horse, nor his pleasure in the legs of a man, but the Lord takes pleasure in those who fear him, in those who hope in his steadfast love.

May the God of hope fill you with all joy and peace in believing, so that by the power of the Holy Spirit you may abound in hope (Rom 15:13).

[Pause. Breathe. Inhale and exhale. Reflect. Listen.]

Give me life according to your word, God!

Journal:

What do you hear God saying to you in these Scripture texts? What do they reveal about God and about you? Converse with God about what you're hearing him say. Verbalize and describe your thoughts, memories that come to mind, questions and emotions, concerns, desires.

Is there a particular word or phrase that disturbs or soothes you?

Do the Scripture texts create a picture or an impression that draws you to linger in exploring and experiencing it?

Choose a word or a phrase from your meditation to write on a slip of paper to carry with you today. Refer to it often throughout the day to remind you of your conversation with God and to continue the conversation all day long. Throughout the day pause to become aware of your thoughts and feelings and will. Ask yourself, "What drives me in this moment? Life according to God's word? Or life according to someone else's word?"

Anticipate that God's words stirred your heart for a reason. He's conversing with you through them. Anticipate that God will bring his word to life in you, to bear fruit in your heart and mind and soul and body. Anticipate that God will reveal the secrets of your heart, for anything that is visible is light. And anticipate that God will cause his words to become a joy and the delight of your heart.

CONTEMPLATE

God is spirit, and those who worship him must worship in spirit and truth. Seek him. Feel your way to him. Reach out. Find him.

Inhale deeply, aware that God *is* in your hidden parts, that it is *his* breath that makes you understand his word. Exhale. Give God the gift that he most desires from you, your exposed and surrendered heart, mind, soul, spirit, and body, your whole self, both outer and inner.

Each time you find that your outer self has pulled your attention away, quietly and gently say the word or phrase you chose and then dive back down deep to the hidden person of your heart to return to the Lord. Bask in him. Rest in perfect love.

At the end of your contemplation, inhale deeply and hold it for a second, aware that you exist in God's abounding grace. Only in God's abounding grace do you exist. In God's abounding grace you are you, the real you, able to worship God in spirit and truth.

2 Cor 9:8 - And ***God is able*** *to make all grace abound to you, so that having all sufficiency in all things at all times,* ***you may*** *abound in every good work.*

Exhale slowly and deeply, anticipating that God's abounding grace, in which you exist and are, will flow around you and through you to enlighten and empower you to love as you have been loved so that you may abound in every good work this day.

Resources:

[1]Intercession: NT:1793<START GREEK>e)ntugxa/nw<END GREEK> entugchano (en-toong-khan'-o); from NT:1722 and NT:5177; to chance upon, i.e. (by implication) confer with; by extension to entreat (in favor or against): (Biblesoft's New Exhaustive Strong's Numbers and Concordance with Expanded Greek-Hebrew Dictionary. Copyright © 1994, 2003, 2006, 2010 Biblesoft, Inc. and International Bible Translators, Inc.)

26 - May the God of Hope Fill You

Prov 3:5 - Trust in the Lord with all your heart, and do not lean on your own understanding.

For most of my life I have leaned on my own understanding to define what I assume is my right to expect to receive from God. And when God didn't comply with my requests and expectations, I judged him to be untrustworthy.

To be free from suffering has been one of my main expectations from God. If I do "A" then I should expect God to do "B" in response. And life should be good. Isn't the Bible full of such promises? It is! Isn't it?

Are you aware of such expectations in your heart?

[Pause. Breathe. Inhale and exhale. Reflect. Listen.]

Ask God to bring the secrets of your heart into the light.

Jer 17:9 - The heart is deceitful above all things, and desperately sick; who can understand it?

Pray: Ask God to prepare your heart and mind and soul to receive his words, to receive truth that will set you free, which will heal and perfect your understanding and knowledge of who God is and who you are.

Ps 119:25-32 - I'm feeling terrible — I couldn't feel worse! Get me on my feet again. You promised, remember? When I told my story, you responded; train me well in your deep wisdom. Help me understand these things inside and out so I can ponder your miracle-wonders. My sad life's dilapidated, a falling-down barn; build me up again by your Word. Barricade the road that goes Nowhere; grace me with your clear revelation. I choose the true road to Somewhere, I post your road signs at every curve and corner. I grasp and cling to whatever you tell me; God, don't let me down! I'll run the course you lay out for me if you'll just show me how. (MSG)

[Murmur and mumble the words. Phrase by phrase. Word by word. Syllable by syllable. Pause. Breathe. Inhale and exhale. Reflect. Listen.]

Journal:

Note how this prayer stirs you today and what you hear God saying to you.

*Deut 12:28 - **Be careful to obey** all these words that I command you, <u>that it may go well with you</u> and with your children after you forever, when you **do what is good and right in the sight of the Lord your God**.*

*Ps 103:17-18 - But <u>the steadfast love of the Lord is from everlasting to everlasting</u> **on those who fear him**, and <u>his righteousness</u> to children's children, **to those who keep his covenant and remember to do his commandments**.*

These Scripture texts appear to be perfect examples of my above formula, don't they?

If <u>you</u> be careful to obey all these words that I command you, ***if*** <u>you</u> do what is good and right in the sight of the Lord your God, ***then*** it will go well with you and with your children after you forever.

If <u>you</u> fear God, ***if*** <u>you</u> keep his covenant, ***if*** <u>you</u> remember to do his commandments, ***then*** the steadfast love of the Lord and his righteousness will be on you from everlasting to everlasting.

[Murmur and mumble the words. Phrase by phrase. Word by word. Syllable by syllable. Take pleasure in making the sounds of the words, getting the feel of the meaning. Experience pleasurable anticipation of taking in what will make you more yourself, the self that God made in his own image and likeness. The self that God made for intimate communion with him. The self that God created for good works, that you should walk in them. Eat God's words. Let God's words become a joy and the delight of your heart.]

Journal:

Are you careful to remember and obey all the words of the commandments written in God's law? Do you do what is good and right in the sight of the Lord your God? Do you fear God? Do you keep his covenant?

Consider the following questions. Do you think the one who has searched you and known you answers the following questions the same way you do?

Upon whose understanding are you leaning when you decide that you can know and understand and will to obey *all* of God's commands in every way in every situation every time?

Upon whose understanding are you leaning when you decide that you can determine what is good and right in the sight of the Lord in every way in every situation every time and that you have actually met his standards each and every moment of your life in order that it will go well with you and your children after you forever?

Upon whose understanding are you leaning when you decide that you do fear God, therefore, you can expect God to see that all goes well with you and yours?

And upon whose understanding are you leaning when you define what "going well" looks and feels like?

Is God's definition of "going well" the same as yours? Or is his understanding and your understanding of the reality of "it going well" two very different things?

Is there, perhaps, a foreign god influencing how you answer these questions? The god of self that leans on his/her own understanding and trusts in his/her own mind?

Prov 16:2 - All the ways of a man are pure in his own eyes, but the Lord weighs the spirit.

Prov 21:2 - Every way of a man is right in his own eyes, but the Lord weighs the heart.

If you be careful to obey all these words that I command you, ***if*** you do what is good and right in the sight of the Lord your God, ***then*** it will go well with you and with your children after you forever.

If you fear God, ***if*** you keep his covenant, ***if*** you remember to do his commandments, ***then*** the steadfast love of the Lord and his righteousness will be on you from everlasting to everlasting.

Jer 10:23 - I know, O Lord, that the way of man is not in himself, that it is not in man who walks to direct his steps. (ESV)

[Murmur and mumble the words. Phrase by phrase. Word by word. Syllable by syllable. Take pleasure in making the sounds of the words, getting the feel of the meaning. Experience pleasurable anticipation of taking in what will make you more yourself, the self that God made in his own image and likeness. The self that God made for intimate communion with him. The self that God created for good works, that you should walk in them. Eat God's words. Let God's words become a joy and the delight of your heart.]

Journal:

So how do we reconcile these Scripture texts?

Is God telling us that we can't direct our steps on the one hand, but on the other hand insisting that we must properly direct our steps if we want his favor? Record your thoughts.

For I tell you that Christ became a servant… "Rejoice, O Gentiles, with his people." … "Praise the Lord, all you Gentiles, and let all the peoples extol him." … "The root of Jesse [Christ Jesus] will come, even he who arises to rule the Gentiles; in him will the Gentiles hope." May the God of hope fill you with all joy and peace in believing, so that by the power of the Holy Spirit you may abound in hope (See Rom 15:8-13).

I tell you

That Christ ***became a servant***

Rejoice, O Gentiles, ***with*** his people

The root of Jesse [Christ Jesus] ***will*** come

Will ***arise***

Will arise ***to rule***

To rule

In him

In him will the Gentiles ***hope*** [trust-expect, confide, and anticipate with pleasure[1]]

May ***the God of hope***

Fill you

Fill you ***with all joy***

And ***peace in believing*** [entrusting your soul and relying on Christ for salvation[2]]

So that

So that ***by the power*** of the Holy Spirit

You may ***abound in hope***.

[Murmur and mumble the words. Phrase by phrase. Word by word. Syllable by syllable. Take pleasure in making the sounds of the words, getting the feel of the meaning. Experience pleasurable anticipation of taking in what will make you more yourself, the self that God made in his own image and likeness. The self that God made for intimate communion with him. The self that God created for good works, that you should walk in them. Eat God's words. Let God's words become a joy and the delight of your heart.]

Journal:

What do you discover about God and his purpose for you and for all of humankind in this Scripture text?

What does this Scripture text say God has done and will do for you and for all humankind?

Let the following words flow over you and through you, deep into the very center of your heart and being. Ask God to open your heart and mind so you can experience the Holy Spirit making known to you the Father and the Son's heart to you.

May the God of hope fill you with all joy and peace in believing, so that by the power of the Holy Spirit you may abound in hope.

Journal:

Record your response to God and Christ Jesus.

Deut 12:28 - Be careful to obey all these words that I command you, that it may go well with you and with your children after you forever, when you do what is good and right in the sight of the Lord your God.

Ps 103:17-18 - But the steadfast love of the Lord is from everlasting to everlasting on those who fear him, and his righteousness to children's children, to those who keep his covenant and remember to do his commandments.

Prov 16:2 - All the ways of a man are pure in his own eyes, but the Lord weighs the spirit.

Prov 21:2 - Every way of a man is right in his own eyes, but the Lord weighs the heart.

Jer 10:23 - I know, O Lord, that the way of man is not in himself, that it is not in man who walks to direct his steps. (ESV)

For I tell you that Christ became a servant… "Rejoice, O Gentiles, with his people." … "Praise the Lord, all you Gentiles, and let all the peoples extol him." … "The root of Jesse [Christ Jesus] will come, even he who arises to rule the Gentiles; in him will the Gentiles hope." May the God of hope fill you with all joy and peace in believ-

ing, so that by the power of the Holy Spirit you may abound in hope (See Rom 15:8-13).

[Pause. Breathe. Inhale and exhale. Reflect. Listen.]

Give me life according to your word, God!

Journal:

What do you hear God saying to you in these Scripture texts? What do they reveal about God and about you? Converse with God about what you're hearing him say. Verbalize and describe your thoughts, memories that come to mind, questions and emotions, concerns, desires.

Is there a particular word or phrase that disturbs or soothes you?

Do the Scripture texts create a picture or an impression that draws you to linger in exploring and experiencing it?

Choose a word or a phrase from your meditation to write on a slip of paper to carry with you today. Refer to it often throughout the day to remind you of your conversation with God and to continue the conversation all day long. Throughout the day pause to become aware of your thoughts and feelings and will. Ask yourself, "What drives me in this moment? Life according to God's word? Or life according to someone else's word?"

Anticipate that God's words stirred your heart for a reason. He's conversing with you through them. Anticipate that God will bring his word to life in you, to bear fruit in your heart and mind and soul and body. Anticipate that God will reveal the secrets of your heart, for anything that is visible is light. And anticipate that God will cause his words to become a joy and the delight of your heart.

CONTEMPLATE

God is spirit, and those who worship him must worship in spirit and truth. Seek him. Feel your way to him. Reach out. Find him.

Inhale deeply, aware that God *is* in your hidden parts, that it is *his* breath that makes you understand his word. Exhale. Give God the gift that he most desires from you, your exposed and surrendered heart, mind, soul, spirit, and body, your whole self, both outer and inner.

Each time you find that your outer self has pulled your attention away, quietly and gently say the word or phrase you chose and then dive back down deep to the hidden person of your heart to return to the Lord. Bask in him. Rest in perfect love.

At the end of your contemplation, inhale deeply and hold it for a second, aware that you exist in God's abounding grace. Only in God's abounding grace do you exist. In God's abounding grace you are you, the real you, able to worship God in spirit and truth.

2 Cor 9:8 - And ***God is able*** *to make all grace abound to you, so that having all sufficiency in all things at all times,* ***you may*** *abound in every good work.*

Exhale slowly and deeply, anticipating that God's abounding grace, in which you exist and are, will flow around you and through you to enlighten and empower you to love as you have been loved so that you may abound in every good work this day.

Resources:

[1]Hope/trust: NT:1679<START GREEK>e)lpi/zw<END GREEK> elpizo (el-pid'-zo); from NT:1680; to expect or confide:

NT:1680<START GREEK>e)lpi/$<END GREEK> elpis (el-pece'); from a primary elpo (to anticipate, usually with pleasure); expectation (abstractly or concretely) or confidence: (Biblesoft's New Exhaustive Strong's Numbers and Concordance with Expanded Greek-Hebrew Dictionary. Copyright © 1994, 2003, 2006, 2010 Biblesoft, Inc. and International Bible Translators, Inc.)

[2]Believing: NT:4100<START GREEK>pisteu/w<END GREEK>

pisteuo (pist-yoo'-o); from NT:4102; to have faith (in, upon, or with respect to, a person or thing), i.e. credit; by implication, to entrust (especially one's spiritual well-being to Christ):

NT:4102<START GREEK>pi/sti$<END GREEK> pistis (pis'-tis); from NT:3982; persuasion, i.e. credence; moral conviction (of religious truth, or the truthfulness of God or a religious teacher), especially reliance upon Christ for salvation; abstractly, constancy in such profession; by extension, the system of religious (Gospel) truth itself:

NT:3982<START GREEK>pei/qw<END GREEK> peitho (pi'-tho); a primary verb; to convince (by argument, true or false); by analogy, to pacify or conciliate (by other fair means); reflexively or passively, to assent (to evidence or authority), to rely (by inward certainty): (Biblesoft's New Exhaustive Strong's Numbers and Concordance with Expanded Greek-Hebrew Dictionary. Copyright © 1994, 2003, 2006, 2010 Biblesoft, Inc. and International Bible Translators, Inc.)

27 – The Way

Pray: Ask God to prepare your heart and mind and soul to receive his words, to receive truth that will set you free, which will heal and perfect your understanding and knowledge of who God is and who you are.

Ps 119:25-32 - My soul clings to the dust; give me life according to your word! When I told of my ways, you answered me; teach me your statutes! Make me understand the way of your precepts, and I will meditate on your wondrous works. My soul melts away for sorrow; strengthen me according to your word! Put false ways far from me and graciously teach me your law! I have chosen the way of faithfulness; I set your rules before me. I cling to your testimonies, O Lord; let me not be put to shame! I will run in the way of your commandments when you enlarge my heart! (ESV)

[Murmur and mumble the words. Phrase by phrase. Word by word. Syllable by syllable. Pause. Breathe. Inhale and exhale. Reflect. Listen.]

Journal:

Note how this prayer stirs you today and what you hear God saying to you.

Jer 10:23 - I know, O Lord, that the way of man is not in himself, that it is not in man who walks to direct his steps. (ESV)

For I tell you that Christ became a servant… "Rejoice, O Gentiles, with his people." … "Praise the Lord, all you Gentiles, and let all the peoples extol him." … "The root of Jesse [Christ Jesus] will come, even he who arises to rule the Gentiles; in him will the Gentiles hope." May the God of hope fill you with all joy and peace in believing, so that by the power of the Holy Spirit you may abound in hope (See Rom 15:8-13).

Ps 18:30 - This God—his way is perfect; the word of the Lord proves true; he is a shield for all those who take refuge in him.

I tell you

That Christ Jesus ***became a servant***

Rejoice

Praise the Lord

All peoples extol him

The root of Jesse [Christ Jesus] ***will come***

In him

Hope

May the ***God of hope*** fill you

Fill you with ***all*** joy and peace in believing

In ***believing***

So that ***by the power of the Holy Spirit***

You may abound in hope

This God-***his way*** is perfect

His way

His ***way***

God's way ***is perfect***

John 14:6 – Jesus said…, "I am the way, and the truth, and the life. No one comes to the Father except through me.

Jesus said, "***I am*** the way."

I am ***the way***

I am the truth

I am ***the truth***

I am the life

I am ***the life***

I

Am

The

Way

This God-***his way*** is perfect

[Murmur and mumble the words. Phrase by phrase. Word by word. Syllable by syllable. Take pleasure in making the sounds of the words, getting the feel of the meaning. Experience pleasurable anticipation of taking in what will make you more yourself, the self that God made in his own image and likeness. The self that God made for intimate communion with him. The self that God created for good works, that you should walk in them. Eat God's words. Let God's words become a joy and the delight of your heart.]

Journal:

What do you discover about God's way?

Scripture says the way of man is not in himself and Christ Jesus has become a servant. Is there a connecting thread running through these two statements? Explain.

Scripture says the way of man is not in himself and God's way is perfect. How does God want you to respond to this revelation?

Jer 10:23 - I know, O Lord, that the way of man is not in himself, that it is not in man who walks to direct his steps. (ESV)

The way to the Father, the way to finding God's favor is not through human effort.

And yet, human effort is required.

Phil 2:12b-13 - ...work out your own salvation with fear and trembling, for it is God who works in you, both to will and to work for his good pleasure.

Work out [accomplish, finish]

Your own salvation [rescue, safety] with fear and trembling

For

For ***it is***

For it is ***God***

For it is God ***who works in you***

In you

Both to ***will*** [to determine]

And to ***work*** [to be active; efficient]

For ***his*** good pleasure [satisfaction, delight, kindness, wish, purpose]

[Murmur and mumble the words. Phrase by phrase. Word by word. Syllable by syllable. Take pleasure in making the sounds of the words, getting the feel of the meaning. Experience pleasurable anticipation of taking in what will make you more yourself, the self that God made in his own image and likeness. The self that God made for intimate communion with him. The self that God created for good works, that you should walk in them. Eat God's words. Let God's words become a joy and the delight of your heart.]

Journal:

What is the relationship between your working out your own salvation and God who works in you both to will and to work for his good pleasure?

What finishing work is God calling you to do in working out your own salvation?

John 6:29 - Jesus answered them, "This is the work of God, that you

believe in him whom he has sent."

This is the work of God

That you ***believe***

That you believe ***in him*** whom he has sent.

Jer 10:23 - I know, O Lord, that the way of man is not in himself, that it is not in man who walks to direct his steps. (ESV)

For I tell you that Christ became a servant… "Rejoice, O Gentiles, with his people." … "Praise the Lord, all you Gentiles, and let all the peoples extol him." … "The root of Jesse [Christ Jesus] will come, even he who arises to rule the Gentiles; in him will the Gentiles hope." May the God of hope fill you with all joy and peace in believing, so that by the power of the Holy Spirit you may abound in hope (See Rom 15:8-13).

John 14:6 – Jesus said…, "I am the way, and the truth, and the life. No one comes to the Father except through me.

Eph Phil 2:12b-13 - …work out your own salvation with fear and trembling, for it is God who works in you, both to will and to work for his good pleasure.

John 6:29 - Jesus answered them, "This is the work of God, that you believe in him whom he has sent."

[Pause. Breathe. Inhale and exhale. Reflect. Listen.]

Give me life according to your word, God!

Journal:

What do you hear God saying to you in these Scripture texts? What do they reveal about God and about you? Converse with God about what you're hearing him say. Verbalize and describe your thoughts, memories that come to mind, questions and emotions, concerns, desires.

Is there a particular word or phrase that disturbs or soothes you?

Do the Scripture texts create a picture or an impression that draws you to linger in exploring and experiencing it?

Choose a word or a phrase from your meditation to write on a slip of paper to carry with you today. Refer to it often throughout the day to remind you of your conversation with God and to continue the conversation all day long. Throughout the day pause to become aware of your thoughts and feelings and will. Ask yourself, "What drives me in this moment? Life according to God's word? Or life according to someone else's word?"

Anticipate that God's words stirred your heart for a reason. He's conversing with you through them. Anticipate that God will bring his word to life in you, to bear fruit in your heart and mind and soul and body. Anticipate that God will reveal the secrets of your heart, for anything that is visible is light. And anticipate that God will cause his words to become a joy and the delight of your heart.

CONTEMPLATE

God is spirit, and those who worship him must worship in spirit and truth. Seek him. Feel your way to him. Reach out. Find him.

Inhale deeply, aware that God *is* in your hidden parts, that it is *his* breath that makes you understand his word. Exhale. Give God the gift that he most desires from you, your exposed and surrendered heart, mind, soul, spirit, and body, your whole self, both outer and inner.

Each time you find that your outer self has pulled your attention away, quietly and gently say the word or phrase you chose and then dive back down deep to the hidden person of your heart to return to the Lord. Bask in him. Rest in perfect love.

At the end of your contemplation, inhale deeply and hold it for a second, aware that you exist in God's abounding grace. Only in God's abounding grace do you exist. In God's abounding grace you are you, the real you, able to worship God in spirit and truth.

*2 Cor 9:8 - And **God is able** to make all grace abound to you, so that having all sufficiency in all things at all times, **you may** abound in every good work.*

Exhale slowly and deeply, anticipating that God's abounding grace, in which you exist and are, will flow around you and through you to enlighten and empower you to love as you have been loved so that you may abound in every good work this day.

28 – The Work of God is that You Believe

Pray: Ask God to prepare your heart and mind and soul to receive his words, to receive truth that will set you free, which will heal and perfect your understanding and knowledge of who God is and who you are.

Ps 119:25-32 - I'm feeling terrible — I couldn't feel worse! Get me on my feet again. You promised, remember? When I told my story, you responded; train me well in your deep wisdom. Help me understand these things inside and out so I can ponder your miracle-wonders. My sad life's dilapidated, a falling-down barn; build me up again by your Word. Barricade the road that goes Nowhere; grace me with your clear revelation. I choose the true road to Somewhere, I post your road signs at every curve and corner. I grasp and cling to whatever you tell me; God, don't let me down! I'll run the course you lay out for me if you'll just show me how. (MSG)

[Murmur and mumble the words. Phrase by phrase. Word by word. Syllable by syllable. Pause. Breathe. Inhale and exhale. Reflect. Listen.]

Journal:

Note how this prayer stirs you today and what you hear God saying to you.

Jer 10:23 - I know, O Lord, that the way of man is not in himself, that it is not in man who walks to direct his steps. (ESV)

Eph Phil 2:12b-13 - …work out your own salvation with fear and trembling, for it is God who works in you, both to will and to work for his good pleasure.

The way of man is not in himself. Christ Jesus has become a servant. The way of man is not in himself. Jesus is the way. Work out your own salvation with fear and trembling. It is God who works in you, both to will and to work for his good pleasure.

How do we work out our own salvation?

Do we turn to the law?

If you be careful to obey all these words that I command you, ***if*** you do what is good and right in the sight of the Lord your God, ***then*** it will go well with you and with your children after you forever.

If you fear God, ***if*** you keep his covenant, ***if*** you remember to do his commandments, ***then*** the steadfast love of the Lord and his righteousness will be on you from everlasting to everlasting.

Or do we turn to God's perfect way, to Jesus?

Eph 2:10 - For we are his workmanship, created in Christ Jesus for good works, which God prepared beforehand, that we should walk in them.

For we are ***his*** workmanship [product; fabric]

Created ***in*** Christ Jesus

For

For ***good works*** [effort; occupation; an act]

Which ***God prepared*** [ordained] beforehand

That ***we should walk*** in them [to tread all around, i.e. walk at large especially as proof of ability; figuratively, to live, deport oneself, follow as a companion or a person bound by a vow or promise; devout worshiper.[1]]

Note that the Scripture text says we are *his* workmanship, not our own. We are created ***in*** Christ Jesus ***for*** good works.

It doesn't say we create ourselves by *doing* good works.

What does this mean?

John 6:28-29 – Then they said to him, "What must we do, to be doing the works of God?" Jesus answered them, "This is the work of God, that you believe in him whom he has sent."

What must ***we*** do?

What must we ***do***?

What must we do, ***to be doing***… ?

What must we do, to be doing ***the works of God***?

Jesus answered, "***This is*** the work of God

That you ***believe*** [persuasion, i.e. credence; moral conviction, esp. reliance upon Christ for salvation; to have faith in; to entrust, esp. one's spiritual well-being to Christ]

This is ***the work of God***

That you believe ***in him whom he sent***

[Murmur and mumble the words. Phrase by phrase. Word by word. Syllable by syllable. Take pleasure in making the sounds of the words, getting the feel of the meaning. Experience pleasurable anticipation of taking in what will make you more yourself, the self that God made in his own image and likeness. The self that God made for intimate communion with him. The self that God created for good works, that you should walk in them. Eat God's words. Let God's words become a joy and the delight of your heart.]

Journal:

Is believing in the one whom God sent the work that you've been toiling at all your life?

Has believing in Christ Jesus, the one whom God sent, been the focus of your effort and occupation?

What specific tasks are involved in the work to believe in him whom God sent?

John 3:34 - For he whom God has sent utters the words of God, for he gives the Spirit without measure.

John 5:19 - So Jesus said to them, "Truly, truly, I say to you, the Son can do nothing of his own accord, but only what he sees the Father doing. For whatever the Father does, that the Son does likewise.

John 7:16-18 - So Jesus answered them, "My teaching is not mine, but his who sent me. If anyone's will is to do God's will, he will know whether the teaching is from God or whether I am speaking on my own authority. The one who speaks on his own authority seeks his own glory, but the one who seeks the glory of him who sent him is true, and in him there is no falsehood.

For he whom God ***has sent***

Utters the ***words of God***

The ***words*** of God

The words ***of God***

For ***he gives the Spirit*** without measure

He gives ***the Spirit***

[Jesus said] My teaching ***is not mine***

My teaching ***is his who sent me***

I seek the glory of ***him who sent me***

There is no falsehood ***in me***

The Son ***can do nothing*** of his own accord

But ***only what he sees*** the Father doing

Whatever the ***Father does***, that

That the ***Son does likewise***

If anyone's ***will***

If anyone's will ***is to do*** God's will

He will ***know*** whether the teaching is from God

[Murmur and mumble the words. Phrase by phrase. Word by word. Syllable by syllable. Take pleasure in making the sounds of the words, getting the feel of the meaning. Experience pleasurable anticipation of taking in what will make you more yourself, the self that God made in his own image and likeness. The self that God made for intimate communion with him. The self that God created for good works, that you should walk in them. Eat God's words. Let God's words become a joy and the delight of your heart.]

Journal:

How did Jesus perfectly demonstrate for us what we're to occupy ourselves with since it is not in humankind to direct our own steps?

Do you believe that Jesus Christ became a servant for *your* benefit?

Are you confident that Christ *has* reconciled you to God by his death? Has your hostile attitude to God been removed? What is your attitude now?

Are you confident that Christ *has* saved you by his life and continues to deliver, provide for and protect *you* in all things at all times?

Are you doing the works of God by entrusting your well-being to the one whom God sent? Are you doing the works of God by entrusting your soul and spirit to the one who does not seek his own glory, but the glory of the one who sent him?

Do you believe and have confidence in the one who does only what he sees his Father doing? Do you follow Christ Jesus as a companion bound by promise? Are you God's devout worshiper as a result of Christ Jesus' relationship with God his Father?

Are you doing the works of God by surrendering all that you are and have to the one whom God sent so *he* can accomplish and perfect everything that concerns you?

Is your will to do God's will?

Are you aware that you are created, and that you are being re-created *in* Christ? As you tread all around your life in this world, are you living proof of Christ's ability to accomplish his Father's work, to perfect everything that concerns you?

As Christ Jesus is bound to his Father - *the Son can do nothing of his own accord, but only what he sees the Father doing* – is it your desire and longing and prayer and hope and confidence that in Christ you also are/will be so bound to God, too?

*May **the God of hope** fill you with all joy and peace <u>in believing</u> so that by the power of the Holy Spirit you may abound in hope.*

Is there something in your deceitful and desperately sick heart that continues to restrain you from receiving with pleasure and believing every word of God?

Ps 18:30 - This God—his way is perfect; the word of the Lord proves true; he is a shield for all those who take refuge in him.

Jer 10:23 - I know, O Lord, that the way of man is not in himself, that it is not in man who walks to direct his steps. (ESV)

For I tell you that Christ became a servant… "Rejoice, O Gentiles, with his people." … "Praise the Lord, all you Gentiles, and let all the peoples extol him." … "The root of Jesse [Christ Jesus] will come, even he who arises to rule the Gentiles; in him will the Gentiles hope." May the God of hope fill you with all joy and peace in believing, so that by the power of the Holy Spirit you may abound in hope (See Rom 15:8-13)

John 3:34 - For he whom God has sent utters the words of God, for he gives the Spirit without measure.

John 5:19 - So Jesus said to them, "Truly, truly, I say to you, the Son can do nothing of his own accord, but only what he sees the Father doing. For whatever the Father does, that the Son does likewise.

[Pause. Breathe. Inhale and exhale. Reflect. Listen.]

Give me life according to your word, God!

Journal:

What do you hear God saying to you in these Scripture texts? What do they reveal about God and about you? Converse with God about what you're hearing him say. Verbalize and describe your thoughts, memories that come to mind, questions and emotions, concerns, desires.

Is there a particular word or phrase that disturbs or soothes you?

Do the Scripture texts create a picture or an impression that draws you to linger in exploring and experiencing it?

Choose a word or a phrase from your meditation to write on a slip of paper to carry with you today. Refer to it often throughout the day to remind you of your conversation with God and to continue the conversation all day long. Throughout the day pause to become aware of your thoughts and feelings and will. Ask yourself, "What drives me in this moment? Life according to God's word? Or life according to someone else's word?"

Anticipate that God's words stirred your heart for a reason. He's conversing with you through them. Anticipate that God will bring his word to life in you, to bear fruit in your heart and mind and soul and body. Anticipate that God will reveal the secrets of your heart, for anything that is visible is light. And anticipate that God will cause his words to become a joy and the delight of your heart.

CONTEMPLATE

God is spirit, and those who worship him must worship in spirit and truth. Seek him. Feel your way to him. Reach out. Find him.

Inhale deeply, aware that God *is* in your hidden parts, that it is *his* breath that makes you understand his word. Exhale. Give God the gift that he most desires from you, your exposed and surrendered heart, mind, soul, spirit, and body, your whole self, both outer and inner.

Each time you find that your outer self has pulled your attention away, quietly and gently say the word or phrase you chose and then dive back down deep to the hidden person of your heart to return to the Lord. Bask in him. Rest in perfect love.

At the end of your contemplation, inhale deeply and hold it for a second, aware that you exist in God's abounding grace. Only in God's abounding grace do you exist. In God's abounding grace you are you, the real you, able to worship God in spirit and truth.

2 Cor 9:8 - And ***God is able*** *to make all grace abound to you, so that having all sufficiency in all things at all times,* ***you may*** *abound in every good work.*

Exhale slowly and deeply, anticipating that God's abounding grace, in which you exist and are, will flow around you and through you to enlighten and empower you to love as you have been loved so that you may abound in every good work this day.

Resources:

[1]We should walk: NT:4043 <START GREEK>peripate/w<END GREEK> peripateo (per-ee-pat-eh'-o); from NT:4012 and NT:3961; to tread all around, i.e. walk at large (especially as proof of ability); figuratively, to live, deport oneself, follow (as a companion or votary): (Biblesoft's New Exhaustive Strong's Numbers and Concordance with Expanded Greek-Hebrew Dictionary. Copyright © 1994, 2003, 2006, 2010 Biblesoft, Inc. and International Bible Translators, Inc.)

29 - Our Inner Nature is Being Renewed

Pray: Ask God to prepare your heart and mind and soul to receive his words, to receive truth that will set you free, which will heal and perfect your understanding and knowledge of who God is and who you are.

Ps 119:25-32 - My soul clings to the dust; give me life according to your word! When I told of my ways, you answered me; teach me your statutes! Make me understand the way of your precepts, and I will meditate on your wondrous works. My soul melts away for sorrow; strengthen me according to your word! Put false ways far from me and graciously teach me your law! I have chosen the way of faithfulness; I set your rules before me. I cling to your testimonies, O Lord; let me not be put to shame! I will run in the way of your commandments when you enlarge my heart! (ESV)

[Murmur and mumble the words. Phrase by phrase. Word by word. Syllable by syllable. Pause. Breathe. Inhale and exhale. Reflect. Listen.]

Journal:

Note how this prayer stirs you today and what you hear God saying to you.

Ps 22:1-2 - My God, my God, why have you forsaken me? Why are you so far from saving me [freeing me, assisting me, relieving me], from the words of my groaning? O my God, I cry by day, but you do not answer, and by night, but I find no rest.

Suffering. It seems that we human beings hate to suffer. Is suffering one of the main reasons we all give for withdrawing from God, for struggling to trust him? Maybe we simply do not understand suffering. As you read the following Scripture texts, think about your own life experience and how you identify with the words and experiences of those who went before you who did receive and believe God's words in spite of suffering.

Ps 22:1-2 - My God, my God, why have you forsaken me? Why are you so far from saving me [freeing me, assisting me, relieving me], from the words of my groaning? O my God, I cry by day, but you do not answer, and by night, but I find no rest.

Ps 22:14-15 - I am poured out like water, and all my bones are out of joint; my heart is like wax; it is melted within my breast; my strength is dried up like a potsherd [piece of pottery], and my tongue sticks to my jaws; you lay me in the dust of death.

Ps 69:9-21, 29 - For zeal for your house has consumed me, and the reproaches of those who reproach you have fallen on me. When I wept and humbled my soul with fasting, it became my reproach. When I made sackcloth my clothing, I became a byword to them. I am the talk of those who sit in the gate, and the drunkards make songs about me.

But as for me, my prayer is to you, O Lord. At an acceptable time, O God, in the abundance of your steadfast love answer me in your saving faithfulness. Deliver me from sinking in the mire; let me be delivered from my enemies and from the deep waters. Let not the flood sweep over me, or the deep swallow me up, or the pit close its mouth over me.

Answer me, O Lord, for your steadfast love is good; according to your abundant mercy, turn to me. Hide not your face from your servant; for I am in distress; make haste to answer me. Draw near to my soul, redeem me; ransom me because of my enemies!

You know my reproach, and my shame and my dishonor; my foes are all known to you. Reproaches have broken my heart, so that I am in despair. I looked for pity, but there was none, and for comforters, but I found none. They gave me poison for food, and for my thirst they gave me sour wine to drink.

But I am afflicted and in pain; let your salvation, O God, set me on high! I will praise the name of God with a song; I will magnify him with thanksgiving.

Luke 22:44 - And being in an agony he prayed more earnestly; and his sweat became like great drops of blood falling down to the ground.

Matt 27:46 - And about the ninth hour Jesus cried out with a loud voice, saying, "Eli, Eli, lema sabachthani?" that is, "My God, my God, why have you forsaken me?"

Luke 23:44-46 - It was now about the sixth hour, and there was darkness over the whole land until the ninth hour, while the sun's light failed. And the curtain of the temple was torn in two. Then Jesus, calling out with a loud voice, said, "Father, into your hands I commit my spirit!" And having said this he breathed his last.

Isa 53:10-12 - Yet it was the will of the Lord to crush him; he has put him to grief; when his soul makes an offering for sin, he shall see his offspring; he shall prolong his days; the will of the Lord shall prosper in his hand. Out of the anguish of his soul he shall see and be satisfied; by his knowledge shall ***the righteous one****, my servant, make many[1] to be accounted righteous [made right[2]], and he shall bear their iniquities. Therefore I will divide him a portion with the many, and he shall divide the spoil with the strong, because he poured out his soul to death and was numbered with the transgressors; yet he bore the sin of many, and makes intercession[3] for the transgressors [those who have broken away from just authority[4]].*

2 Cor 4:16-18 - So we do not lose heart. Though our outer nature is wasting away, our inner nature is being renewed day by day. For this slight momentary affliction is preparing for us an eternal weight of glory beyond all comparison, as we look not to the things that are seen but to the things that are unseen. For the things that are seen are transient, but the things that are unseen are eternal.

Phil 3:8-11 - Indeed, I count everything as loss because of the surpassing worth of knowing Christ Jesus my Lord. For his sake I have suffered the loss of all things and count them as rubbish, in order that I may gain Christ and be found in him, not having a righteousness of my own that comes from the law, but that which comes through faith in [of] Christ, the righteousness from God that depends on faith— that I may know him and the power of his resurrection, and may share his sufferings, becoming like him in his death, that by any means possible I may attain the resurrection from the dead.

Phil 3:9 - not having my righteousness, which [is] of law, but that which [is] ***through faith of Christ[5]*** *— the righteousness that is of God by the faith, (YLT)*

1 John 3:2 - Beloved, we are God's children now, and what we will be has not yet appeared; but we know that when he appears we shall be like him, because we shall see him as he is.

[Murmur and mumble the words. Phrase by phrase. Word by word. Syllable by syllable. Take pleasure in making the sounds of the words, getting the feel of the meaning. Experience pleasurable anticipation of taking in what will make you more yourself, the self that God made in his own image and likeness. The self that God made for intimate communion with him. The self that God created for good works, that you should walk in them. Eat God's words. Let God's words become a joy and the delight of your heart.]

Journal:

Record your thoughts on how you tend to respond to suffering and how these men who have gone before you responded to suffering.

During times when you've suffered, were you looking to things that are seen, things that are transient?

Were you able, at some point, to shift from looking to things that are seen to things that are unseen, to things that are eternal?

In the midst of your suffering were you able to recall and hope in the things that you know about God's character? The abundance of his steadfast love. His saving faithfulness. His abundant mercy. That he accounts you righteous with the righteousness that comes from God that depends on the faith of Christ. That he intercedes for you. That he bears your iniquities even when you don't yet believe.

In your agony did you withdraw from God [break away from just authority]? Or did you snuggle ever more closely in his embrace? Were you able to pray as David and as Jesus prayed to their God and Father even in the midst of suffering?

Ps 69:29 - But I am afflicted and in pain; let your salvation [deliverance, aid, victory prosperity[6]], O God, set me on high! I will praise the name of God with a song; I will magnify him with thanksgiving.

[Pause. Breathe. Inhale and exhale. Reflect. Listen.]

Give me life according to your word, God!

Journal:

What do you hear God saying to you in these Scripture texts? What do they reveal about God and about you? Converse with God about what you're hearing him say. Verbalize and describe your thoughts, memories that come to mind, questions and emotions, concerns, desires.

Is there a particular word or phrase that disturbs or soothes you?

Do the Scripture texts create a picture or an impression that draws you to linger in exploring and experiencing it?

Choose a word or a phrase from your meditation to write on a slip of paper to carry with you today. Refer to it often throughout the day to remind you of your conversation with God and to continue the conversation all day long. Throughout the day pause to become aware of your thoughts and feelings and will. Ask yourself, "What drives me in this moment? Life according to God's word? Or life according to someone else's word?"

Anticipate that God's words stirred your heart for a reason. He's conversing with you through them. Anticipate that God will bring his word to life in you, to bear fruit in your heart and mind and soul and body. Anticipate that God will reveal the secrets of your heart, for anything that is visible is light. And anticipate that God will cause his words to become a joy and the delight of your heart.

CONTEMPLATE

God is spirit, and those who worship him must worship in spirit and truth. Seek him. Feel your way to him. Reach out. Find him.

You exist in God's abounding grace. Only in God's abounding grace do you exist. In God's abounding grace you are you, the real you, able to worship God in spirit and truth.

*2 Cor 9:8 - And **God is able** to make all grace abound to you, so that having all sufficiency in all things at all times, **you may** abound in every good work.*

Anticipate that God's abounding grace, in which you exist and are, will flow around you and through you to enlighten and empower you to love as you have been loved so that you may abound in every good work this day.

Resources:

[1]Many: OT:7227 <START HEBREW>br^<END HEBREW> rab (rab); by contracted from OT:7231; abundant (in quantity, size, age, number, rank, quality):

OT:7231 <START HEBREW>bb^r*<END HEBREW> rabab (raw-bab'); a primitive root; properly, to cast together [compare OT:7241], i.e. increase, especially in number; also (as denominative from OT:7233) to multiply by the myriad:

OT:7233 <START HEBREW>hb*b*r=<END HEBREW> rebabah (reb-aw-baw'); from OT:7231; abundance (in number), i.e. (specifically) a myriad (whether definite or indefinite): (Biblesoft's New Exhaustive Strong's Numbers and Concordance with Expanded Greek-Hebrew Dictionary. Copyright © 1994, 2003, 2006, 2010 Biblesoft, Inc. and International Bible Translators, Inc.)

[2]To be accounted righteous: OT:6663 <START HEBREW>qd^x-*<END HEBREW> tsadaq (tsaw-dak'); a primitive root; to be (causatively, make) right (in a moral or forensic sense): (Biblesoft's New Exhaustive Strong's Numbers and Concordance with Expanded Greek-Hebrew Dictionary. Copyright © 1994, 2003, 2006, 2010 Biblesoft, Inc. and International Bible Translators, Inc.)

[3]Made intercession for: OT:6293 <START HEBREW>ug^P*<END HEBREW> paga` (paw-gah'); a primitive root; to impinge, by accident or violence, or (figuratively) by importunity: (Biblesoft's New Exhaustive Strong's Numbers and Concordance with Expanded Greek-Hebrew Dictionary. Copyright © 1994, 2003, 2006, 2010 Biblesoft, Inc. and International Bible Translators, Inc.)

Impinge: To strike, hit, or dash on, upon, or against something; to touch on or upon; have an effect; to make inroads or encroach on or upon the property or rights of another. (from Webster's Dictionary)

Importunity: persistence in requesting or demanding. (from Webster's Dictionary.)

[4]Transgressors: OT:6586 <START HEBREW>uv^P*<END HEBREW> pasha` (paw-shah'); a primitive root [identical with OT:6585 through the idea of expansion]; to break away (from just authority), i.e. trespass, apostatize, quarrel: (Biblesoft's New Exhaustive Strong's Numbers and Concordance with Expanded Greek-Hebrew Dictionary. Copyright © 1994, 2003, 2006, 2010 Biblesoft, Inc. and International Bible Translators, Inc.)

[5]Of Christ: NT:5548<START GREEK>xri/w<END GREEK> chrio (khree'-o); probably akin to NT:5530 through the idea of contact; to smear or rub with oil, i.e. (by implication) to consecrate to an office or religious service:

NT:5530<START GREEK>xra/omai<END GREEK> chraomai (khrah'-om-ahee); middle voice of a primary verb (perhaps rather from NT:5495, to handle); to furnish what is needed; (give an oracle, "graze" [touch slightly], light upon, etc.), i.e. (by implication) to employ or (by extension) to act towards one in a given manner: (Biblesoft's New Exhaustive Strong's Numbers and Concordance with Expanded Greek-Hebrew Dictionary. Copyright © 1994, 2003, 2006, 2010 Biblesoft, Inc. and International Bible Translators, Inc.)

[6]Your salvation: OT:3444 <START HEBREW>hu*Wvy=<END HEBREW> yeshuw`ah (yesh-oo'-aw); feminine passive participle of OT:3467; something saved, i.e. (abstractly) deliverance; hence, aid, victory, prosperity:

OT:3467 <START HEBREW>uv^y*<END HEBREW> yasha` (yaw-shah'); a primitive root; properly, to be open, wide or free, i.e. (by implication) to be safe; causatively, to free or succor: (Biblesoft's New Exhaustive Strong's Numbers and Concordance with Expanded Greek-Hebrew Dictionary. Copyright © 1994, 2003, 2006, 2010 Biblesoft, Inc. and International Bible Translators, Inc.)

30 - Out of the Anguish of His Soul

Pray: Ask God to prepare your heart and mind and soul to receive his words, to receive truth that will set you free, which will heal and perfect your understanding and knowledge of who God is and who you are.

Ps 119:25-32 - I'm feeling terrible — I couldn't feel worse! Get me on my feet again. You promised, remember? When I told my story, you responded; train me well in your deep wisdom. Help me understand these things inside and out so I can ponder your miracle-wonders. My sad life's dilapidated, a falling-down barn; build me up again by your Word. Barricade the road that goes Nowhere; grace me with your clear revelation. I choose the true road to Somewhere, I post your road signs at every curve and corner. I grasp and cling to whatever you tell me; God, don't let me down! I'll run the course you lay out for me if you'll just show me how. (MSG)

[Murmur and mumble the words. Phrase by phrase. Word by word. Syllable by syllable. Pause. Breathe. Inhale and exhale. Reflect. Listen.]

Journal:

Note how this prayer stirs you today and what you hear God saying to you.

Ps 22:1-2 - My God, my God, why have you forsaken me? Why are you so far from saving me [freeing me, assisting me, relieving me], from the words of my groaning? O my God, I cry by day, but you do not answer, and by night, but I find no rest.

Isa 53:10-12 - Yet it was the will of the Lord to crush him; he has put him to grief; when his soul makes an offering for sin, he shall see his offspring; he shall prolong his days; the will of the Lord shall prosper in his hand. Out of the anguish of his soul he shall see and be satisfied; by his knowledge shall the righteous one, my servant, make many to be accounted righteous, and he shall bear their iniquities. Therefore I will divide him a portion with the many, and he shall divide the spoil with the strong, because he poured out his soul to death and was numbered with the transgressors; yet he bore the sin of many, and makes intercession for the transgressors.

Yet it was ***the will*** of the Lord

It was the will of the Lord ***to crush him***

The Lord has ***put him to grief***

Out of the anguish of his soul he shall see and be satisfied.

[Murmur and mumble the words. Phrase by phrase. Word by word. Syllable by syllable. Take pleasure in making the sounds of the words, getting the feel of the meaning. Experience pleasurable anticipation of taking in what will make you more yourself, the self that God made in his own image and likeness. The self that God made for intimate communion with him. The self that God created for good works, that you should walk in them. Eat God's words. Let God's words become a joy and the delight of your heart.]

Journal:

How do you respond to these words? If these words refer to you as well as to Jesus Christ, does your response change?

It was the will of the Lord to crush ***me***.

The Lord has put ***me*** to grief.

In my family's experience of deep grief, I withdrew from God. I judged God, accusing him of failing to love us, of being negligent because he failed to protect and save us. He is all-powerful, all-knowing, present everywhere at once, yet he didn't bother to do a thing to prevent the accident that took my father's life when I was just a kid. God failed us. I held that against God for years, and it caused me to withdraw from him, even though, at the same time, I tried desperately to please him so he wouldn't take anyone or anything else that I cherished away from me. My heart was far from him. The heart is deceitful and desperately sick!

I found that I had to forgive God for being willing to crush me, for being willing to put me to grief before I could begin to come close to him again. And then God ever so tenderly began to probe my heart and mind to reveal that it was actually me that needed forgiveness, that it was my heart that was deceitful and desperately sick.

As I became aware of my arrogant, unreasonable judgment of God, I expected God to be angry and punish me and even destroy me for slandering his name. But I had no idea what Perfect Love is or what Perfect Love does or what Perfect Love does not do. Instead of doing what I expected, he sent Jesus Christ as his servant, to serve me, to help me, to draw me back to himself. To wake me up. Christ never ceases to make intercession, no matter the depth and height and width and breadth of my transgression and sin.

He makes intercession for the transgressors.

Intercession: To impinge by importunity. To strike, hit, or dash on, upon, or against something; to touch on or upon; have an effect; to make inroads or encroach on or upon the property or rights of another by persistence in repeatedly, urgently urging, requesting or demanding.[1]

Jesus Christ never failed me in all those years when I was hurt and angry, finding fault with God, rejecting him, and withdrawing from him. Jesus Christ never ceased to strike against the evil one's lies that held me captive. He never ceased to touch upon my stone-hard heart, begging me to open up and listen. Though I had no idea of his tireless intercession for me, he consistently made inroads through his persistence in requesting and demanding my release, as he himself bore each and every errant word and thought and action of mine. His faithfulness obtained release and forgiveness for me. His faithfulness in death reconciled me to God. His faithfulness in life continues to save me and give me life moment by moment to this day.

Only in looking back, after Christ Jesus had turned my heart back to God, so that I woke up, so that I began to earnestly seek God, did I discover how abundant and abounding God's steadfast love and his saving faithfulness through Christ Jesus is. How tirelessly God persisted in requesting and demanding that I come and reason together with him through Christ Jesus!

I have no idea what foreign god I'd been so terrified of, seeking to please and appease in order to avoid suffering and death. But I do know that it was not the God of Abraham, Isaac, Jacob, Moses and David. It was not the Father of Jesus Christ.

Out of the ***anguish*** of his soul

He ***shall see***

And ***be satisfied***

Do you lose heart in the midst of disappointment and failure and loss and pain and doubt and grief?

Do you receive any comfort from the promise that the suffering you endure now is actually slight and momentary in comparison to what will come out of the anguish of your soul?

Do you trust that you shall see and be satisfied?

Ps 66:10, 12 - For you, O God, have tested us; you have tried us as silver is tried. …we went through fire and through water; yet you have brought us out to a place of abundance.

Does the realization that much of our suffering now is related to our outer nature wasting away and our inner nature being renewed day by day soothe, calm and relieve you?

Do we suffer more intensely and for longer periods if we attempt to cling to that which is wasting away?

2 Cor 4:16-18 - So we do not lose heart. Though our outer nature is wasting away, <u>our inner nature is being renewed day by day</u>. For this slight momentary affliction is preparing for us an eternal weight of glory beyond all comparison, as we look not to the things that are seen but to the things that are unseen. For the things that are seen *are transient, but the things that are unseen are eternal.*

Phil 3:8-11 - Indeed, I count everything as loss because of the surpassing worth of knowing Christ Jesus my Lord. For his sake I have suffered the loss of all things and count them as rubbish, in order that I may gain Christ and be found in him, not having a righteousness of my own that comes from the law, but that which comes through faith in [of] Christ, the righteousness from God that depends on faith— that I may know him and the power of his resurrection, and may share his sufferings, becoming like him in his death, that by any means possible I may attain the resurrection from the dead.

Do we suffer more intensely and for longer periods if what we long for is not aligned with what God longs for us?

That I may ***gain Christ***

What do you long to gain?

That I may be ***found in him***

The righteousness ***from God***

That I may ***know him*** and the ***power of his resurrection***

That I may ***share his sufferings***

That I may ***become like him*** in his death

That by any means possible I may attain the ***resurrection from the dead***.

Ps 138:8 - The Lord will perfect that which concerns me; Your mercy, O Lord, endures forever; Do not forsake the works of Your hands. (NKJV)

[Murmur and mumble the words. Phrase by phrase. Word by word. Syllable by syllable. Take pleasure in making the sounds of the words, getting the feel of the meaning. Experience pleasurable anticipation of taking in what will make you more yourself, the self that God made in his own image and likeness. The self that God made for intimate communion with him. The self that God created for good works, that you should walk in them. Eat God's words. Let God's words become a joy and the delight of your heart.]

Journal:

What do you discover about God and about yourself in these Scripture texts?

Do you count everything as loss because of the surpassing worth of knowing Christ Jesus your Lord?

Do you want to know him?

Do you want to know the power of his resurrection?

Do you want to share his sufferings, becoming like him in his death?

Perhaps I lean on my own understanding when I fix my eyes on my suffering rather than on the mercy and steadfast love of God which endures forever. I lean on my own understanding when I withdraw from God rather than pressing in close in the midst of my anguish. I lean on my own understanding when I think of my loss or the grave rather than of gaining Christ and of God setting me on high. I lean on my own understanding when I always ask God to spare me from suffering or remove it, rather than asking him to let me share his sufferings.

I trust in the Lord with all my heart when I entrust my soul to him even in the midst of my anguish, confident that somehow, some time, out of the anguish of my soul I *shall* see and be satisfied because what God is doing in my inner nature far outweighs what is so painful in my outer nature. He is preparing for me an eternal weight of glory beyond all comparison.

*1 John 3:2 - Beloved, we <u>are</u> God's children <u>now</u>, and what we will be has not yet appeared; but we know that when he appears **we shall be like him**, because **we shall see him as he is**.*

Ps 22:1-2 - My God, my God, why have you forsaken me? Why are you so far from saving me [freeing me, assisting me, relieving me], from the words of my groaning? O my God, I cry by day, but you do not answer, and by night, but I find no rest.

Isa 53:10-12 - Yet it was the will of the Lord to crush him; he has put him to grief; when his soul makes an offering for sin, he shall see his offspring; he shall prolong his days; the will of the Lord shall prosper in his hand. Out of the anguish of his soul he shall see and be satisfied; by his knowledge shall the righteous one, my servant, make many to be accounted righteous, and he shall bear their iniquities. Therefore I will divide him a portion with the many, and he shall divide the spoil with the strong, because he poured out his soul to death and was numbered with the transgressors; yet he bore the sin of many, and makes intercession for the transgressors.

[Pause. Breathe. Inhale and exhale. Reflect. Listen.]

Give me life according to your word, God!

Journal:

What do you hear God saying to you in these Scripture texts? What do they reveal about God and about you? Converse with God about what you're hearing him say. Verbalize and describe your thoughts, memories that come to mind, questions and emotions, concerns, desires.

Is there a particular word or phrase that disturbs or soothes you?

Do the Scripture texts create a picture or an impression that draws you to linger in exploring and experiencing it?

Choose a word or a phrase from your meditation to write on a slip of paper to carry with you today. Refer to it often throughout the day to remind you of your conversation with God and to continue the conversation all day long. Throughout the day pause to become aware of your thoughts and feelings and will. Ask yourself, "What drives me in this moment? Life according to God's word? Or life according to someone else's word?"

Anticipate that God's words stirred your heart for a reason. He's conversing with you through them. Anticipate that God will bring his word to life in you, to bear fruit in your heart and mind and soul and body. Anticipate that God will reveal the secrets of your heart, for anything that is visible is light. And anticipate that God will cause his words to become a joy and the delight of your heart.

CONTEMPLATE

God is spirit, and those who worship him must worship in spirit and truth. Seek him. Feel your way to him. Reach out. Find him.

Inhale deeply, aware that God *is* in your hidden parts, that it is *his* breath that makes you understand his word. Exhale. Give God the gift that he most desires from you, your exposed and surrendered heart, mind, soul, spirit, and body, your whole self, both outer and inner.

Each time you find that your outer self has pulled your attention away, quietly and gently say the word or phrase you chose and then dive back down deep to the hidden person of your heart to return to the Lord. Bask in him. Rest in perfect love.

At the end of your contemplation, inhale deeply and hold it for a second, aware that you exist in God's abounding grace. Only in God's abounding grace do you exist. In God's abounding grace you are you, the real you, able to worship God in spirit and truth.

*2 Cor 9:8 - And **God is able** to make all grace abound to you, so that having all sufficiency in all things at all times, **you may** abound in every good work.*

Exhale slowly and deeply, anticipating that God's abounding grace, in which you exist and are, will flow around you and through you to enlighten and empower you to love as you have been loved so that you may abound in every good work this day.

Resources:

[1]Made intercession for: OT:6293 <START HEBREW>ug^P*<END HEBREW> paga` (paw-gah'); a primitive root; to impinge, by accident or violence, or (figuratively) by importunity: (Biblesoft's New Exhaustive Strong's Numbers and Concordance with Expanded Greek-Hebrew Dictionary. Copyright © 1994, 2003, 2006, 2010 Biblesoft, Inc. and International Bible Translators, Inc.)

Impinge: To strike, hit, or dash on, upon, or against something; to touch on or upon; have an effect; to make inroads or encroach on or upon the property or rights of another. (from Webster's Dictionary)

Importunity: persistence in requesting or demanding. (from Webster's Dictionary.)

31 - As It Goes Well with Your Soul

Pray: Ask God to prepare your heart and mind and soul to receive his words, to receive truth that will set you free, which will heal and perfect your understanding and knowledge of who God is and who you are.

Ps 119:25-32 - My soul clings to the dust; give me life according to your word! When I told of my ways, you answered me; teach me your statutes! Make me understand the way of your precepts, and I will meditate on your wondrous works. My soul melts away for sorrow; strengthen me according to your word! Put false ways far from me and graciously teach me your law! I have chosen the way of faithfulness; I set your rules before me. I cling to your testimonies, O Lord; let me not be put to shame! I will run in the way of your commandments when you enlarge my heart! (ESV)

[Murmur and mumble the words. Phrase by phrase. Word by word. Syllable by syllable. Pause. Breathe. Inhale and exhale. Reflect. Listen.]

Journal:

Note how this prayer stirs you today and what you hear God saying to you.

3 John 2 - Beloved, I pray that all may go well with you and that you may be in good health, as it goes well with your soul.

Beloved, I pray that ***all may go well*** with you…

…and that you may be in good health…

As…

As it ***goes well***…

As it goes well ***with your soul***.

[Murmur and mumble the words. Phrase by phrase. Word by word. Syllable by syllable. Take pleasure in making the sounds of the words, getting the feel of the meaning. Experience pleasurable anticipation of taking in what will make you more yourself, the self that

God made in his own image and likeness. The self that God made for intimate communion with him. The self that God created for good works, that you should walk in them. Eat God's words. Let God's words become a joy and the delight of your heart.]

Journal:

What is your soul?

Are you concerned about your soul? Or are you mostly concerned with other things so that you're seldom even aware of your soul?

Are you consumed with concern for things like your physical body, your financial success, your favor with people, excellence in your endeavors, etc.?

Is God perhaps more concerned with your soul while you are more concerned about all of these other things?

What is your soul?

Soul: breath, i.e. (by implication) spirit, abstractly or concretely the animal sentient principle only[1]

As it goes well with your ***soul***.

As it goes well with your breath.

As it goes well with your spirit.

As it goes well with your perception through the senses.

As it goes well with your capacity of feeling or perception.

As it goes well with your consciousness.

As it goes will with your soul.

Beloved, I pray that all may go well with you and that you may be in good health, ***as*** it goes well with your soul.

Is God saying that our soul's well-being is his priority? Is he saying that he wants us to make our soul our priority, too? Does our soul's well-being set the precedent for well-being in everything else?

Does well-being mean that we never experience loss of power and control, loss of safety and security, loss of esteem and affection in our outer self in our existence in this world? Or can well-being only be truly experienced in the hidden person of the heart? Consider the Apostle Paul's testimony.

2 Cor 12:10 - For the sake of Christ, then, I am content with weaknesses, insults, hardships, persecutions, and calamities. For when I am weak, then I am strong.

Phil 4:11-13 - Not that I am speaking of being in need, for I have learned in whatever situation I am to be content. I know how to be brought low, and I know how to abound. In any and every circumstance, I have learned the secret of facing plenty and hunger, abundance and need. I can do all things through him who strengthens me.

For the ***sake of Christ***

I am content with weakness, insults, hardships, persecutions, and calamities

I am content. I take pleasure. I think well of, i.e. approve.[2]

For the ***sake of Christ***

For ***when***

For when ***I am weak***

Then

Then ***I am strong***

I have learned

I have learned in ***whatever situation*** I am

To be content

Content. Self-complacent.[3]

I can do all things

I can do all things ***through him*** who strengthens me.

[Murmur and mumble the words. Phrase by phrase. Word by word. Syllable by syllable. Take pleasure in making the sounds of the words, getting the feel of the meaning. Experience pleasurable anticipation of taking in what will make you more yourself, the self that God made in his own image and likeness. The self that God made for intimate communion with him. The self that God created for good works, that you should walk in them. Eat God's words. Let God's words become a joy and the delight of your heart.]

Journal:

Is your thought routinely, "For the sake of Christ," or more often, "For my sake,"?

What do you think the learning process was for Apostle Paul to be content in any and all situations?

Do you regularly ask God to help you learn to live in this same state of contentment, self-complacency?

Christ Jesus is the channel, the means, the way by which we have strength to be content in all situations. How do we find our way into this channel, into relationship with The Way?

As you read the following Scripture texts note knowledge and understanding and desires and actions that impact your soul's well-being. Might the Apostle Paul have meditated on these words in his work to learn to be content in every situation for the sake of Christ? Is there one that you are willing to acknowledge and/or pray regularly?

Job 33:4 - The Spirit of God has made me, and the breath of the Almighty gives me life.

Job 34:14-15 - If he should set his heart to it and gather to himself his spirit and his breath, all flesh would perish together, and man would return to dust.

Ps 31:5 - Into your hand I commit my spirit; you have redeemed me, O Lord, faithful God.

Ps 51:10-12 - Create in me a clean heart, O God, and renew a right spirit within me. Cast me not away from your presence, and take not your Holy Spirit from me. Restore to me the joy of your salvation, and uphold me with a willing spirit.

Ps 104:29-30 - When you hide your face, they are dismayed; when you take away their breath, they die and return to their dust. When you send forth your Spirit, they are created, and you renew the face of the ground.

Ps 139:7-12 - Where shall I go from your Spirit? Or where shall I flee from your presence? If I ascend to heaven, you are there! If I make my bed in Sheol, you are there! If I take the wings of the morning and dwell in the uttermost parts of the sea, even there your hand shall lead me, and your right hand shall hold me. If I say, "Surely the darkness shall cover me, and the light about me be night," even the darkness is not dark to you; the night is bright as the day, for darkness is as light with you.

Ps 142:3a - When my spirit faints within me, you know my way!

Ps 143:10 - Teach me to do your will, for you are my God! Let your good Spirit lead me on level ground!

Prov 3:5-6 - Trust in the Lord with all your heart, and do not lean on your own understanding. In all your ways acknowledge him, and he will make straight your paths.

3 John 2 - Beloved, I pray that all may go well with you and that you may be in good health, as it goes well with your soul.

[Pause. Breathe. Inhale and exhale. Reflect. Listen.]

Give me life according to your word, God!

Journal:

What do you hear God saying to you in these Scripture texts? What do they reveal about God and about you? Converse with God about what you're hearing him say. Verbalize and describe your thoughts, memories that come to mind, questions and emotions, concerns, desires.

Is there a particular word or phrase that disturbs or soothes you?

Do the Scripture texts create a picture or an impression that draws you to linger in exploring and experiencing it?

Choose a word or a phrase from your meditation to write on a slip of paper to carry with you today. Refer to it often throughout the day to remind you of your conversation with God and to continue the conversation all day long. Throughout the day pause to become aware of your thoughts and feelings and will. Ask yourself, "What drives me in this moment? Life according to God's word? Or life according to someone else's word?"

Anticipate that God's words stirred your heart for a reason. He's conversing with you through them. Anticipate that God will bring his word to life in you, to bear fruit in your heart and mind and soul and body. Anticipate that God will reveal the secrets of your heart, for anything that is visible is light. And anticipate that God will cause his words to become a joy and the delight of your heart.

CONTEMPLATE

God is spirit, and those who worship him must worship in spirit and truth. Seek him. Feel your way to him. Reach out. Find him.

Inhale deeply, aware that God *is* in your hidden parts, that it is *his* breath that makes you understand his word. Exhale. Give God the gift that he most desires from you, your exposed and surrendered heart, mind, soul, spirit, and body, your whole self, both outer and inner.

Each time you find that your outer self has pulled your attention away, quietly and gently say the word or phrase you chose and then dive back down deep to the hidden person of your heart to return to the Lord. Bask in him. Rest in perfect love.

At the end of your contemplation, inhale deeply and hold it for a second, aware that you exist in God's abounding grace. Only in God's abounding grace do you exist. In God's abounding grace you are you, the real you, able to worship God in spirit and truth.

2 Cor 9:8 - And ***God is able*** *to make all grace abound to you, so that having all sufficiency in all things at all times,* ***you may*** *abound in every good work.*

Exhale slowly and deeply, anticipating that God's abounding grace, in which you exist and are, will flow around you and through you to enlighten and empower you to love as you have been loved so that you may abound in every good work this day.

Resources:

[1]Soul: NT:5590<START GREEK>yuxh/<END GREEK> psuche (psoo-khay'); from NT:5594; breath, i.e. (by implication) spirit, abstractly or concretely (the animal sentient principle only; thus distinguished on the one hand from NT:4151, which is the rational and

immortal soul; and on the other from NT:2222, which is mere vitality, even of plants: these terms thus exactly correspond respectively to the Hebrew OT:5315, OT:7307 and OT:2416):

NT:5594<START GREEK>yu/xw<END GREEK> psucho (psoo'-kho); a primary verb; to breathe (voluntarily but gently, thus differing on the one hand from NT:4154, which denotes properly a forcible respiration; and on the other from the base of NT:109, which refers properly to an inanimate breeze), i.e. (by implication of reduction of temperature by evaporation) to chill (figuratively): (Biblesoft's New Exhaustive Strong's Numbers and Concordance with Expanded Greek-Hebrew Dictionary. Copyright © 1994, 2003, 2006 Biblesoft, Inc. and International Bible Translators, Inc.)

[2]Content/take pleasure in: NT:2106 <START GREEK>eu)doke/w<END GREEK> eudokeo (yoo-dok-eh'-o); from NT:2095 and NT:1380; to think well of, i.e. approve (an act); specially, to approbate (a person or thing): (Biblesoft's New Exhaustive Strong's Numbers and Concordance with Expanded Greek-Hebrew Dictionary. Copyright © 1994, 2003, 2006, 2010 Biblesoft, Inc. and International Bible Translators, Inc.)

[3]Content: NT:842<START GREEK>au)ta/rkh$<END GREEK> autarkes (ow-tar'-kace); from NT:846 and NT:714; self-complacent, i.e. contented: (Biblesoft's New Exhaustive Strong's Numbers and Concordance with Expanded Greek-Hebrew Dictionary. Copyright © 1994, 2003, 2006, 2010 Biblesoft, Inc. and International Bible Translators, Inc.)

32 - Made Alive in the Spirit

Pray: Ask God to prepare your heart and mind and soul to receive his words, to receive truth that will set you free, which will heal and perfect your understanding and knowledge of who God is and who you are.

Ps 119:25-32 - I'm feeling terrible — I couldn't feel worse! Get me on my feet again. You promised, remember? When I told my story, you responded; train me well in your deep wisdom. Help me understand these things inside and out so I can ponder your miracle-wonders. My sad life's dilapidated, a falling-down barn; build me up again by your Word. Barricade the road that goes Nowhere; grace me with your clear revelation. I choose the true road to Somewhere, I post your road signs at every curve and corner. I grasp and cling to whatever you tell me; God, don't let me down! I'll run the course you lay out for me if you'll just show me how. (MSG)

[Murmur and mumble the words. Phrase by phrase. Word by word. Syllable by syllable. Pause. Breathe. Inhale and exhale. Reflect. Listen.]

Journal:

Note how this prayer stirs you today and what you hear God saying to you.

If I look more carefully into Scripture, it seems that God says suffering is mandatory. Suffering is mandatory for *all* of us. Suffering seems to be necessary in order for God to reveal my true self, the hidden person of my heart, my spirit self, my soul. Even his own, beloved Son was not spared from suffering.

Matt 16:21-23 - From that time Jesus began to show his disciples that he ***must*** *go to Jerusalem and suffer many things from the elders and chief priests and scribes, and be killed, and on the third day be raised. And Peter took him aside and began to rebuke him, saying, "Far be it from you, Lord! This shall never happen to you." But he turned and said to Peter, "Get behind me, Satan! You are a* *hindrance to me. For you are not setting your mind on the things of God, but on the things of man."*

He ***must***... ***suffer*** many things... and be ***killed*** ...and be ***raised***. He ***must***.

Is this a life pattern that *all* of humanity must experience in order to become our true selves, the selves that God made in his image and likeness? The self that God made for intimate communion with him? The self that he created for good works, that we should walk in them? Is suffering a requirement so that it *will* go well with our soul, with our spirit? Suffer many things. Die. Be raised.

1 Peter 3:18 - For Christ also suffered once for sins, the righteous for the unrighteous, that he might bring us to God, being put to death in the flesh but made alive in the spirit

1 Pet 4:1 - Since therefore Christ suffered in the flesh, arm yourselves with the same way of thinking, for whoever has suffered in the flesh has ceased from sin, so as to live for the rest of the time in the flesh no longer for human passions but for the will of God.

1 Peter 4:19 - Therefore let those who suffer according to God's will entrust their souls to a faithful Creator while doing good.

Suffer.

Suffer ***for sins***. Suffer for breaking away, withdrawing, rebelling, and becoming independent and lawless.

Be put to ***death*** in the ***flesh***.

Be made ***alive*** in the ***spirit***.

Bring us to God.

Bring those who broke away, withdrew, rebelled, and became independent and lawless ***to God***.

Since therefore

Since therefore ***Christ suffered***

Since therefore Christ suffered in the ***flesh***

Since therefore Christ suffered in the flesh, ***arm yourself***. Equip yourself. Take every thought captive to obey Christ (2 Cor 10:5).

Equip yourself. Arm yourself with ***the same way of thinking***.

Arm yourself with the same way of thinking ***for***...

For ***whoever has suffered***

Whoever has suffered ***in the flesh***...

Whoever has suffered in the flesh ***has ceased from sin***. Has ceased from withdrawing, breaking away, rebelling, becoming independent and lawless.

No longer live for human passions. But ***live*** for the will of God.

Live for the ***will of God.***

[Murmur and mumble the words. Phrase by phrase. Word by word. Syllable by syllable. Take pleasure in making the sounds of the words, getting the feel of the meaning. Experience pleasurable anticipation of taking in what will make you more yourself, the self that God made in his own image and likeness. The self that God made for intimate communion with him. The self that God created for good works, that you should walk in them. Eat God's words. Let God's words become a joy and the delight of your heart.]

Journal:

Record your thoughts about what this text is saying about suffering, sin, dying, and living.

Do we get so absorbed in the pain and fear of suffering, sin, and death that we are ignorant of the God of hope who fills us with all joy and peace in believing, so that by the power of the Holy Spirit we may abound in hope?

Live. Live for the will of God. Made alive in the spirit. How can we become absorbed in living for the will of God?

How does living for the will of God impact our well-being?

[Pause. Breathe. Inhale and exhale. Reflect. Listen.]

Give me life according to your word, God!

Journal:

What do you hear God saying to you in these Scripture texts? What do they reveal about God and about you? Converse with God about what you're hearing him say. Verbalize and describe your thoughts, memories that come to mind, questions and emotions, concerns, desires.

Is there a particular word or phrase that disturbs or soothes you?

Do the Scripture texts create a picture or an impression that draws you to linger in exploring and experiencing it?

Choose a word or a phrase from your meditation to write on a slip of paper to carry with you today. Refer to it often throughout the day to remind you of your conversation with God and to continue the conversation all day long. Throughout the day pause to become aware of your thoughts and feelings and will. Ask yourself, "What drives me in this moment? Life according to God's word? Or life according to someone else's word?"

Anticipate that God's words stirred your heart for a reason. He's conversing with you through them. Anticipate that God will bring his word to life in you, to bear fruit in your heart and mind and soul and body. Anticipate that God will reveal the secrets of your heart, for anything that is visible is light. And anticipate that God will cause his words to

become a joy and the delight of your heart.

CONTEMPLATE

God is spirit, and those who worship him must worship in spirit and truth. Seek him. Feel your way to him. Reach out. Find him.

You exist in God's abounding grace. Only in God's abounding grace do you exist. In God's abounding grace you are you, the real you, able to worship God in spirit and truth.

2 Cor 9:8 - And ***God is able*** *to make all grace abound to you, so that having all sufficiency in all things at all times,* ***you may*** *abound in every good work.*

Anticipate that God's abounding grace, in which you exist and are, will flow around you and through you to enlighten and empower you to love as you have been loved so that you may abound in every good work this day.

33 - It is Christ Who Lives in Me

Pray: Ask God to prepare your heart and mind and soul to receive his words, to receive truth that will set you free, which will heal and perfect your understanding and knowledge of who God is and who you are.

Ps 119:25-32 - My soul clings to the dust; give me life according to your word! When I told of my ways, you answered me; teach me your statutes! Make me understand the way of your precepts, and I will meditate on your wondrous works. My soul melts away for sorrow; strengthen me according to your word! Put false ways far from me and graciously teach me your law! I have chosen the way of faithfulness; I set your rules before me. I cling to your testimonies, O Lord; let me not be put to shame! I will run in the way of your commandments when you enlarge my heart! (ESV)

[Murmur and mumble the words. Phrase by phrase. Word by word. Syllable by syllable. Pause. Breathe. Inhale and exhale. Reflect. Listen.]

Journal:

Note how this prayer stirs you today and what you hear God saying to you.

1 Peter 3:18 - For Christ also suffered once for sins, the righteous for the unrighteous, that he might bring us to God, being put to death in the flesh but made alive in the spirit,

Put to death ***in the flesh***

But made alive ***in the spirit***

The mystery of being put to death in the flesh but made alive in the spirit cannot be understood by the intellect. It cannot be accomplished or experienced through human will or effort.

Rom 6:7 - For one who has died has been set free from sin.

Gal 2:20 - I have been crucified with Christ. It is no longer I who live, but Christ who lives in me. And the life I now live in the flesh I live by faith in the Son of God, who loved me and gave himself for me.

One who ***has died***

One who has died has been ***set free*** [to show or regard as just or innocent]

One who has died has been set free ***from sin*** [missing the mark and so not sharing in the prize]

[Murmur and mumble the words. Phrase by phrase. Word by word. Syllable by syllable. Take pleasure in making the sounds of the words, getting the feel of the meaning. Experience pleasurable anticipation of taking in what will make you more yourself, the self that God made in his own image and likeness. The self that God made for intimate communion with him. The self that God created for good works, that you should walk in them. Eat God's words. Let God's words become a joy and the delight of your heart.]

Journal:

Do you have a deep longing to be set free? What do you want to be set free from?

Deep inside, do you have a sense that you somehow miss the mark? That somehow you just don't quite measure up? That somehow there's a separation between you and others, and you're missing something vital? That you're not complete?

How liberating it would be to vanquish those failures and worries and insecurities!

Rom 6:7 - For one who has died has been set free from sin.

How does dying liberate us? Is this Scripture text speaking of literal, physical death or a different kind of death?

I ***have died***

I have been ***crucified with Christ***

It is no longer I who live, but ***Christ who lives in me***

And the life ***I now live*** in the flesh

In the flesh. The body, as opposed to the soul or spirit, or as the symbol of what is external; human nature, with its frailties, physically or morally and passions.[1]

Gal 2:20 - with Christ I have been crucified, and live no more do I, and Christ doth live in me; and that which I now live in the flesh — in the faith I live of the Son of God, who did love me and did give himself for me; (YLT)

Live no more do I

And **Christ doth live in me**

In the faith I live ***of the Son of God***

Who did ***love me***

And did ***give himself for me***

[Murmur and mumble the words. Phrase by phrase. Word by word. Syllable by syllable. Take pleasure in making the sounds of the words, getting the feel of the meaning. Experience pleasurable anticipation of taking in what will make you more yourself, the self that God made in his own image and likeness. The self that God made for intimate communion with him. The self that God created for good works, that you should walk in them. Eat God's words. Let God's words become a joy and the delight of your heart.]

Journal:

Who is the "I" that Apostle Paul says lives no more? Who is the "I" that died? Who is the "I" that has been crucified with Christ?

Are you fearful of living no more?

Are you fearful of Christ living in you? Are you fearful of living in the faith of the Son of God who did love you and give himself for you?

What does it mean to live in the faith *of* the Son of God? Note the emphasis on the faith *of* the Son of God, rather than your faith in your ability to produce or have faith in Christ.

Faith: NT:4102 <START GREEK>pi/sti$<END GREEK> pistis (pis'-tis); from NT:3982; persuasion, i.e. credence; moral conviction (of religious truth, or the truthfulness of God or a religious teacher), especially reliance upon Christ for salvation; abstractly, constancy in such profession; by extension, the system of religious (Gospel) truth itself:

NT:3982 <START GREEK>pei/qw<END GREEK> peitho (pi'-tho); a primary verb; to convince (by argument, true or false); by analogy, to pacify or conciliate (by other fair means); reflexively or passively, to assent (to evidence or authority), to rely (by inward certainty)[2]

Persuasion. Credence. Moral conviction. To be convinced by argument, true or false. To pacify or conciliate. To assent to evidence or authority. To rely by *inward* certainty. To rely upon Christ for salvation.

As you ponder the definition of faith, do you hear the back and forth, the give and take nature of the process of an individual developing faith? Like a relationship is formed in the process of receiving and relying upon the faith of Christ?

What is the faith of the Son of God?

What evidence do you have of the complete faith that Christ Jesus has in his Father, God?

Do you make time and space for Christ Jesus to persuade you and convince you of his love for you in doing whatever it takes so that he can draw you to his Father?

What are these Scripture texts revealing about your outer nature and your inner nature, your body and your soul and spirit?

What is this death that the Apostle Paul is describing? Is it literal, physical death? Or is it referring to our outer and inner natures?

Have you died? Is this death in the flesh a one-time occurrence? Or is it an ongoing process of renewal, moment by moment?

Have you been set free from sin? Explain.

1 Peter 3:18 - For Christ also suffered once for sins, the righteous for the unrighteous, that he might bring us to God, being put to death in the flesh but made alive in the spirit

Rom 6:7 - For one who has died has been set free from sin.

Gal 2:20 - I have been crucified with Christ. It is no longer I who live, but Christ who lives in me. And the life I now live in the flesh I live by faith in the Son of God, who loved me and gave himself for me.

[Pause. Breathe. Inhale and exhale. Reflect. Listen.]

Give me life according to your word, God!

Journal:

What do you hear God saying to you in these Scripture texts? What do they reveal about God and about you? Converse with God about what you're hearing him say. Verbalize and describe your thoughts, memories that come to mind, questions and emotions, concerns, desires.

Is there a particular word or phrase that disturbs or soothes you?

Do the Scripture texts create a picture or an impression that draws you to linger in exploring and experiencing it?

Choose a word or a phrase from your meditation to write on a slip of paper to carry with you today. Refer to it often throughout the day to remind you of your conversation with God and to continue the conversation all day long. Throughout the day pause to become aware of your thoughts and feelings and will. Ask yourself, "What drives me in this moment? Life according to God's word? Or life according to someone else's word?"

Anticipate that God's words stirred your heart for a reason. He's conversing with you through them. Anticipate that God will bring his word to life in you, to bear fruit in your heart and mind and soul and body. Anticipate that God will reveal the secrets of your heart, for anything that is visible is light. And anticipate that God will cause his words to become a joy and the delight of your heart.

CONTEMPLATE

God is spirit, and those who worship him must worship in spirit and truth. Seek him. Feel your way to him. Reach out. Find him.

You exist in God's abounding grace. Only in God's abounding grace do you exist. In God's abounding grace you are you, the real you, able to worship God in spirit and truth.

*2 Cor 9:8 - And **God is able** to make all grace abound to you, so that having all sufficiency in all things at all times, **you may** abound in every good work.*

Anticipate that God's abounding grace, in which you exist and are, will flow around you and through you to enlighten and empower you to love as you have been loved so that you may abound in every good work this day.

Resources:

[1]Flesh: NT:4561 <START GREEK>sa/rc<END GREEK> sarx (sarx); probably from the base of NT:4563; flesh (as stripped of the skin), i.e. (strictly) the meat of an animal (as food), or (by extension) the body (as opposed to the soul [or spirit], or as the symbol of what is external, or as the means of kindred), or (by implication) human nature (with its frailties [physically or morally] and passions), or (specifically) a human being (as such): (Biblesoft's New Exhaustive Strong's Numbers and Concordance with Expanded Greek-Hebrew Dictionary. Copyright © 1994, 2003, 2006, 2010 Biblesoft, Inc. and International Bible Translators, Inc.)

[2]*(Biblesoft's New Exhaustive Strong's Numbers and Concordance with Expanded Greek-Hebrew Dictionary. Copyright © 1994, 2003, 2006, 2010 Biblesoft, Inc. and International Bible Translators, Inc.)*

34 – We Regard No One According to the Flesh

Pray: Ask God to prepare your heart and mind and soul to receive his words, to receive truth that will set you free, which will heal and perfect your understanding and knowledge of who God is and who you are.

Ps 119:25-32 - My soul clings to the dust; give me life according to your word! When I told of my ways, you answered me; teach me your statutes! Make me understand the way of your precepts, and I will meditate on your wondrous works. My soul melts away for sorrow; strengthen me according to your word! Put false ways far from me and graciously teach me your law! I have chosen the way of faithfulness; I set your rules before me. I cling to your testimonies, O Lord; let me not be put to shame! I will run in the way of your commandments when you enlarge my heart! (ESV)

[Murmur and mumble the words. Phrase by phrase. Word by word. Syllable by syllable. Pause. Breathe. Inhale and exhale. Reflect. Listen.]

Journal:

Note how this prayer stirs you today and what you hear God saying to you.

1 Peter 3:18 - For Christ also suffered once for sins, the righteous for the unrighteous, that he might bring us to God, being put to death in the flesh but made alive in the spirit,

Put to death ***in the flesh***

But made alive ***in the spirit***

Gal 2:20 - I have been crucified with Christ. It is no longer I who live, but Christ who lives in me. And the life I now live in the flesh I live by faith in the Son of God, who loved me and gave himself for me.

I have been crucified with Christ

The life ***I now live*** in the flesh

I live ***by faith***

I life by faith ***in the Son of God***

Who loved me

Who gave himself for me

Gal 6:14-15 - But far be it from me to boast except in the cross of our Lord Jesus Christ, by which the world has been crucified to me, and I to the world. For neither circumcision counts for anything, nor uncircumcision, but a new creation.

Far be it from me to ***boast***

Except

Except ***in the cross*** of our Lord Jesus Christ

In the cross ***of our Lord Jesus Christ***

In the cross

The world has been crucified [to impale, to extinguish or subdue passion or selfishness] ***to me***

In the cross of our Lord Jesus Christ

In the cross

I have been crucified [to impale, to extinguish or subdue passion or selfishness] ***to the world***

In the cross of our Lord Jesus Christ, ***the world has been*** crucified ***to me***

In the cross of our Lord Jesus Christ, ***I have been*** crucified ***to the world***

Crucified

Selfishness

Selfishness ***extinguished or subdued***

Crucified

Selfish passion

Selfish passion ***extinguished or subdued***

New

A ***new creation***

Crucified

The ***world*** to me

Crucified

I to the world

Crucified

To impale. To pierce through. ***To make helpless***.

To extinguish or subdue passion or selfishness

In the cross of our Lord Jesus Christ

A ***new*** creation

A new ***creation***

[Murmur and mumble the words. Phrase by phrase. Word by word. Syllable by syllable. Take pleasure in making the sounds of the words, getting the feel of the meaning. Experience pleasurable anticipation of taking in what will make you more yourself, the self that God made in his own image and likeness. The self that God made for intimate communion with him. The self that God created for good works, that you should walk in them. Eat God's words. Let God's words become a joy and the delight of your heart.]

Journal:

Through Christ Jesus, are your passions and selfishness being made helpless, subdued and extinguished?

What is Christ's role and what is your role in making helpless, subduing and extinguishing the passions of your flesh and your selfishness?

Describe what it means to be crucified with Jesus Christ and to be made a new creation, being put to death in the flesh, but made alive in the spirit.

Eph 2:10 - For we are his workmanship, created in Christ Jesus for good works, which God prepared beforehand, that we should walk in them.

A ***new creation***

His workmanship

Created ***in Christ Jesus***

Extinguish or subdue passion or selfishness in the flesh, but made alive in the spirit.

2 Cor 5:16-21 - From now on, therefore, we regard no one according to the flesh. Even though we once regarded Christ according to the flesh, we regard him thus no longer. Therefore, if anyone is in Christ, he is a new creation. The old has passed away; behold, the new has come. All this is from God, who through Christ reconciled us to himself and gave us the ministry of reconciliation; that is, in Christ God was reconciling the world to himself, not counting their trespasses against them, and entrusting to us the message of reconciliation. Therefore, we are ambassadors for Christ, God making his appeal through us. We implore you on behalf of Christ, be reconciled to God. For our sake he made him to be sin who knew no sin, so that in him we might become the righteousness of God.

From now on

We regard [know; see] ***no one*** according to the flesh [as opposed to soul or spirit]

Therefore, if anyone ***is in Christ***

He is ***a new creation***.

The old has ***passed away***

The new ***has come***

All this

All this ***is from God***

Who ***through Christ*** reconciled us to himself

In Christ God was reconciling ***the world*** to himself

Not counting their trespasses against them

That in him ***we might become*** the righteousness of God

[Murmur and mumble the words. Phrase by phrase. Word by word. Syllable by syllable. Take pleasure in making the sounds of the words, getting the feel of the meaning. Experience pleasurable anticipation of taking in what will make you more yourself, the self that God made in his own image and likeness. The self that God made for intimate communion with him. The self that God created for good works, that you should walk in them. Eat God's words. Let God's words become a joy and the delight of your heart.]

Journal:

How will your view of yourself and all of humankind change when you begin to *know and see no one according to the flesh*?

How will your view of yourself and all of humankind change when you begin to see yourself and all of humankind as having been *reconciled to God through Christ, God not counting our trespasses against us*?

Is it possible to *know and see no one according to the flesh* only after the world has been crucified to you, and you have been crucified to the world? Is it possible to *know and see no one according to the flesh* until you are a *new* creation?

Rom 6:7 - For one who has died has been set free from sin.

Gal 2:20 - I have been crucified with Christ. It is no longer I who live, but Christ who lives in me. And the life I now live in the flesh I live by faith in the Son of God, who loved me and gave himself for me.

Gal 6:14-15 - But far be it from me to boast except in the cross of our Lord Jesus Christ, by which the world has been crucified to me, and I to the world. For neither circumcision counts for anything, nor uncircumcision, but a new creation.

Eph 2:10 - For we are his workmanship, created in Christ Jesus for good works, which God prepared beforehand, that we should walk in them.

2 Cor 5:16-21 - From now on, therefore, we regard no one according to the flesh. ...if anyone is in Christ, he is a new creation. ...All this is from God, who through Christ reconciled us to himself and gave us the ministry of reconciliation; that is, in Christ God was reconciling the world to himself, not counting their trespasses against them, and entrusting to us the message of reconciliation. ...We implore you on behalf of Christ, be reconciled to God. For our sake he made him to be sin who knew no sin, so that in him we might become the righteousness of God.

[Pause. Breathe. Inhale and exhale. Reflect. Listen.]

Give me life according to your word, God!

Journal:

What do you hear God saying to you in these Scripture texts? What do they reveal about God and about you? Converse with God about what you're hearing him say. Verbalize and describe your thoughts, memories that come to mind, questions and emotions, concerns, desires.

Is there a particular word or phrase that disturbs or soothes you?

Do the Scripture texts create a picture or an impression that draws you to linger in exploring and experiencing it?

Choose a word or a phrase from your meditation to write on a slip of paper to carry with you today. Refer to it often throughout the day to remind you of your conversation with God and to continue the conversation all day long. Throughout the day pause to become aware of your thoughts and feelings and will. Ask yourself, "What drives me in this moment? Life according to God's word? Or life according to someone else's word?"

Anticipate that God's words stirred your heart for a reason. He's conversing with you through them. Anticipate that God will bring his word to life in you, to bear fruit in your heart and mind and soul and body. Anticipate that God will reveal the secrets of your heart, for anything that is visible is light. And anticipate that God will cause his words to become a joy and the delight of your heart.

CONTEMPLATE

God is spirit, and those who worship him must worship in spirit and truth. Seek him. Feel your way to him. Reach out. Find him.

You exist in God's abounding grace. Only in God's abounding grace do you exist. In God's abounding grace you are you, the real you, able to worship God in spirit and truth.

*2 Cor 9:8 - And **God is able** to make all grace abound to you, so that having all sufficiency in all things at all times, **you may** abound in every good work.*

Anticipate that God's abounding grace, in which you exist and are, will flow around you and through you to enlighten and empower you to love as you have been loved so that you may abound in every good work this day.

35 – Let Your Good Spirit Lead Me

Pray: Ask God to prepare your heart and mind and soul to receive his words, to receive truth that will set you free, which will heal and perfect your understanding and knowledge of who God is and who you are.

Ps 119:25-32 - I'm feeling terrible — I couldn't feel worse! Get me on my feet again. You promised, remember? When I told my story, you responded; train me well in your deep wisdom. Help me understand these things inside and out so I can ponder your miracle-wonders. My sad life's dilapidated, a falling-down barn; build me up again by your Word. Barricade the road that goes Nowhere; grace me with your clear revelation. I choose the true road to Somewhere, I post your road signs at every curve and corner. I grasp and cling to whatever you tell me; God, don't let me down! I'll run the course you lay out for me if you'll just show me how. (MSG)

[Murmur and mumble the words. Phrase by phrase. Word by word. Syllable by syllable. Pause. Breathe. Inhale and exhale. Reflect. Listen.]

Journal:

Note how this prayer stirs you today and what you hear God saying to you.

Gal 6:14-15 - But far be it from me to boast except in the cross of our Lord Jesus Christ, by which the world has been crucified to me, and I to the world. For neither circumcision counts for anything, nor uncircumcision, but a new creation.

Eph 2:10 - For we are his workmanship, created in Christ Jesus for good works, which God prepared beforehand, that we should walk in them.

The cross of our Lord Jesus Christ

By which

By which the world has been ***crucified*** to me, and I to the world

A ***new creation***

His workmanship

Created ***in Christ Jesus***

Extinguish or subdue passion or selfishness in the flesh, but made alive in the spirit.

Made alive ***in the spirit***

Luke 9:23 - And he said to all, "If anyone would come after me, let him deny himself and take up his cross daily and follow me.

If

If ***anyone***

If anyone would ***come after me***

Let him

Deny himself

Take up his cross

Daily

Follow ***me***

What does it mean to come after Jesus Christ?

Rom 8:13 - For if you live according to the flesh you will die, but if by the Spirit you put to death the deeds of the body, you will live.

Col 3:5 - Put to death therefore what is earthly in you: sexual immorality, impurity, passion, evil desire, and covetousness, which is idolatry.

By the Spirit

You ***put to death***

By the Spirit

You put to death the ***deeds of the body***

By the Spirit you put to death what is earthly in you

By the Spirit you put to death sexual immorality, impurity, passion, evil desire, and covetousness, which is idolatry.

By the Spirit

[Murmur and mumble the words. Phrase by phrase. Word by word. Syllable by syllable. Take pleasure in making the sounds of the words, getting the feel of the meaning. Experience pleasurable anticipation of taking in what will make you more yourself, the self that God made in his own image and likeness. The self that God made for intimate communion with him. The self that God created for good works, that you should walk in them. Eat God's words. Let God's words become a joy and the delight of your heart.]

Journal:

Have you been crucified with Christ? Have your passions all been impaled? Has your selfishness been subdued or extinguished?

Is this impaling, subduing, and extinguishing of selfish passions a one-time event or a moment by moment process?

Do you come after Christ Jesus?

What does this Scripture text mean when it says, By the Spirit you put to death the deeds of the body? What action can you take to put to death what is earthly in you by the Spirit?

What did David do, the man God described as "a man after my heart, who will do all my will"? (Acts 13:22)

Ps 119:36-37 - <u>Incline my heart</u> to your testimonies, and not to selfish gain! <u>Turn my eyes</u> from looking at worthless things; and <u>give me life in your ways</u>.

Ps 119:112 - <u>I incline my heart</u> to perform your statutes forever, to the end.

Ps 141:4 - <u>Do not let my heart incline</u> to any evil, to busy myself with wicked deeds in company with men who work iniquity, and let me not *eat of their delicacies!*

Ps 31:5 - Into your hand I commit my spirit; you have redeemed me, O Lord, faithful God.

Ps 51:10-12 - Create in me a clean heart, O God, and renew a right spirit within me. Cast me not away from your presence, and take not your Holy Spirit from me. Restore to me the joy of your salvation, and uphold me with a willing spirit.

Ps 143:10 - Teach me to do your will, for you are my God! Let your good Spirit lead me on level ground!

[Murmur and mumble the words. Phrase by phrase. Word by word. Syllable by syllable. Take pleasure in making the sounds of the words, getting the feel of the meaning. Experience pleasurable anticipation of taking in what will make you more yourself, the self that God made in his own image and likeness. The self that God made for intimate communion with him. The self that God created for good works, that you should walk in them. Eat God's words. Let God's words become a joy and the delight of your heart.]

Journal:

Choose one of David's prayers that you desire to become true in your heart and mind and soul and spirit and life. Trust that God will do it even as you agree to incline your heart to agree and participate with him in accomplishing it.

Gal 6:14-15 - But far be it from me to boast except in the cross of our Lord Jesus Christ, by which the world has been crucified to me, and I to the world. For neither circumcision counts for anything, nor uncircumcision, but a new creation.

Eph 2:10 - For we are his workmanship, created in Christ Jesus for good works, which God prepared beforehand, that we should walk in them.

Luke 9:23 - And he said to all, "If anyone would come after me, let him deny himself and take up his cross daily and follow me.

Rom 8:13 - For if you live according to the flesh you will die, but if by the Spirit you put to death the deeds of the body, you will live.

Ps 143:10 - Teach me to do your will, for you are my God! Let your good Spirit lead me on level ground!

[Pause. Breathe. Inhale and exhale. Reflect. Listen.]

Give me life according to your word, God!

Journal:

What do you hear God saying to you in these Scripture texts? What do they reveal about God and about you? Converse with God about what you're hearing him say. Verbalize and describe your thoughts, memories that come to mind, questions and emotions, concerns, desires.

Is there a particular word or phrase that disturbs or soothes you?

Do the Scripture texts create a picture or an impression that draws you to linger in exploring and experiencing it?

Choose a word or a phrase from your meditation to write on a slip of paper to carry with you today. Refer to it often throughout the day to remind you of your conversation with God and to continue the conversation all day long. Throughout the day pause to become aware of your thoughts and feelings and will. Ask yourself, "What drives me in this moment? Life according to God's word? Or life according to someone else's word?"

Anticipate that God's words stirred your heart for a reason. He's conversing with you through them. Anticipate that God will bring his word to life in you, to bear fruit in your heart and mind and soul and body. Anticipate that God will reveal the secrets of your heart, for anything that is visible is light. And anticipate that God will cause his words to become a joy and the delight of your heart.

CONTEMPLATE

God is spirit, and those who worship him must worship in spirit and truth. Seek him. Feel your way to him. Reach out. Find him.

You exist in God's abounding grace. Only in God's abounding grace do you exist. In God's abounding grace you are you, the real you, able to worship God in spirit and truth.

*2 Cor 9:8 - And **God is able** to make all grace abound to you, so that having all sufficiency in all things at all times, **you may** abound in every good work.*

Anticipate that God's abounding grace, in which you exist and are, will flow around you and through you to enlighten and empower you to love as you have been loved so that you may abound in every good work this day.

36 – Entrust Your Soul to a Faithful Creator

Pray: Ask God to prepare your heart and mind and soul to receive his words, to receive truth that will set you free, which will heal and perfect your understanding and knowledge of who God is and who you are.

Ps 119:25-32 - My soul clings to the dust; give me life according to your word! When I told of my ways, you answered me; teach me your statutes! Make me understand the way of your precepts, and I will meditate on your wondrous works. My soul melts away for sorrow; strengthen me according to your word! Put false ways far from me and graciously teach me your law! I have chosen the way of faithfulness; I set your rules before me. I cling to your testimonies, O Lord; let me not be put to shame! I will run in the way of your commandments when you enlarge my heart! (ESV)

[Murmur and mumble the words. Phrase by phrase. Word by word. Syllable by syllable. Pause. Breathe. Inhale and exhale. Reflect. Listen.]

Journal:

Note how this prayer stirs you today and what you hear God saying to you.

Luke 9:23 - And he said to all, "If anyone would come after me, let him deny himself and take up his cross daily and follow me.

What does it mean to deny yourself?

Luke 9:23 - And he said unto all, 'If any one doth will to come after me, let him <u>disown himself</u>, and take up his cross daily, and follow me; (YLT)

Luke 9:23 - He said to all of them, "Those who want to come with me must <u>say no to the things they want</u>, pick up their crosses every day, and follow me. (God's Word)

Luke 9:23-24 - Then he told them what they could expect for themselves: "Anyone who intends to come with me <u>has to let me lead</u>. You're not in the driver's seat — I am. Don't run from suffering; embrace it. <u>Follow me and I'll show you how</u>. <u>Self-help is no help at all</u>.

Self-sacrifice is the way, my way, to finding yourself, your true self. (MSG)

[Murmur and mumble the words. Phrase by phrase. Word by word. Syllable by syllable. Take pleasure in making the sounds of the words, getting the feel of the meaning. Experience pleasurable anticipation of taking in what will make you more yourself, the self that God made in his own image and likeness. The self that God made for intimate communion with him. The self that God created for good works, that you should walk in them. Eat God's words. Let God's words become a joy and the delight of your heart.]

Journal:

What do these Scripture texts say to you about what it means to deny yourself?

Are you willing to deny yourself?

Are you willing to embrace suffering?

Self-sacrifice is the way, my way, to finding yourself, your true self. Are you interested in finding your true self?

What has God done to show us how to deny ourselves?

Titus 2:11-14 - For the grace of God has appeared, bringing salvation for all people, training us to renounce ungodliness and worldly passions, and to live self-controlled, upright, and godly lives in the present age, waiting for our blessed hope, the appearing of the glory of our great God and Savior Jesus Christ, who gave himself for us to redeem us from all lawlessness and to purify for himself a people for his own possession who are zealous for good works.

For the ***grace of God*** has appeared

Bringing salvation [defense, defender, rescue, safety physically or morally]

Bringing salvation for ***all*** people

For the ***grace of God*** has appeared

Training us [educate, discipline]

Training us ***to renounce*** ungodliness and worldly passions

Training us to contradict, disavow, disown, reject, renounce, give up ungodliness and worldly passions

For the ***grace of God*** has appeared

Training us

Training us ***to live***

Training us to live self-controlled [with sound mind, moderately], upright [equitable, just], and godly [well-reverent] lives ***in the present age***

Waiting

Waiting ***for our blessed hope***, the appearing of the glory of our great God and Savior Jesus Christ

Waiting

For our blessed hope, our Savior Jesus Christ who gave himself ***to redeem us*** from all lawlessness

Waiting

For our blessed hope, our Savior Jesus Christ who gave himself ***to purify for himself*** a people for his own possession who are zealous for good works

For the grace of God ***has appeared***

[Murmur and mumble the words. Phrase by phrase. Word by word. Syllable by syllable. Take pleasure in making the sounds of the words, getting the feel of the meaning. Experience pleasurable anticipation of taking in what will make you more yourself, the self that God made in his own image and likeness. The self that God made for intimate communion with him. The self that God created for good works, that you should walk in them. Eat God's words. Let God's words become a joy and the delight of your heart.]

Journal:

Have you surrendered what you want to God? Have you agreed to do your life God's way?

What does being in training under the grace of God look like in your life? In the world at large? What does suffering have to do with being in training under the grace of God?

1 Peter 4:19 - Therefore let those who suffer according to God's will entrust their souls to a faithful Creator while doing good.

Therefore let those who ***suffer*** according to God's will…

Ps 138:8 - The Lord will fulfill his purpose for me; your steadfast love, O Lord, endures forever. Do not forsake the work of your hands.

Prov 19:21 - Many are the plans in the mind of a man, but it is the purpose of the Lord that will stand.

Therefore

Therefore let those who suffer according to ***God's will***

Entrust.

Entrust. Assign the care of. Turn over for safekeeping

Entrust their ***souls***…

Entrust their *souls* to a ***faithful Creator*** while doing good [in well-doing, virtuous]

*Ps 18:30 - This God—**his way** is perfect; the **word of the Lord** proves true; he is a shield for all those who take refuge in him.*

[Murmur and mumble the words. Phrase by phrase. Word by word. Syllable by syllable. Take pleasure in making the sounds of the words, getting the feel of the meaning. Experience pleasurable anticipation of taking in what will make you more yourself, the self that God made in his own image and likeness. The self that God made for intimate communion with him. The self that God created for good works, that you should walk in them. Eat God's words. Let God's words become a joy and the delight of your heart.]

Journal:

Have you taken refuge in God? Do you flee to God for protection? Do you confide in God? Why or why not?

Luke 9:23 - And he said to all, "If anyone would come after me, let him deny himself and take up his cross daily and follow me.

Titus 2:11-12 - For the grace of God has appeared, bringing salvation for all people, training us to renounce ungodliness and worldly passions, and to live self-controlled, upright, and godly lives in the present age

1 Peter 4:19 - Therefore let those who suffer according to God's will entrust their souls to a faithful Creator while doing good.

Ps 18:30 - This God—his way is perfect; the word of the Lord proves true; he is a shield for all those who take refuge in him.

[Pause. Breathe. Inhale and exhale. Reflect. Listen.]

Give me life according to your word, God!

Journal:

What do you hear God saying to you in these Scripture texts? What do they reveal about God and about you? Converse with God about what you're hearing him say. Verbalize and describe your thoughts, memories that come to mind, questions and emotions, concerns, desires.

Is there a particular word or phrase that disturbs or soothes you?

Do the Scripture texts create a picture or an impression that draws you to linger in exploring and experiencing it?

Choose a word or a phrase from your meditation to write on a slip of

paper to carry with you today. Refer to it often throughout the day to remind you of your conversation with God and to continue the conversation all day long. Throughout the day pause to become aware of your thoughts and feelings and will. Ask yourself, "What drives me in this moment? Life according to God's word? Or life according to someone else's word?"

Anticipate that God's words stirred your heart for a reason. He's conversing with you through them. Anticipate that God will bring his word to life in you, to bear fruit in your heart and mind and soul and body. Anticipate that God will reveal the secrets of your heart, for anything that is visible is light. And anticipate that God will cause his words to become a joy and the delight of your heart.

CONTEMPLATE

God is spirit, and those who worship him must worship in spirit and truth. Seek him. Feel your way to him. Reach out. Find him.

You exist in God's abounding grace. Only in God's abounding grace do you exist. In God's abounding grace you are you, the real you, able to worship God in spirit and truth.

2 Cor 9:8 - And ***God is able*** *to make all grace abound to you, so that having all sufficiency in all things at all times,* ***you may*** *abound in every good work.*

Anticipate that God's abounding grace, in which you exist and are, will flow around you and through you to enlighten and empower you to love as you have been loved so that you may abound in every good work this day.

37 - Set Your Mind on the Things of God

Pray: Ask God to prepare your heart and mind and soul to receive his words, to receive truth that will set you free, which will heal and perfect your understanding and knowledge of who God is and who you are.

Ps 119:25-32 - I'm feeling terrible — I couldn't feel worse! Get me on my feet again. You promised, remember? When I told my story, you responded; train me well in your deep wisdom. Help me understand these things inside and out so I can ponder your miracle-wonders. My sad life's dilapidated, a falling-down barn; build me up again by your Word. Barricade the road that goes Nowhere; grace me with your clear revelation. I choose the true road to Somewhere, I post your road signs at every curve and corner. I grasp and cling to whatever you tell me; God, don't let me down! I'll run the course you lay out for me if you'll just show me how. (MSG)

[Murmur and mumble the words. Phrase by phrase. Word by word. Syllable by syllable. Pause. Breathe. Inhale and exhale. Reflect. Listen.]

Journal:

Note how this prayer stirs you today and what you hear God saying to you.

Prov 3:5 - Trust in the Lord with all your heart, and do not lean on your own understanding.

Matt 16:21-23 - From that time Jesus began to show his disciples that he must go to Jerusalem and suffer many things from the elders and chief priests and scribes, and be killed, and on the third day be raised. And Peter took him aside and began to rebuke him, saying, "Far be it from you, Lord! This shall never happen to you." But he turned and said to Peter, "Get behind me, Satan! You are a hindrance to me. For you are not setting your mind on the things of God, but on the things of man."

This shall never happen to you!

At least Peter was thinking of Jesus. How often I think only of me. How often I cry, "This shall never happen to *me*! Why is this happening to *me*? Make it go away!" My focus is always on myself, my plans and purposes and desires. No! ***I*** shouldn't have to suffer. ***I*** shouldn't have to experience deprivation. ***I*** shouldn't have to experience failure. ***I*** shouldn't have to die. ***I*** shouldn't have to turn over my soul to the care of another for safekeeping. These things should never happen to *me or to those I care about*!

Was Peter thinking of Jesus? Or was he thinking of himself, how he himself would be impacted if/when Jesus was killed? Was he thinking about how his own dreams and expectations would be affected?

Why? Why do unpleasant, painful, horrific things happen to us? Didn't Jesus take our place in suffering so we wouldn't have to?

Jesus said to Peter, "Get behind me, ***Satan***!"

You are a ***hindrance*** to me.

You are a ***snare*** to me. You are the ***cause*** of displeasure and sin to me.

You are ***not*** setting your mind on the things of God, but on the things of man.

You are ***setting your mind*** on… You are leaning… You are mentally disposed, more or less earnestly, in a certain direction…

You are ***leaning***…

To the ***things of God***.

To the ***things of man***.

[Murmur and mumble the words. Phrase by phrase. Word by word. Syllable by syllable. Take pleasure in making the sounds of the words, getting the feel of the meaning. Experience pleasurable anticipation of taking in what will make you more yourself, the self that God made in his own image and likeness. The self that God made for intimate communion with him. The self that God created for good works, that you should walk in them. Eat God's words. Let God's words become a joy and the delight of your heart.]

Journal:

How are you leaning?

Many are the plans in the mind of a man, but it is the purpose of the Lord that will stand. (Prov 19:21)

Jer 17:9 - The heart is deceitful above all things, and desperately sick; who can understand it?

Job 13:23 - How many are my iniquities and my sins? Make me know my transgression and my sin.

Make me know, God! Make me ***know*** how I'm withdrawing from you! ***Make me know*** how I am a cause of displeasure to you. Make me know how I'm a hindrance to you in accomplishing your purpose for me. Make me know how I am leaning.

Pause for a moment. Become aware of what you're feeling and thinking in relation to suffering and death. Might God be saying to you as he said to Peter, "Get behind me, Satan"? Are you leaning toward the things of God or the things of man?

You are a ***hindrance*** to me.

You are a ***snare*** to me.

You are ***not setting your mind*** on the ***things of God***

You ***are setting your mind*** on the ***things of man***.

[Murmur and mumble the words. Phrase by phrase. Word by word. Syllable by syllable. Take pleasure in making the sounds of the words, getting the feel of the meaning. Experience pleasurable anticipation of taking in what will make you more yourself, the self that God made in his own image and likeness. The self that God made for intimate communion with him. The self that God created for good works, that you should walk in them. Eat God's words. Let God's words become a joy and the delight of your heart.]

Journal:

What are you setting your mind on? On your soul? Your spirit? Your breath? The things of God?

Are you, by the Spirit, consistently putting to death what is earthly in you? Are you eagerly participating in being trained by the grace of God to renounce ungodliness and worldly passions and to live a self-controlled, upright and godly life?

Are you setting your mind on the comfort or passions of your physical body and mind? Are you setting your mind on things pertaining to this world? The things of man, approval, belonging, success, fame, power, etc.?

Are you setting your mind on things that are seen and transient, or on things that are unseen and eternal?

To what or whom are you entrusting your soul? To what or whom are you assigning the care of your soul? To what or whom are you turning your soul over for safekeeping? Are you in step with God's purpose? Or are you opposed to God's purpose? How can you know?

Col 3:2 - Set your minds on things that are above, not on things that are on earth.

Ps 119:36-37- Incline my heart to your testimonies, and not to selfish gain! Turn my eyes from looking at worthless things; and give me life in your ways.

I have learned to appreciate how the psalmists turn God's commands into a prayer. I think that's the most powerful way for us to set our minds on the things of God and to do the work of God, to believe in him whom he has sent, to put to death what is earthly in us, and to be trained by the grace of God.

There is something really perverted in me that is convinced that I must somehow obey rules and dig deep into my well of self-discipline in order to deny my selfish interests and please God.

So when I read, *Set your minds on things that are above, not on things that are on earth,* my first reaction is to try to think of a plan of action to train and discipline my thoughts to bring them into alignment with the command. Then I rack my brain to figure out, what are the things that are above that I'm supposed to set my mind on? I feel defeated before I even get started.

But David's response is to pray. To believe that the one whom God sent will hear and answer and fulfill God's purpose and perfect everything that concerns him.

Isn't that refreshing? Doesn't that cause hope to swell within your heart? The responsibility is not yours to accomplish.

Incline (to stretch or spread out, to bend away, to have a particular disposition or bent of mind, will, etc., to give a tendency, make willing, influence.)

Incline ***my heart***

Bend my heart

Influence my heart

Make my heart willing

Give my heart the disposition and tendency to life in your ways.

Incline my heart ***to your testimonies***, and not to selfish gain!

Turn my eyes from looking at worthless things

And ***give me life***

And give me life ***in your ways***.

David asks God to create in his heart what God reveals that he wants from David. But David doesn't expect that God will make his request reality without any effort from David. David commits his heart to God. He commits to work in partnership with God so that working together with God his heart will become inclined to God's commandments and God's ways.

Note how the psalmist asks God to incline his heart to God's word, then follows up stating his own intention and desire to do exactly what he's asked God to do for him.

Ps 119:112 - I incline my heart to perform your statutes forever, to the end.

I

I incline

I incline ***my heart***

I incline my heart ***to perform*** your statutes forever, to the end.

[Murmur and mumble the words. Phrase by phrase. Word by word. Syllable by syllable. Take pleasure in making the sounds of the words, getting the feel of the meaning. Experience pleasurable anticipation of taking in what will make you more yourself, the self that God made in his own image and likeness. The self that God made for intimate communion with him. The self that God created for good works, that you should walk in them. Eat God's words. Let God's words become a joy and the delight of your heart.]

Journal:

Will you try the psalmists' method of understanding and obeying God's commands?

[Pause. Breathe. Inhale and exhale. Reflect. Listen.]

Give me life according to your word, God!

Journal:

What do you hear God saying to you in these Scripture texts? What do they reveal about God and about you? Converse with God about what you're hearing him say. Verbalize and describe your thoughts, memories that come to mind, questions and emotions, concerns, desires.

Is there a particular word or phrase that disturbs or soothes you?

Do the Scripture texts create a picture or an impression that draws you to linger in exploring and experiencing it?

Choose a word or a phrase from your meditation to write on a slip of paper to carry with you today. Refer to it often throughout the day to remind you of your conversation with God and to continue the conversation all day long. Throughout the day pause to become aware of your thoughts and feelings and will. Ask yourself, "What drives me in this moment? Life according to God's word? Or life according to someone else's word?"

Anticipate that God's words stirred your heart for a reason. He's conversing with you through them. Anticipate that God will bring his word to life in you, to bear fruit in your heart and mind and soul and body. Anticipate that God will reveal the secrets of your heart, for anything that is visible is light. And anticipate that God will cause his words to become a joy and the delight of your heart.

CONTEMPLATE

God is spirit, and those who worship him must worship in spirit and truth. Seek him. Feel your way to him. Reach out. Find him.

You exist in God's abounding grace. Only in God's abounding grace do you exist. In God's abounding grace you are you, the real you, able to worship God in spirit and truth.

*2 Cor 9:8 - And **God is able** to make all grace abound to you, so that having all sufficiency in all things at all times, **you may** abound in every good work.*

Anticipate that God's abounding grace, in which you exist and are, will flow around you and through you to enlighten and empower you to love as you have been loved so that you may abound in every good work this day.

38 - Take Hold of That Which is Truly Life

Pray: Ask God to prepare your heart and mind and soul to receive his words, to receive truth that will set you free, which will heal and perfect your understanding and knowledge of who God is and who you are.

Ps 119:25-32 - My soul clings to the dust; give me life according to your word! When I told of my ways, you answered me; teach me your statutes! Make me understand the way of your precepts, and I will meditate on your wondrous works. My soul melts away for sorrow; strengthen me according to your word! Put false ways far from me and graciously teach me your law! I have chosen the way of faithfulness; I set your rules before me. I cling to your testimonies, O Lord; let me not be put to shame! I will run in the way of your commandments when you enlarge my heart! (ESV)

[Murmur and mumble the words. Phrase by phrase. Word by word. Syllable by syllable. Pause. Breathe. Inhale and exhale. Reflect. Listen.]

Journal:

Note how this prayer stirs you today and what you hear God saying to you.

Matt 16:22-23 - And Peter took him aside and began to rebuke him, saying, "Far be it from you, Lord! This shall never happen to you." But he turned and said to Peter, "Get behind me, Satan! You are a hindrance to me. For you are not setting your mind on the things of God, but on the things of man."

Prov 10:28 - The hope of the righteous brings joy, but the expectation of the wicked will perish.

What expectations do you have that are the cause of displeasure and sin? What are you setting your mind on?

Ps 10:3-4 - For the wicked [to be, do or declare wrong; disturb, violate] boasts of the desires of his soul, and the one greedy [covetous] for gain curses and renounces the Lord. In the pride of his face the wicked does not seek him; all his thoughts are, "There is no God."

Prov 23:4-5 - Do not overwork to be rich [to accumulate, to grow]; Because of your own understanding, cease! Will you set your eyes on that which is not? For riches certainly make themselves wings; They fly away like an eagle toward heaven. (NKJV)

Luke 12:15 - And he said to them, "Take care, and be on your guard against all covetousness, for one's life does not consist in the abundance of his possessions."

1 Tim 6:9-10 - But those who desire to be rich [wealthy] fall into temptation, into a snare, into many senseless and harmful desires that plunge people into ruin and destruction. For the love [greed] of money is a root of all kinds of evils. It is through this craving that some have wandered away from the faith and pierced themselves with many pangs.

1 John 2:16-17- For all that is in the world— the desires of the flesh and the desires of the eyes and pride in possessions—is not from the Father but is from the world. And the world is passing away along with its desires, but whoever does the will of God abides forever.

Do not ***overwork*** to be rich

Will you set your eyes ***on that which is not***?

One's ***life does not consist*** in the abundance of his possessions

Those who ***desire*** [to will, to intend]

Those who desire to be rich ***fall into temptation***

Into ***a snare***, into many ***senseless and harmful desires***

That plunge people into ***ruin and destruction***

It is through this craving that some have ***wandered away from the faith***

And ***pierced themselves*** with many pangs

All that is in the ***world***

The ***desires*** [lust; to set the heart on; a longing especially for what is forbidden] ***of the flesh***

The ***desires*** [lust] ***of the eyes***

Pride [braggart; self-confidence] ***in possessions***

Is not from the Father

But ***is from*** the world

And the world is passing away ***along with its desires*** [lust]

But whoever does the will of God ***abides forever***

Because of your ***own understanding, cease***!

Take care

And ***be on your guard*** against all covetousness

For the love of money is ***a root of all kinds of evils*** [intrinsically worthless]

[Murmur and mumble the words. Phrase by phrase. Word by word. Syllable by syllable. Take pleasure in making the sounds of the words, getting the feel of the meaning. Experience pleasurable anticipation of taking in what will make you more yourself, the self that God made in his own image and likeness. The self that God made for intimate communion with him. The self that God created for good works, that you should walk in them. Eat God's words. Let God's words become a joy and the delight of your heart.]

Ask God to bring the secrets of your heart into the light.

Journal:

Take care. Be on your guard against all covetousness. Are you aware of covetousness rooted deep in your deceitful and desperately sick heart?

What longings drive you? Doing the will of God? Lust of the flesh? Lust of the eyes? Confidence in possessions?

Is it riches themselves that are problematic?

Do you know the difference between what is real and lasting and what is fleeting and unsatisfying and worthless? What do you seek in order to satisfy your longings?

What did the psalmist seek to satisfy his longings?

Ps 90:14 - Satisfy us in the morning with your steadfast love, that we may rejoice and be glad all our days.

Satisfy us [to fill full; gratify completely]

Satisfy us ***in the morning***

With your ***steadfast love***

Satisfy us

That we may rejoice and be glad ***all our days***

[Murmur and mumble the words. Phrase by phrase. Word by word. Syllable by syllable. Take pleasure in making the sounds of the words, getting the feel of the meaning. Experience pleasurable anticipation of taking in what will make you more yourself, the self that God made in his own image and likeness. The self that God made for intimate communion with him. The self that God created for good works, that you should walk in them. Eat God's words. Let God's words become a joy and the delight of your heart.]

Journal:

Do you go to bed each night and wake up each morning simply (and yet so very profoundly) asking that God satisfy you with his steadfast love so that you may rejoice and be glad?

Are you familiar with God's satisfying steadfast love?

Ps 36:7-9 - How precious is your steadfast love, O God! The children of mankind take refuge in the shadow of your wings. They feast on the abundance of your house, and you give them drink from the river of your delights. For with you is the fountain of life; in your light do we see light.

How ***precious***

How precious is ***your steadfast love***, O God!

The children of mankind ***take refuge*** in the shadow of your wings.

They feast on the abundance of your house

And you give them drink from the ***river of your delights***.

For with you is the ***fountain of life***

In your light do we see light.

How does God respond to those who ask to be satisfied with his steadfast love?

Ps 91:14-16 - "Because he holds fast to me in love, I will deliver him; I will protect him, because he knows my name. When he calls to me, I will answer him; I will be with him in trouble; I will rescue him and honor him. With long life I will satisfy him and show him my salvation."

Because he ***holds fast*** [to cling, join, to love, to delight in]

Because he holds fast to me in love

I will ***deliver*** him

Because he knows my name

I will ***protect*** him

I will ***answer*** him when he calls to me

I will ***be with*** him in trouble

I will ***rescue*** him

I will ***honor*** him

With long life I will ***satisfy*** him

I will ***show*** him my salvation

[Murmur and mumble the words. Phrase by phrase. Word by word.

Syllable by syllable. Take pleasure in making the sounds of the words, getting the feel of the meaning. Experience pleasurable anticipation of taking in what will make you more yourself, the self that God made in his own image and likeness. The self that God made for intimate communion with him. The self that God created for good works, that you should walk in them. Eat God's words. Let God's words become a joy and the delight of your heart.]

Journal:

What does God's steadfast love look like as he responds to your request that he satisfy you with his steadfast love?

Matt 16:22-23 - And Peter took him aside and began to rebuke him, saying, "Far be it from you, Lord! This shall never happen to you." But he turned and said to Peter, "Get behind me, Satan! You are a hindrance to me. For you are not setting your mind on the things of God, but on the things of man."

Prov 10:28 - The hope of the righteous brings joy, but the expectation of the wicked will perish.

Luke 12:15 - And he said to them, "Take care, and be on your guard against all covetousness, for one's life does not consist in the abundance of his possessions."

1 John 2:16-17- For all that is in the world— the desires of the flesh and the desires of the eyes and pride in possessions—is not from the Father but is from the world. And the world is passing away along with its desires, but whoever does the will of God abides forever.

Ps 90:14 - Satisfy us in the morning with your steadfast love, that we may rejoice and be glad all our days.

[Pause. Breathe. Inhale and exhale. Reflect. Listen.]

Give me life according to your word, God!

Journal:

What do you hear God saying to you in these Scripture texts? What do they reveal about God and about you? Converse with God about what you're hearing him say. Verbalize and describe your thoughts, memories that come to mind, questions and emotions, concerns, desires.

Is there a particular word or phrase that disturbs or soothes you?

Do the Scripture texts create a picture or an impression that draws you to linger in exploring and experiencing it?

Choose a word or a phrase from your meditation to write on a slip of paper to carry with you today. Refer to it often throughout the day to remind you of your conversation with God and to continue the conversation all day long. Throughout the day pause to become aware of your thoughts and feelings and will. Ask yourself, "What drives me in this moment? Life according to God's word? Or life according to someone else's word?"

Anticipate that God's words stirred your heart for a reason. He's conversing with you through them. Anticipate that God will bring his word to life in you, to bear fruit in your heart and mind and soul and body. Anticipate that God will reveal the secrets of your heart, for anything that is visible is light. And anticipate that God will cause his words to become a joy and the delight of your heart.

CONTEMPLATE

God is spirit, and those who worship him must worship in spirit and truth. Seek him. Feel your way to him. Reach out. Find him.

You exist in God's abounding grace. Only in God's abounding grace do you exist. In God's abounding grace you are you, the real you, able to worship God in spirit and truth.

*2 Cor 9:8 - And **God is able** to make all grace abound to you, so that having all sufficiency in all things at all times, **you may** abound in every good work.*

Anticipate that God's abounding grace, in which you exist and are, will flow around you and through you to enlighten and empower you to love as you have been loved so that you may abound in every good work this day.

39 - God Richly Provides Us with Everything

Pray: Ask God to prepare your heart and mind and soul to receive his words, to receive truth that will set you free, which will heal and perfect your understanding and knowledge of who God is and who you are.

Ps 119:25-32 - I'm feeling terrible — I couldn't feel worse! Get me on my feet again. You promised, remember? When I told my story, you responded; train me well in your deep wisdom. Help me understand these things inside and out so I can ponder your miracle-wonders. My sad life's dilapidated, a falling-down barn; build me up again by your Word. Barricade the road that goes Nowhere; grace me with your clear revelation. I choose the true road to Somewhere, I post your road signs at every curve and corner. I grasp and cling to whatever you tell me; God, don't let me down! I'll run the course you lay out for me if you'll just show me how. (MSG)

[Murmur and mumble the words. Phrase by phrase. Word by word. Syllable by syllable. Pause. Breathe. Inhale and exhale. Reflect. Listen.]

Journal:

Note how this prayer stirs you today and what you hear God saying to you.

Prov 10:28 - The hope of the righteous brings joy, but the expectation of the wicked will perish.

Luke 12:15 - And he said to them, "Take care, and be on your guard against all covetousness, for one's life does not consist in the abundance of his possessions."

Do we know the difference between what is real and lasting and what is fleeting and unsatisfying and worthless?

Jesus Christ knew the difference.

Are we looking to the wrong source to fulfill our desires? Are we listening to, and responding to, and believing the words of an imposter who makes empty promises, and speaks lies?

Luke 4:5-8 - And the devil took him [Christ] up and showed him all the kingdoms of the world in a moment of time, and said to him, "To you I will give all this authority and their glory, for it has been delivered [yielded up, surrendered] to me, and I give it to whom I will. If you, then, will worship me, it will all be yours."

And Jesus answered him, "It is written, "'You shall worship the Lord your God, and him only shall you serve.'"

The ***devil***

Showed him all the kingdoms ***of the world***

To you ***I will give*** all this authority and their glory

For ***it has been delivered*** [yielded up, surrendered] to me

If you will worship me

If you ***will worship*** me [to kiss, like a dog licking his master's hand; to fawn or crouch to, i.e. prostrate oneself in homage; do reverence to, adore]

If you will worship ***me***

Then it will ***all be yours***

[Murmur and mumble the words. Phrase by phrase. Word by word. Syllable by syllable. Take pleasure in making the sounds of the words, getting the feel of the meaning. Experience pleasurable anticipation of taking in what will make you more yourself, the self that God made in his own image and likeness. The self that God made for intimate communion with him. The self that God created for good works, that you should walk in them. Eat God's words. Let God's words become a joy and the delight of your heart.]

Journal:

To whose authority do you yield? Who do you worship?

What drives your desire, craving and toil?

Christ declared:

Luke 10:22 - All things have been handed over to me ***by my Father****, and no one knows who the Son is except the Father, or who the Father is except the Son and anyone to whom the Son chooses to reveal him."*

Note the difference between the words that the devil used (Luke 4:5-8) and the words Jesus used (Luke 10:22) regarding their authority.

The devil specifically mentions that he has authority over all the kingdoms of the world. He is very vague about who and how all was delivered, yielded up, surrendered to him. And he certainly does not disclose the temporary nature of all his kingdoms.

1 John 2:17 - And the world is passing away along with its desires, but whoever does the will of God abides forever.

Jesus, on the other hand, boldly claims that all things have been handed over to him, which signifies much more than the kingdoms of the world that are passing away. He very clearly states that it is his Father who handed all things over to him.

Do you know who the Father is? Has the Son of God revealed the Father to you? Or are you getting your knowledge of God from other sources?

Ps 139:1 - O Lord, you have searched me and known me!

Journal:

Ask God to help you see as he sees.

"What do you see and find when you search and examine me, Lord? What do you know about me? What do I not know about myself?"

"For what do I labor and toil and weary myself, Lord? Is it worth my effort and tears and time?"

"What do I work to acquire, Lord?"

"What do I desire and crave, Lord?"

"What do I love most of all?"

"What cravings entice and ensnare me? What senseless and harmful desires plunge me into ruin and destruction, Lord?"

Prov 23:4-5 - Do not overwork to be rich [to accumulate, to grow]; Because of your own understanding, cease! Will you set your eyes on that which is not? For riches certainly make themselves wings; They fly away like an eagle toward heaven. (NKJV)

Cease!

Cease from thine own intelligence!

Cease from thine own understanding!

Will you set your eyes on that which is not?

Will you set your eyes on that which is an illusion?

All things

All things have been handed over ***to me*** by my Father

1 Tim 6:17-19 - As for the rich in this present age, charge them not to be haughty, nor to set their hopes on the uncertainty of riches, but on God, who richly provides us with everything to enjoy. They are to do good, to be rich in good works, to be generous and ready to share, thus storing up treasure for themselves as a good foundation for the future, so that they may take hold of that which is truly life.

Set your ***hope***

Set your hope ***on God***.

Set your hope on God, who ***richly provides***

Set your hope on God, who richly provides us with ***everything to enjoy***.

...take hold of that which is ***truly life***.

Journal:

What are you grasping and taking hold of? Are you settling for the uncertainty of the riches of this present age? Or are you taking hold of that which is truly life?

Ps 141:4 - Do not let my heart incline to any evil, to busy myself with wicked deeds in company with men who work iniquity, and let me not eat of their delicacies!

Ps 119:40 - Behold, I long for your precepts; in your righteousness give me life!

Do not let

Do not let ***my heart incline***

Do not let my heart incline ***to any evil*** [to spoil, literally by breaking to pieces; figuratively, to make or be good for nothing, i.e. bad physically, socially or morally]

In ***your*** righteousness

In your righteousness ***give me life!***

[Murmur and mumble the words. Phrase by phrase. Word by word. Syllable by syllable. Take pleasure in making the sounds of the words, getting the feel of the meaning. Experience pleasurable anticipation of taking in what will make you more yourself, the self that God made in his own image and likeness. The self that God made for intimate communion with him. The self that God created for good works, that you should walk in them. Eat God's words. Let God's words become a joy and the delight of your heart.]

Luke 12:15 - And he said to them, "Take care, and be on your guard against all covetousness, for one's life does not consist in the abundance of his possessions."

And Jesus answered him, "It is written, "'You shall worship the Lord your God, and him only shall you serve.'"

1 Tim 6:17-19 - As for the rich in this present age, charge them not to be haughty, nor to set their hopes on the uncertainty of riches, but on God, who richly provides us with everything to enjoy. They are to do good, to be rich in good works, to be generous and ready to share, thus storing up treasure for themselves as a good foundation for the future, so that they may take hold of that which is truly life.

Ps 141:4 - Do not let my heart incline to any evil, to busy myself with wicked deeds in company with men who work iniquity, and let me not eat of their delicacies!

Ps 119:40 - Behold, I long for your precepts; in your righteousness give me life!

[Pause. Breathe. Inhale and exhale. Reflect. Listen.]

Give me life according to your word, God!

Journal:

What do you hear God saying to you in these Scripture texts? What do they reveal about God and about you? Converse with God about what you're hearing him say. Verbalize and describe your thoughts, memories that come to mind, questions and emotions, concerns, desires.

Is there a particular word or phrase that disturbs or soothes you?

Do the Scripture texts create a picture or an impression that draws you to linger in exploring and experiencing it?

Choose a word or a phrase from your meditation to write on a slip of paper to carry with you today. Refer to it often throughout the day to remind you of your conversation with God and to continue the conversation all day long. Throughout the day pause to become aware of your thoughts and feelings and will. Ask yourself, "What drives me in this moment? Life according to God's word? Or life according to someone else's word?"

Anticipate that God's words stirred your heart for a reason. He's conversing with you through them. Anticipate that God will bring his word to life in you, to bear fruit in your heart and mind and soul and body. Anticipate that God will reveal the secrets of your heart, for anything that is visible is light. And anticipate that God will cause his words to become a joy and the delight of your heart.

CONTEMPLATE

God is spirit, and those who worship him must worship in spirit and truth. Seek him. Feel your way to him. Reach out. Find him.

You exist in God's abounding grace. Only in God's abounding grace do you exist. In God's abounding grace you are you, the real you, able to worship God in spirit and truth.

2 Cor 9:8 - And ***God is able*** *to make all grace abound to you, so that having all sufficiency in all things at all times,* ***you may*** *abound in every good work.*

Anticipate that God's abounding grace, in which you exist and are, will flow around you and through you to enlighten and empower you to love as you have been loved so that you may abound in every good work this day.

40 - Your Words, the Delight of My Heart

Pray: Ask God to prepare your heart and mind and soul to receive his words, to receive truth that will set you free, which will heal and perfect your understanding and knowledge of who God is and who you are.

Ps 119:25-32 - My soul clings to the dust; give me life according to your word! When I told of my ways, you answered me; teach me your statutes! Make me understand the way of your precepts, and I will meditate on your wondrous works. My soul melts away for sorrow; strengthen me according to your word! Put false ways far from me and graciously teach me your law! I have chosen the way of faithfulness; I set your rules before me. I cling to your testimonies, O Lord; let me not be put to shame! I will run in the way of your commandments when you enlarge my heart! (ESV)

[Murmur and mumble the words. Phrase by phrase. Word by word. Syllable by syllable. Pause. Breathe. Inhale and exhale. Reflect. Listen.]

Journal:

Note how this prayer stirs you today and what you hear God saying to you.

Prov 28:26 - Whoever trusts in his own mind is a fool, but he who walks in wisdom will be delivered.

Matt 16:23 - But he turned and said to Peter, "Get behind me, Satan! You are a hindrance to me. For you are not setting your mind on the things of God, but on the things of man."

What is the antidote to all our senseless and harmful desires that are the cause of displeasure and sin?

He who walks ***in wisdom*** will be delivered.

He who is wise in mind, word and act ***will be*** delivered.

He who has or shows good judgment will be ***delivered***.

He who is ***enlightened*** will be delivered.

Prov 28:26 - Whoever trusts in his own mind is a fool, but he who walks in wisdom will be delivered.

[Murmur and mumble the words. Phrase by phrase. Word by word. Syllable by syllable. Take pleasure in making the sounds of the words, getting the feel of the meaning. Experience pleasurable anticipation of taking in what will make you more yourself, the self that God made in his own image and likeness. The self that God made for intimate communion with him. The self that God created for good works, that you should walk in them. Eat God's words. Let God's words become a joy and the delight of your heart.]

Journal:

Record your thoughts, feelings, and questions as you seek to understand God's words regarding wisdom and deliverance. How do you get wisdom in order to be delivered? What does wisdom deliver you from?

Prov 24:13-14 - My son, eat honey, for it is good, and the drippings of the honeycomb are sweet to your taste. Know that wisdom is such to your soul; if you find it, there will be a future, and your hope will not be cut off.

My son, eat honey, for ***it is good***.

And the drippings of the honeycomb are ***sweet to your taste***.

Honey is good.

Sweet to your taste.

Know

Know that **wisdom**

Know that wisdom ***is such*** to your soul.

Wisdom is such to ***your soul***.

Wisdom is such to your breath.

Wisdom is such to your spirit. Your perception. Your consciousness.

Wisdom.

Wisdom is sweet to your ***soul*** as honey is sweet to your ***taste***.

If...

If you find it... If you find ***wisdom***...

...there ***will be*** a future.

If you find ***wisdom*** your hope will not be cut off.

[Murmur and mumble the words. Phrase by phrase. Word by word. Syllable by syllable. Take pleasure in making the sounds of the words, getting the feel of the meaning. Experience pleasurable anticipation of taking in what will make you more yourself, the self that God made in his own image and likeness. The self that God made for intimate communion with him. The self that God created for good works, that you should walk in them. Eat God's words. Let God's words become a joy and the delight of your heart.]

Journal:

Have you experienced this wisdom that is sweet to your soul as honey is sweet to your taste?

If you find wisdom. Is wisdom difficult to find?

How do we find wisdom? Note what David says.

Ps 19:8-11 - the precepts of the Lord are right, rejoicing the heart; the commandment of the Lord is pure, enlightening the eyes; the fear of the Lord is clean, enduring forever; the rules of the Lord are true, and righteous altogether. More to be desired are they than gold, even much fine gold; sweeter also than honey and drippings of the honeycomb. Moreover, by them is your servant warned; in keeping them there is great reward.

In Old Testament times, as at present, honey was rare enough to be considered a luxury (Gen 43:11; 1 Kings 14:3).[1]

Journal:

Do you consider wisdom to be a luxury? Do you long for wisdom and seek for it? Are you willing to give up other things in order to get wisdom?

As a symbol, honey stands for abundance (Ex 3:8; 13:5; 33:3), the believer's delight in God's word (Ps 19:10; 119:103), and the rightness of God's word to His people (Ezek 3:3).[1]

Ps 119:103 - How sweet are your words to my taste, sweeter than honey to my mouth!

Wisdom. A luxury. Abundance. Delight. Rightness.

How ***sweet***

How sweet ***are your words*** to my taste…

Your words…***sweeter than honey*** to my mouth.

Your ***words***

[Murmur and mumble the words. Phrase by phrase. Word by word. Syllable by syllable. Take pleasure in making the sounds of the words, getting the feel of the meaning. Experience pleasurable anticipation of taking in what will make you more yourself, the self that God made in his own image and likeness. The self that God made for intimate communion with him. The self that God created for good works, that you should walk in them. Eat God's words. Let God's words become a joy and the delight of your heart.]

Journal:

Have you shared the psalmist's experience in tasting the sweetness of God's words?

The prophet Jeremiah stated:

Jer 15:16 - Your words were found, and I ate them, and your words became to me a joy and the delight of my heart, for I am called by your name, O Lord, God of hosts.

Have you personally experienced God's words like the prophet describes? A joy? The delight of your heart?

Your words

Your ***words***

Your words were ***found***.

I ate your words.

Your words ***became to me*** a joy and the delight of my heart

[Murmur and mumble the words. Phrase by phrase. Word by word. Syllable by syllable. Take pleasure in making the sounds of the words, getting the feel of the meaning. Experience pleasurable anticipation of taking in what will make you more yourself, the self that God made in his own image and likeness. The self that God made for intimate communion with him. The self that God created for good works, that you should walk in them. Eat God's words. Let God's words become a joy and the delight of your heart.]

Journal:

Do you seek God's words in order to find them?

Have you found God's words?

Do you eat God's words? Do you take God's words into your mouth and chew them and swallow them? Digest them to take in what will make you more yourself?

Your words ***became to me*** a joy and the delight of my heart

Became to me…

For

For ***I am called***

For I am called ***by your name***, O Lord, God of hosts.

Ps 44:20-21 - If we had forgotten the name of our God or spread out our hands to a foreign god, would not God discover this? For he knows the secrets of the heart.

Do you trust that God will never fail to search you? Do you trust that God will never fail to discover and expose the secrets of your heart? Do you trust that God will never fail to test you and try you? Do you trust that God will never fail to bring you out to a place of abundance?

Ps 66:10, 12 - For you, O God, have tested us; you have tried us as silver is tried. ...we went through fire and through water; yet you have brought us out to a place of abundance.

[Murmur and mumble the words. Phrase by phrase. Word by word. Syllable by syllable. Take pleasure in making the sounds of the words, getting the feel of the meaning. Experience pleasurable anticipation of taking in what will make you more yourself, the self that God made in his own image and likeness. The self that God made for intimate communion with him. The self that God created for good works, that you should walk in them. Eat God's words. Let God's words become a joy and the delight of your heart.]

Journal:

At what point did God's words become a joy and delight to the prophet Jeremiah's heart?

Do you know who you are? Do you know whose you are? Do you know whose name you are called by?

Do you consider seeking and knowing the name that you are called by, worth whatever your time and effort to know might cost you?

Do you consider wisdom to be worth whatever it might cost you to find it, and taste it, and eat it, and be delivered by it?

I need not tell the Reader that the honey and the honey-comb of scripture, means somewhat infinitely higher than the mere food of the body. The land of Canaan, which was a type of the gospel church, was promised to flow with milk and honey: and hence the gospel call was to buy wine and milk without money and without price. Ezek 20:6; Isa 55:1. <u>Christ is himself the honey and the honey-comb</u>, for his flesh is meat indeed, and his blood is drink indeed. His word is sweet unto my taste (said one of old) yea, sweeter than honey to my mouth. Ps 119:103, so that when Solomon recommends the honey *and the honey-comb, the Holy Ghost shews from other scriptures this is meant concerning Christ and his salvation.*[2]

Christ himself is the honey and the honeycomb.

Prov 28:26 - Whoever trusts in his own mind is a fool, but he who walks in wisdom will be delivered.

Prov 24:13-14 - My son, eat honey, for it is good, and the drippings of the honeycomb are sweet to your taste. Know that wisdom is such to your soul; if you find it, there will be a future, and your hope will not be cut off.

Jer 15:16 - Your words were found, and I ate them, and your words became to me a joy and the delight of my heart, for I am called by your name, O Lord, God of hosts.

[Pause. Breathe. Inhale and exhale. Reflect. Listen.]

Give me life according to your word, God!

Journal:

What do you hear God saying to you in these Scripture texts? What do they reveal about God and about you? Converse with God about what you're hearing him say. Verbalize and describe your thoughts, memories that come to mind, questions and emotions, concerns, desires.

Is there a particular word or phrase that disturbs or soothes you?

Do the Scripture texts create a picture or an impression that draws you to linger in exploring and experiencing it?

Choose a word or a phrase from your meditation to write on a slip of paper to carry with you today. Refer to it often throughout the day to remind you of your conversation with God and to continue the conversation all day long. Throughout the day pause to become aware of your thoughts and feelings and will. Ask yourself, "What drives me in this moment? Life according to God's word? Or life according to someone else's word?"

Anticipate that God's words stirred your heart for a reason. He's conversing with you through them. Anticipate that God will bring his word to life in you, to bear fruit in your heart and mind and soul and body. Anticipate that God will reveal the secrets of your heart, for anything that is visible is light. And anticipate that God will cause his words to become a joy and the delight of your heart.

CONTEMPLATE

God is spirit, and those who worship him must worship in spirit and truth. Seek him. Feel your way to him. Reach out. Find him.

You exist in God's abounding grace. Only in God's abounding grace do you exist. In God's abounding grace you are you, the real you, able to worship God in spirit and truth.

*2 Cor 9:8 - And **God is able** to make all grace abound to you, so that having all sufficiency in all things at all times, **you may** abound in every good work.*

Anticipate that God's abounding grace, in which you exist and are, will flow around you and through you to enlighten and empower you to love as you have been loved so that you may abound in every good work this day.

Resources:

[1]International Standard Bible Encyclopaedia, Electronic Database Copyright © 1996, 2003, 2006 by Biblesoft, Inc. All rights reserved.

[2]from Hawker's Poor Man's Commentary. Biblesoft Formatted Electronic Database Copyright © 2014 by Biblesoft, Inc. All rights reserved.

41 - In Christ are Hidden All the Treasures

Pray: Ask God to prepare your heart and mind and soul to receive his words, to receive truth that will set you free, which will heal and perfect your understanding and knowledge of who God is and who you are.

Ps 119:25-32 - I'm feeling terrible — I couldn't feel worse! Get me on my feet again. You promised, remember? When I told my story, you responded; train me well in your deep wisdom. Help me understand these things inside and out so I can ponder your miracle-wonders. My sad life's dilapidated, a falling-down barn; build me up again by your Word. Barricade the road that goes Nowhere; grace me with your clear revelation. I choose the true road to Somewhere, I post your road signs at every curve and corner. I grasp and cling to whatever you tell me; God, don't let me down! I'll run the course you lay out for me if you'll just show me how. (MSG)

[Murmur and mumble the words. Phrase by phrase. Word by word. Syllable by syllable. Pause. Breathe. Inhale and exhale. Reflect. Listen.]

Journal:

Note how this prayer stirs you today and what you hear God saying to you.

Prov 24:13-14 - My son, eat honey, for it is good, and the drippings of the honeycomb are sweet to your taste. Know that wisdom is such to your soul; if you find it, there will be a future, and your hope will not be cut off.

Wisdom.

If you find wisdom.

If you find wisdom, ***there will be*** a future.

If you find wisdom, ***your hope*** will not be cut off.

Col 2:3 - in [Christ] are hidden all the treasures of wisdom and knowledge.

In Christ

In Christ are ***hidden*** [concealed away, secret, treasured]

In Christ are hidden ***all***

In Christ are hidden all the ***treasures***

In Christ are hidden all the treasures of **wisdom**

In Christ are hidden all the treasures of *wisdom* ***and knowledge***

All treasures of wisdom and knowledge

Hidden

Concealed away

Secret

Treasured

In Christ.

[Murmur and mumble the words. Phrase by phrase. Word by word. Syllable by syllable. Take pleasure in making the sounds of the words, getting the feel of the meaning. Experience pleasurable anticipation of taking in what will make you more yourself, the self that God made in his own image and likeness. The self that God made for intimate communion with him. The self that God created for good works, that you should walk in them. Eat God's words. Let God's words become a joy and the delight of your heart.]

Journal:

If you desire to get wisdom, who must you seek to find and know?

What are the hidden treasures of wisdom in Christ?

What are the hidden treasures of knowledge in Christ?

How do we seek for the treasures of wisdom and knowledge that are hidden in Christ? How can we find him and them?

How do the hidden treasures of wisdom and knowledge in Christ compare with the treasures of the world?

Are you willing to seek the treasures of wisdom and knowledge that are hidden in Christ regardless of what your efforts in seeking and finding might cost you?

How does one seek the treasures of wisdom and knowledge that are hidden in Christ?

Prov 25:2-3 - It is the glory of God to conceal things, but the glory of kings is to search things out. As the heavens for height, and the earth for depth, so the heart of kings is unsearchable.

1 Cor 2:9-10 - But, as it is written, "What no eye has seen, nor ear heard, nor the heart of man imagined, what God has prepared for those who love him"— these things God has revealed to us through the Spirit. For the Spirit searches everything, even the depths of God.

1 Cor 2:14 - The natural person does not accept the things of the Spirit of God, for they are folly to him, and he is not able to understand them because they are spiritually discerned.

It is the glory of God to ***conceal*** things

But the glory of kings is to ***search things out***

As the heavens for ***height***, and the earth for ***depth***

So the ***heart***

So the heart of kings is ***unsearchable***

[Murmur and mumble the words. Phrase by phrase. Word by word.

Syllable by syllable. Take pleasure in making the sounds of the words, getting the feel of the meaning. Experience pleasurable anticipation of taking in what will make you more yourself, the self that God made in his own image and likeness. The self that God made for intimate communion with him. The self that God created for good works, that you should walk in them. Eat God's words. Let God's words become a joy and the delight of your heart.]

Journal:

Has God concealed the wisdom and knowledge that you long for in the depths of your heart which is impossible for you, in your natural self, to search out and understand?

Why do you think God conceals things (wisdom and knowledge) so that we must search them out rather than simply handing them over to us in a gift basket?

Perhaps Christ Jesus is like a gift basket that God has graciously given to us, but we've not yet discovered how to get to know him and relate to him.

No ***eye*** has seen

No ***ear*** has heard

No ***heart*** of man has imagined

What God has prepared for those who love him

These things

These things God has revealed to us ***through the Spirit***

For ***the Spirit***

For the Spirit ***searches*** everything

The Spirit searches ***everything*** - the unsearchable heart of humankind

Even the ***depths of God***

The Spirit searches everything

The ***natural person*** does not accept the things of the Spirit of God

The ***things of the Spirit of God*** are folly [silly, absurd] to the natural person

The natural person ***is not able to understand*** the things of the Spirit of God

Because the things of the Spirit of God are ***spiritually discerned***

[Murmur and mumble the words. Phrase by phrase. Word by word. Syllable by syllable. Take pleasure in making the sounds of the words, getting the feel of the meaning. Experience pleasurable anticipation of taking in what will make you more yourself, the self that God made in his own image and likeness. The self that God made for intimate communion with him. The self that God created for good works, that you should walk in them. Eat God's words. Let God's words become a joy and the delight of your heart.]

Journal:

Are you living and thinking from your natural self, or do you have spiritual discernment?

How do we get and develop spiritual discernment?

Ps 143:10 - Teach me to do your will, for <u>*you are my God*</u>*! Let your good Spirit lead me on level ground!*

Ps 25:4-5 - Make me to know your ways, O Lord; teach me your paths. Lead me in your truth and teach me, for <u>*you are the God of my salvation*</u>*; for you I wait all the day long.*

Ps 25:8-9 - <u>*Good and upright is the Lord*</u>*; therefore he instructs sinners in the way. He leads the humble in what is right, and teaches the humble his way.*

Ps 25:12-13a - Who is the man who <u>*fears the Lord*</u>*? Him will he instruct in the way that he should choose. His soul shall abide in well-being…*

Heb 13:20-21 - Now may <u>*the God of peace*</u> *who brought again from*

the dead our Lord Jesus, the great shepherd of the sheep, by the blood of the eternal covenant, equip you with everything good that you may do his will, working in us that which is pleasing in his sight, through Jesus Christ, to whom be glory forever and ever. Amen.

1 John 2:26-27 - I write these things to you about those who are trying to deceive you. But the anointing that you received from him abides in you, and you have no need that anyone should teach you. But as his anointing teaches you about everything—and is true and is no lie, just as it has taught you—abide in him.

[Murmur and mumble the words. Phrase by phrase. Word by word. Syllable by syllable. Take pleasure in making the sounds of the words, getting the feel of the meaning. Experience pleasurable anticipation of taking in what will make you more yourself, the self that God made in his own image and likeness. The self that God made for intimate communion with him. The self that God created for good works, that you should walk in them. Eat God's words. Let God's words become a joy and the delight of your heart.]

Journal:

You are my God. There is no knowledge that the natural person can gather and no effort that the natural person can take to get or develop spiritual discernment, other than surrender with a willingness to wait quietly for God. It begins with God. It begins with knowing God and responding to God. Is God your God?

Do you know the God of your salvation?

Are you aware of him working in you, teaching you, guiding you?

Prov 24:13-14 - My son, eat honey, for it is good, and the drippings of the honeycomb are sweet to your taste. Know that wisdom is such to your soul; if you find it, there will be a future, and your hope will not be cut off.

Col 2:3 - in [Christ] are hidden all the treasures of wisdom and knowledge.

Cor 2:9-10 - But, as it is written, "What no eye has seen, nor ear heard, nor the heart of man imagined, what God has prepared for those who love him"— these things God has revealed to us through the Spirit. For the Spirit searches everything, even the depths of God.

1 Cor 2:14 - The natural person does not accept the things of the Spirit of God, for they are folly to him, and he is not able to understand them because they are spiritually discerned.

Ps 69:13 - But as for me, my prayer is to you, O Lord. At an acceptable time, O God, in the abundance of your steadfast love answer me in your saving faithfulness.

[Pause. Breathe. Inhale and exhale. Reflect. Listen.]

Give me life according to your word, God!

Journal:

What do you hear God saying to you in these Scripture texts? What do they reveal about God and about you? Converse with God about what you're hearing him say. Verbalize and describe your thoughts, memories that come to mind, questions and emotions, concerns, desires.

Is there a particular word or phrase that disturbs or soothes you?

Do the Scripture texts create a picture or an impression that draws you to linger in exploring and experiencing it?

Choose a word or a phrase from your meditation to write on a slip of paper to carry with you today. Refer to it often throughout the day to remind you of your conversation with God and to continue the conversation all day long. Throughout the day pause to become aware of your thoughts and feelings and will. Ask yourself, "What drives me in this moment? Life according to God's word? Or life according to someone else's word?"

Anticipate that God's words stirred your heart for a reason. He's conversing with you through them. Anticipate that God will bring his word to life in you, to bear fruit in your heart and mind and soul and body. Anticipate that God will reveal the secrets of your heart, for anything that is visible is light. And anticipate that God will cause his words to become a joy and the delight of your heart.

CONTEMPLATE

God is spirit, and those who worship him must worship in spirit and truth. Seek him. Feel your way to him. Reach out. Find him.

You exist in God's abounding grace. Only in God's abounding grace do you exist. In God's abounding grace you are you, the real you, able to worship God in spirit and truth.

2 Cor 9:8 - And ***God is able*** *to make all grace abound to you, so that having all sufficiency in all things at all times,* ***you may*** *abound in every good work.*

Anticipate that God's abounding grace, in which you exist and are, will flow around you and through you to enlighten and empower you to love as you have been loved so that you may abound in every good work this day.

42 – The Natural Person and the Spirit of God

Pray: Ask God to prepare your heart and mind and soul to receive his words, to receive truth that will set you free, which will heal and perfect your understanding and knowledge of who God is and who you are.

Ps 119:25-32 - My soul clings to the dust; give me life according to your word! When I told of my ways, you answered me; teach me your statutes! Make me understand the way of your precepts, and I will meditate on your wondrous works. My soul melts away for sorrow; strengthen me according to your word! Put false ways far from me and graciously teach me your law! I have chosen the way of faithfulness; I set your rules before me. I cling to your testimonies, O Lord; let me not be put to shame! I will run in the way of your commandments when you enlarge my heart! (ESV)

[Murmur and mumble the words. Phrase by phrase. Word by word. Syllable by syllable. Pause. Breathe. Inhale and exhale. Reflect. Listen.]

Journal:

Note how this prayer stirs you today and what you hear God saying to you.

1 Cor 3:18-20 - Let no one deceive himself. If anyone among you thinks that he is wise in this age, let him become a fool that he may become wise. For the wisdom of this world is folly with God. For it is written, "He catches the wise in their craftiness," and again, "The Lord knows the thoughts of the wise, that they are futile."

Jer 9:23-24 - Thus says the Lord: "Let not the wise man boast in his wisdom, let not the mighty man boast in his might, let not the rich man boast in his riches, but let him who boasts boast in this, that he understands and knows me, that I am the Lord who practices steadfast love, justice, and righteousness in the earth. For in these things I delight, declares the Lord."

Let no one ***deceive himself***.

[Pause. Breathe. Inhale and exhale. Reflect. Listen.]

Ask God to bring the secrets of your heart into the light.

Journal:

Have you deceived yourself into thinking that you are wise or mighty or rich? Are you trusting an illusion?

Who do you turn to for answers when deciding on a course of action, or a word to speak, or a thought to entertain, or a need to have met, or a craving to address?

If ***you think*** you are wise,

If you think you are wise, ***then become a fool***

Do you think you are wise? What knowledge and experiences and successes, relationships, freedoms, possessions, etc. cause you to think that you are wise?

If you think you are wise in this age, ***become a fool***.

Fool: to shut the mouth; a secret or "mystery" (through the idea of silence imposed by initiation into religious rites[1])

Become a ***fool***.

Shut the mouth.

Become silent.

A secret or "mystery"; silence

If anyone among you thinks that he is wise in this age, let him ***become a fool*** that he may become wise.

Let him become a fool ***that he may become*** wise.

For...

The ***wisdom of this world*** is folly with God. The wisdom of this world lacks understanding. The wisdom of this world lacks sense. The wisdom of this world lacks rational conduct with God.

The Lord knows that the thoughts of the wise in this age are ***futile***.

The thoughts of the wise in this age are futile. Worthless. Untrustworthy. Trifling. Unimportant. Ineffective. Vain. When it comes to knowing and understanding and interacting with God the wisdom of this age is ineffective.

Are your thoughts futile? Worthless? Untrustworthy? Trifling? Unimportant? Ineffective? Vain? Do you know and understand and interact with God? Do you have a desire for God's wisdom and knowledge?

A secret.

Mystery.

Become silent before the Lord.

[Murmur and mumble the words. Phrase by phrase. Word by word. Syllable by syllable. Take pleasure in making the sounds of the words, getting the feel of the meaning. Experience pleasurable anticipation of taking in what will make you more yourself, the self that God made in his own image and likeness. The self that God made for intimate communion with him. The self that God created for good works, that you should walk in them. Eat God's words. Let God's words become a joy and the delight of your heart.]

Ask God to bring the secrets of your heart into the light.

Let him who boasts boast ***in this***,

...that he understands and knows ***me***, that ***I am*** the Lord...

Let him who boasts boast that he ***understands*** and ***knows*** me...

...that he ***understands***...

...and ***knows***

...me...

...that he knows that ***I am the Lord***...

I am the Lord

I am the Lord who practices ***steadfast love***...

I am the Lord

Jonah 2:8 - Those who pay regard to vain idols forsake their hope of steadfast love.

I am the Lord who practices ***steadfast love***...

Those who pay ***regard.*** A firm, fixed look. Consideration. Attention. Concern. Respect. Affection.

Those who pay regard to ***vain idols***

Forsake. Oppose. Give up. Renounce. Abandon.

Those who pay regard to vain idols forsake ***their hope of steadfast love***.

I am the Lord who practices ***steadfast love***...

Those who pay regard to vain idols forsake the Lord who ***practices*** steadfast love.

Those who pay regard to vain idols forsake the Lord, ***their hope*** of steadfast love.

Those who pay regard to vain idols ***withdraw and break away*** from the Lord, their hope of steadfast love.

[Murmur and mumble the words. Phrase by phrase. Word by word. Syllable by syllable. Take pleasure in making the sounds of the words, getting the feel of the meaning. Experience pleasurable anticipation of taking in what will make you more yourself, the self that God made in his own image and likeness. The self that God made

for intimate communion with him. The self that God created for good works, that you should walk in them. Eat God's words. Let God's words become a joy and the delight of your heart.]

Journal:

Who or what do you regard? Who or what is the recipient of your firm, fixed look? Who or what has priority of your consideration, attention, concern, respect and/or affection?

By regarding another have you renounced the one who practices steadfast love? Have you unknowingly abandoned your hope of steadfast love by regarding another?

Do you consider all the treasures of wisdom and knowledge that are hidden in Christ worth whatever it might cost you to seek and find them?

I am the Lord who ***practices*** steadfast love...

Who practices... To do or engage in frequently or usually; to make a habit or custom of.

I am the Lord who makes a habit of ***steadfast*** love...

I am the Lord who has a custom of ***justice***...

I am the Lord who makes a habit of ***righteousness*** in the earth.

For in these things – steadfast love, justice, and righteousness – ***I delight***.

Is it possible for you and me to know the Lord? Is it possible for you and me to understand the Lord? Is it possible for you and me to hope in his steadfast love?

Know that God is Lord. Know that we are **not** Lord. Know that no one and nothing else is Lord. God is Lord. It is the purpose of the Lord that will stand (Prov 19:21). There is no wisdom, no understanding, no advice that can succeed against the Lord (Prov 21:30).

1 Cor 2:14 - The natural person does not accept the things of the Spirit of God, for they are folly to him, and he is not able to understand them because they are spiritually discerned.

1 Cor 3:18-20 - Let no one deceive himself. If anyone among you thinks that he is wise in this age, let him become a fool that he may become wise. For the wisdom of this world is folly with God. For it is written, "He catches the wise in their craftiness," and again, "The Lord knows the thoughts of the wise, that they are futile."

Jer 9:23-24 - Thus says the Lord: "Let not the wise man boast in his wisdom, let not the mighty man boast in his might, let not the rich man boast in his riches, but let him who boasts boast in this, that he understands and knows me, that I am the Lord who practices steadfast love, justice, and righteousness in the earth. For in these things I delight, declares the Lord."

[Pause. Breathe. Inhale and exhale. Reflect. Listen.]

Give me life according to your word, God!

Journal:

What do you hear God saying to you in these Scripture texts? What do they reveal about God and about you? Converse with God about what you're hearing him say. Verbalize and describe your thoughts, memories that come to mind, questions and emotions, concerns, desires.

Is there a particular word or phrase that disturbs or soothes you?

Do the Scripture texts create a picture or an impression that draws you to linger in exploring and experiencing it?

Choose a word or a phrase from your meditation to write on a slip of paper to carry with you today. Refer to it often throughout the day to remind you of your conversation with God and to continue the conversation all day long. Throughout the day pause to become aware of your thoughts and feelings and will. Ask yourself, "What drives me in this moment? Life according to God's word? Or life according to someone else's word?"

Anticipate that God's words stirred your heart for a reason. He's conversing with you through them. Anticipate that God will bring his word to life in you, to bear fruit in your heart and mind and soul and body. Anticipate that God will reveal the secrets of your heart, for anything that is visible is light. And anticipate that God will cause his words to become a joy and the delight of your heart.

CONTEMPLATE

God is spirit, and those who worship him must worship in spirit and truth. Seek him. Feel your way to him. Reach out. Find him.

You exist in God's abounding grace. Only in God's abounding grace do you exist. In God's abounding grace you are you, the real you, able to worship God in spirit and truth.

2 Cor 9:8 - And ***God is able*** *to make all grace abound to you, so that having all sufficiency in all things at all times,* ***you may*** *abound in every good work.*

Anticipate that God's abounding grace, in which you exist and are, will flow around you and through you to enlighten and empower you to love as you have been loved so that you may abound in every good work this day.

Resources:

[1]Fool: NT:3466<START GREEK>musth/rion<END GREEK> musterion (moos-tay'-ree-on); from a derivative of muo (to shut the mouth); a secret or "mystery" (through the idea of silence imposed by initiation into religious rites): (Biblesoft's New Exhaustive Strong's Numbers and Concordance with Expanded Greek-Hebrew Dictionary. Copyright © 1994, 2003, 2006 Biblesoft, Inc. and International Bible Translators, Inc.)

43 – You Will Find that You Know God

Pray: Ask God to prepare your heart and mind and soul to receive his words, to receive truth that will set you free, which will heal and perfect your understanding and knowledge of who God is and who you are.

Ps 119:25-32 - I'm feeling terrible — I couldn't feel worse! Get me on my feet again. You promised, remember? When I told my story, you responded; train me well in your deep wisdom. Help me understand these things inside and out so I can ponder your miracle-wonders. My sad life's dilapidated, a falling-down barn; build me up again by your Word. Barricade the road that goes Nowhere; grace me with your clear revelation. I choose the true road to Somewhere, I post your road signs at every curve and corner. I grasp and cling to whatever you tell me; God, don't let me down! I'll run the course you lay out for me if you'll just show me how. (MSG)

[Murmur and mumble the words. Phrase by phrase. Word by word. Syllable by syllable. Pause. Breathe. Inhale and exhale. Reflect. Listen.]

Journal:

Note how this prayer stirs you today and what you hear God saying to you.

Jer 9:23-24 - Thus says the Lord: "Let not the wise man boast in his wisdom, let not the mighty man boast in his might, let not the rich man boast in his riches, but let him who boasts boast in this, that he understands and knows me, that I am the Lord who practices steadfast love, justice, and righteousness in the earth. For in these things I delight, declares the Lord."

Let him who boasts ***boast in this***

That he understands and knows ***me***

That I am the Lord ***who practices steadfast*** love in the earth

That I am the Lord ***who practices justice*** in the earth

That I am the Lord ***who practices righteousness*** in the earth

For in these things ***I delight***, declares the Lord

How can we ever boldly and honestly boast that we understand and know the Lord?

Prov 2:1-6 - My child, listen to what I say and remember what I command you. Listen carefully to wisdom; set your mind on understanding. Cry out for wisdom, and beg for understanding. Search for it like silver, and hunt for it like hidden treasure. Then you will understand respect for the Lord, and you will find that you know God. Only the Lord gives wisdom; he gives knowledge and understanding. (NCV)

My child…

My child, ***listen***…

Make a conscious effort to pay close attention. Take advice.

Shut your mouth. Be silent. A secret or "mystery".

Listen ***carefully***… [acting or working in a thoughtful, painstaking way, accurately, thoroughly; close attention, great concern, guarding against error]

Remember. Hide. Hoard. Protect my commands within you.

Treasure my commands within you. ***Remember***.

Listen carefully to wisdom; ***set your mind on*** understanding. Be earnestly, mentally disposed to understand.

Cry out for wisdom.

Beg for understanding.

Search for it like silver.

Hunt for it like hidden treasure.

Then…

Then you ***will understand***

Then you will understand ***respect for the Lord***

Respect for the Lord

Then...

Then you will ***find***. You will discover. You will experience. You will realize.

Then you will find that you ***know God***.

Only...

Only ***the Lord***...

Only the Lord ***gives*** wisdom.

The Lord ***gives*** knowledge.

The Lord ***gives*** understanding.

Only the Lord.

Cry out for wisdom. ***Beg*** for understanding. ***Search*** for it like silver. ***Hunt*** for it like hidden treasure.

Then

You will find that ***you know God***.

[Murmur and mumble the words. Phrase by phrase. Word by word. Syllable by syllable. Take pleasure in making the sounds of the words, getting the feel of the meaning. Experience pleasurable anticipation of taking in what will make you more yourself, the self that God made in his own image and likeness. The self that God made for intimate communion with him. The self that God created for good works, that you should walk in them. Eat God's words. Let God's words become a joy and the delight of your heart.]

Journal:

Are you willing to follow this advice?

Jer 9:23-24 - Thus says the Lord: "Let not the wise man boast in his wisdom, let not the mighty man boast in his might, let not the rich man boast in his riches, but let him who boasts boast in this, that he understands and knows me, that I am the Lord who practices steadfast love, justice, and righteousness in the earth. For in these things I delight, declares the Lord."

Prov 2:1-6 - My child, listen to what I say and remember what I command you. Listen carefully to wisdom; set your mind on understanding. Cry out for wisdom, and beg for understanding. Search for it like silver, and hunt for it like hidden treasure. Then you will understand respect for the Lord, and you will find that you know God. Only the Lord gives wisdom; he gives knowledge and understanding. (NCV)

[Pause. Breathe. Inhale and exhale. Reflect. Listen.]

Give me life according to your word, God!

Journal:

What do you hear God saying to you in these Scripture texts? What do they reveal about God and about you? Converse with God about what you're hearing him say. Verbalize and describe your thoughts, memories that come to mind, questions and emotions, concerns, desires.

Is there a particular word or phrase that disturbs or soothes you?

Do the Scripture texts create a picture or an impression that draws you to linger in exploring and experiencing it?

Choose a word or a phrase from your meditation to write on a slip of paper to carry with you today. Refer to it often throughout the day to remind you of your conversation with God and to continue the conversation all day long. Throughout the day pause to become aware of your thoughts and feelings and will. Ask yourself, "What drives me in this moment? Life according to God's word? Or life according to someone else's word?"

Anticipate that God's words stirred your heart for a reason. He's conversing with you through them. Anticipate that God will bring his word to life in you, to bear fruit in your heart and mind and soul and body. Anticipate that God will reveal the secrets of your heart, for anything that is visible is light. And anticipate that God will cause his words to become a joy and the delight of your heart.

CONTEMPLATE

God is spirit, and those who worship him must worship in spirit and truth. Seek him. Feel your way to him. Reach out. Find him.

You exist in God's abounding grace. Only in God's abounding grace do you exist. In God's abounding grace you are you, the real you, able to worship God in spirit and truth.

*2 Cor 9:8 - And **God is able** to make all grace abound to you, so that having all sufficiency in all things at all times, **you may** abound in every good work.*

Anticipate that God's abounding grace, in which you exist and are, will flow around you and through you to enlighten and empower you to love as you have been loved so that you may abound in every good work this day.

44 - To You, O Humankind, Wisdom Calls

Pray: Ask God to prepare your heart and mind and soul to receive his words, to receive truth that will set you free, which will heal and perfect your understanding and knowledge of who God is and who you are.

Ps 119:25-32 - My soul clings to the dust; give me life according to your word! When I told of my ways, you answered me; teach me your statutes! Make me understand the way of your precepts, and I will meditate on your wondrous works. My soul melts away for sorrow; strengthen me according to your word! Put false ways far from me and graciously teach me your law! I have chosen the way of faithfulness; I set your rules before me. I cling to your testimonies, O Lord; let me not be put to shame! I will run in the way of your commandments when you enlarge my heart! (ESV)

[Murmur and mumble the words. Phrase by phrase. Word by word. Syllable by syllable. Pause. Breathe. Inhale and exhale. Reflect. Listen.]

Journal:

Note how this prayer stirs you today and what you hear God saying to you.

Col 2:3 - in [Christ] are hidden all the treasures of wisdom and knowledge.

As you read Proverbs 8 note all the treasures that are hidden in Christ. Highlight, underline, or circle all that you find.

Does not wisdom call? Does not understanding raise her voice? On the heights beside the way, at the crossroads she takes her stand; beside the gates in front of the town, at the entrance of the portals she cries aloud: "To you, O men, I call, and my cry is to the children of man. O simple ones, learn prudence; O fools, learn sense. Hear, for I will speak noble things, and from my lips will come what is right, for my mouth will utter truth; wickedness is an abomination to my lips. All the words of my mouth are righteous; there is nothing twisted or crooked in them. They are all straight to him who under-

stands, and right to those who find knowledge.

Take my instruction instead of silver, and knowledge rather than choice gold, for wisdom is better than jewels, and all that you may desire cannot compare with her. "I, wisdom, dwell with prudence, and I find knowledge and discretion. The fear of the Lord is hatred of evil. Pride and arrogance and the way of evil and perverted speech I hate. I have counsel and sound wisdom; I have insight; I have strength. By me kings reign, and rulers decree what is just; by me princes rule, and nobles, all who govern justly. I love those who love me, and those who seek me diligently find me. Riches and honor are with me, enduring wealth and righteousness. My fruit is better than gold, even fine gold, and my yield than choice silver. I walk in the way of righteousness, in the paths of justice, granting an inheritance to those who love me, and filling their treasuries.

"The Lord possessed me at the beginning of his work, the first of his acts of old. Ages ago I was set up, at the first, before the beginning of the earth. When there were no depths I was brought forth, when there were no springs abounding with water. Before the mountains had been shaped, before the hills, I was brought forth, before he had made the earth with its fields, or the first of the dust of the world. When he established the heavens, I was there; when he drew a circle on the face of the deep, when he made firm the skies above, when he established the fountains of the deep, when he assigned to the sea its limit, so that the waters might not transgress his command, when he marked out the foundations of the earth, then I was beside him, like a master workman, and I was daily his delight, rejoicing before him always, rejoicing in his inhabited world and delighting in the children of man.

"And now, O sons, listen to me: blessed are those who keep my ways. Hear instruction and be wise, and do not neglect it. Blessed is the one who listens to me, watching daily at my gates, waiting beside my doors. For whoever finds me finds life and obtains favor from the Lord, but he who fails to find me injures himself; all who hate me love death."

[Murmur and mumble the words. Phrase by phrase. Word by word. Syllable by syllable. Take pleasure in making the sounds of the words, getting the feel of the meaning. Experience pleasurable anticipation of taking in what will make you more yourself, the self that God made in his own image and likeness. The self that God made for intimate communion with him. The self that God created for good works, that you should walk in them. Eat God's words. Let God's words become a joy and the delight of your heart.]

Journal:

Jot down the treasures of wisdom that are hidden in Christ that especially stirred you as you read. Which do you especially want to seek and find for yourself?

[Pause. Breathe. Inhale and exhale. Reflect. Listen.]

Give me life according to your word, God!

Journal:

What do you hear God saying to you in these Scripture texts? What do they reveal about God and about you? Converse with God about what you're hearing him say. Verbalize and describe your thoughts, memories that come to mind, questions and emotions, concerns, desires.

Is there a particular word or phrase that disturbs or soothes you?

Do the Scripture texts create a picture or an impression that draws you to linger in exploring and experiencing it?

Choose a word or a phrase from your meditation to write on a slip of paper to carry with you today. Refer to it often throughout the day to remind you of your conversation with God and to continue the conversation all day long. Throughout the day pause to become aware of your thoughts and feelings and will. Ask yourself, "What drives me in this moment? Life according to God's word? Or life according to someone else's word?"

Anticipate that God's words stirred your heart for a reason. He's conversing with you through them. Anticipate that God will bring his word to life in you, to bear fruit in your heart and mind and soul and body. Anticipate that God will reveal the secrets of your heart, for anything that is visible is light. And anticipate that God will cause his words to become a joy and the delight of your heart.

CONTEMPLATE

God is spirit, and those who worship him must worship in spirit and truth. Seek him. Feel your way to him. Reach out. Find him.

You exist in God's abounding grace. Only in God's abounding grace do you exist. In God's abounding grace you are you, the real you, able to worship God in spirit and truth.

2 Cor 9:8 - And ***God is able*** *to make all grace abound to you, so that having all sufficiency in all things at all times,* ***you may*** *abound in every good work.*

Anticipate that God's abounding grace, in which you exist and are, will flow around you and through you to enlighten and empower you to love as you have been loved so that you may abound in every good work this day.

45 - Whoever Finds Me Finds Life

Pray: Ask God to prepare your heart and mind and soul to receive his words, to receive truth that will set you free, which will heal and perfect your understanding and knowledge of who God is and who you are.

Ps 119:25-32 - I'm feeling terrible — I couldn't feel worse! Get me on my feet again. You promised, remember? When I told my story, you responded; train me well in your deep wisdom. Help me understand these things inside and out so I can ponder your miracle-wonders. My sad life's dilapidated, a falling-down barn; build me up again by your Word. Barricade the road that goes Nowhere; grace me with your clear revelation. I choose the true road to Somewhere, I post your road signs at every curve and corner. I grasp and cling to whatever you tell me; God, don't let me down! I'll run the course you lay out for me if you'll just show me how. (MSG)

[Murmur and mumble the words. Phrase by phrase. Word by word. Syllable by syllable. Pause. Breathe. Inhale and exhale. Reflect. Listen.]

Journal:

Note how this prayer stirs you today and what you hear God saying to you.

Col 2:3 - in [Christ] are hidden all the treasures of wisdom and knowledge.

Review Proverbs 8. See #44.

Wisdom does not leave us to stumble around, helplessly, hopelessly seeking for what cannot be found.

Wisdom ***calls***.

Understanding ***raises her voice***.

She takes her stand beside the way, at the crossroads, beside the gates in front of the town, at the entrance of the portals. Everywhere that people tread, wisdom ***cries aloud***.

*Prov 8:4 - To you, O men, **I call**, and my cry is to the children of man.*

*Ps 50:1 - The Mighty One, God the Lord, **speaks and summons** the earth from the rising of the sun to its setting.*

[Murmur and mumble the words. Phrase by phrase. Word by word. Syllable by syllable. Take pleasure in making the sounds of the words, getting the feel of the meaning. Experience pleasurable anticipation of taking in what will make you more yourself, the self that God made in his own image and likeness. The self that God made for intimate communion with him. The self that God created for good works, that you should walk in them. Eat God's words. Let God's words become a joy and the delight of your heart.]

Journal:

What do you discover about God in these Scripture texts?

What do you discover about yourself? Do you anticipate that you will hear God and wisdom and understanding? Do you intentionally listen?

Prov 8:4-9, 34 - "To you, O men, I call, and my cry is to the children of man. O simple ones, learn prudence; O fools, learn sense. Hear, for I will speak noble things, and from my lips will come what is right, for my mouth will utter truth; wickedness is an abomination to my lips. All the words of my mouth are righteous; there is nothing twisted or crooked in them. They are all straight to him who understands, and right to those who find knowledge. Blessed is the one who listens to me, watching daily at my gates, waiting beside my doors.

O simple ones, ***learn*** [get knowledge or skill by study, experience, or instruction, to acquire as a habit or attitude]

O simple ones, learn ***prudence*** [exercise sound judgment in practical matters, esp. as concerns one's own interests]

O fools, learn ***sense*** [the ability to think or reason soundly, wisdom]

Hear

Hear, for ***I will*** speak noble things, and from my lips ***will come*** what is right, for my mouth ***will utter*** truth

All ***the words of my mouth*** are righteous

They are all straight to him ***who understands***, and right to those ***who find knowledge***.

O sons, ***listen***

Listen ***to me***

Blessed. ***Happy***.

Blessed are those who ***keep*** my ways.

Keep: a primitive root; properly, to hedge about (as with thorns), i.e. guard; generally, to protect, attend to, etc.[1]

Happy are those who hedge about as with thorns **my ways**.

Happy are those who ***guard*** my ways.

Happy are those who ***protect*** my ways.

Happy are those who ***attend to*** my ways.

Blessed are those who keep ***my ways***.

Ways: a road (as trodden); figuratively, a course of life or mode of action[2]

Happy are those who guard, protect, and attend to ***my*** course of life and ***my*** mode of action.

[Murmur and mumble the words. Phrase by phrase. Word by word. Syllable by syllable. Take pleasure in making the sounds of the words, getting the feel of the meaning. Experience pleasurable anticipation of taking in what will make you more yourself, the self that God made in his own image and likeness. The self that God made for intimate communion with him. The self that God created for good works, that you should walk in them. Eat God's words. Let God's words become a joy and the delight of your heart.]

Journal:

What do you discover about God in these Scripture texts? What does he want for you?

What do you discover about yourself? Are you interested, even passionate about God's word and his ways? Do you seek them, gather them to yourself, guard them, and attend to them more carefully and faithfully than you attend to anything else?

Hear instruction

And

Be wise

And

Do not ***neglect*** it.

Neglect: a primitive root; to loosen; by implication, to expose, dismiss; figuratively, absolve[3]

Do not loosen your guard, protection, and attention to ***my*** ways. Do not expose [lay open to danger, attack, ridicule, etc.] or dismiss ***my*** ways.

Blessed [happy] is the one who ***listens***

Blessed [happy] is the one who listens ***to me***

Blessed is the one who listens to me, ***watching daily*** at my gates, ***waiting*** beside my doors.

Hear

And ***be wise***

And ***do not neglect*** it

For

Whoever

For whoever ***finds me***

For whoever finds me ***finds life***

And

Obtains favor from the Lord

[Murmur and mumble the words. Phrase by phrase. Word by word.

Syllable by syllable. Take pleasure in making the sounds of the words, getting the feel of the meaning. Experience pleasurable anticipation of taking in what will make you more yourself, the self that God made in his own image and likeness. The self that God made for intimate communion with him. The self that God created for good works, that you should walk in them. Eat God's words. Let God's words become a joy and the delight of your heart.]

Journal:

What do you discover about God in these Scripture texts? What does he want for you?

What do you discover about yourself? Do you want the same things for yourself that God wants for you?

Col 2:3 - in [Christ] are hidden all the treasures of wisdom and knowledge.

Prov 8:4 - To you, O men, I call, and my cry is to the children of man.

Ps 50:1 - The Mighty One, God the Lord, speaks and summons the earth from the rising of the sun to its setting.

Prov 8:4-9, 34 - "To you, O men, I call, and my cry is to the children of man. O simple ones, learn prudence; O fools, learn sense. Hear, for I will speak noble things, and from my lips will come what is right, for my mouth will utter truth; wickedness is an abomination to my lips. All the words of my mouth are righteous; there is nothing twisted or crooked in them. They are all straight to him who understands, and right to those who find knowledge. Blessed is the one who listens to me, watching daily at my gates, waiting beside my doors.

[Pause. Breathe. Inhale and exhale. Reflect. Listen.]

Give me life according to your word, God!

Journal:

What do you hear God saying to you in these Scripture texts? What do they reveal about God and about you? Converse with God about what you're hearing him say. Verbalize and describe your thoughts, memories that come to mind, questions and emotions, concerns, desires.

Is there a particular word or phrase that disturbs or soothes you?

Do the Scripture texts create a picture or an impression that draws you to linger in exploring and experiencing it?

Choose a word or a phrase from your meditation to write on a slip of paper to carry with you today. Refer to it often throughout the day to remind you of your conversation with God and to continue the conversation all day long. Throughout the day pause to become aware of your thoughts and feelings and will. Ask yourself, "What drives me in this moment? Life according to God's word? Or life according to someone else's word?"

Anticipate that God's words stirred your heart for a reason. He's conversing with you through them. Anticipate that God will bring his word to life in you, to bear fruit in your heart and mind and soul and body. Anticipate that God will reveal the secrets of your heart, for anything that is visible is light. And anticipate that God will cause his words to become a joy and the delight of your heart.

CONTEMPLATE

God is spirit, and those who worship him must worship in spirit and truth. Seek him. Feel your way to him. Reach out. Find him.

You exist in God's abounding grace. Only in God's abounding grace do you exist. In God's abounding grace you are you, the real you, able to worship God in spirit and truth.

2 Cor 9:8 - And ***God is able*** *to make all grace abound to you, so that having all sufficiency in all things at all times,* ***you may*** *abound in every good work.*

Anticipate that God's abounding grace, in which you exist and are, will flow around you and through you to enlighten and empower you to love as you have been loved so that you may abound in every good work this day.

Resources:

[1]Keep: OT:8104 <START HEBREW>rm^v*<END HEBREW> shamar (shaw-mar'); a primitive root; properly, to hedge about (as with thorns), i.e. guard; generally, to protect, attend to, etc.: (Biblesoft's New Exhaustive Strong's Numbers and Concordance with Expanded Greek-Hebrew Dictionary. Copyright © 1994, 2003, 2006, 2010 Biblesoft, Inc. and International Bible Translators, Inc.)

[2]Ways: OT:1870 <START HEBREW>Er#D#<END HEBREW> derek (deh'-rek); from OT:1869; a road (as trodden); figuratively, a course of life or mode of action, (Biblesoft's New Exhaustive Strong's Numbers and Concordance with Expanded Greek-Hebrew Dictionary. Copyright © 1994, 2003, 2006, 2010 Biblesoft, Inc. and International Bible Translators, Inc.)

[3]Neglect: OT:6544 <START HEBREW>ur^P*<END HEBREW> para` (paw-rah'); a primitive root; to loosen; by implication, to expose, dismiss; figuratively, absolve, begin: (Biblesoft's New Exhaustive Strong's Numbers and Concordance with Expanded Greek-Hebrew Dictionary. Copyright © 1994, 2003, 2006, 2010 Biblesoft, Inc. and International Bible Translators, Inc.)

Also Webster's dictionary.

46 - The Word Became Flesh

Pray: Ask God to prepare your heart and mind and soul to receive his words, to receive truth that will set you free, which will heal and perfect your understanding and knowledge of who God is and who you are.

Ps 119:25-32 - I'm feeling terrible — I couldn't feel worse! Get me on my feet again. You promised, remember? When I told my story, you responded; train me well in your deep wisdom. Help me understand these things inside and out so I can ponder your miracle-wonders. My sad life's dilapidated, a falling-down barn; build me up again by your Word. Barricade the road that goes Nowhere; grace me with your clear revelation. I choose the true road to Somewhere, I post your road signs at every curve and corner. I grasp and cling to whatever you tell me; God, don't let me down! I'll run the course you lay out for me if you'll just show me how. (MSG)

[Murmur and mumble the words. Phrase by phrase. Word by word. Syllable by syllable. Pause. Breathe. Inhale and exhale. Reflect. Listen.]

Journal:

Note how this prayer stirs you today and what you hear God saying to you.

*Col 2:3 - in [Christ] are **hidden** all the treasures of wisdom and knowledge.*

*Prov 8:4 - To you, O men, **I call**, and my cry is to the children of man.*

*Ps 50:1 - The Mighty One, God the Lord, **speaks and summons** the earth from the rising of the sun to its setting.*

Wisdom's story

"The Lord possessed me at the beginning of his work, the first of his acts of old.

Ages ago I was set up, at the first, before the beginning of the earth. When there were no depths I was brought forth, when there were no springs abounding with water. Before the mountains had been shaped, before the hills, I was brought forth, before he had made the earth with its fields, or the first of the dust of the world.

When he established the heavens, I was there; when he drew a circle on the face of the deep, when he made firm the skies above, when he established the fountains of the deep, when he assigned to the sea its limit, so that the waters might not transgress his command, when he marked out the foundations of the earth, then I was beside him, like a master workman, and I was daily his delight, rejoicing before him always, rejoicing in his inhabited world and delighting in the children of man. (Prov 8:21-31)

Gen 1:1-3 - In the beginning, God created the heavens and the earth. The earth was without form and void, and darkness was over the face of the deep. And the Spirit of God was hovering over the face of the waters. ***And God said****, "Let there be light," and there was light.*

John 1:1-5 - In the beginning was the ***Word****, and the* ***Word*** *was with God, and the* ***Word*** *was God.* ***He*** *was in the beginning with God. All things were made through* ***him****, and without* ***him*** *was not any thing made that was made.* ***In him*** *was* ***life****, and the life was the* ***light*** *of men. The light shines in the darkness, and the darkness has not overcome it.*

John 1:14-18 - And the ***Word became flesh*** *and dwelt among us, and we have seen his glory, glory as of the only Son from the Father, full of grace and truth. (John [the Baptist] bore witness about him, and cried out, "This was he of whom I said, 'He who comes after me ranks before me, because he was before me.'") And from his fullness we have all received, grace upon grace. For the law was given through Moses; grace and truth came through Jesus Christ. No one has ever seen God; the only God, who is at the Father's side, he has made him known.*

The Lord possessed me [Wisdom] at ***the beginning of his work***, the first of his acts of old.

Ages ago I was set up, at the first, ***before the beginning*** of the earth.

In the ***beginning***

Was the ***Word***, and the ***Word*** *was* with God, and the ***Word*** was God

He was

He was ***in the beginning*** with God

The earth was **without form** and **void**

When he established the heavens, ***I was there***; when he drew a circle on the face of the deep, when he made firm the skies above, when he established the fountains of the deep, when he assigned to the sea its limit, so that the waters might not transgress his command, when he marked out the foundations of the earth, ***then I was beside him, like a master workman***, and ***I was daily his delight***, rejoicing before him always, ***rejoicing in his inhabited world and delighting in the children of man.***

All things were made ***through him***

In him

In him ***was life***

And God said, "Let there be ***light,***" and ***there was light***.

The life was ***the light of men***

The life

The life was the ***light of men***

The ***light shines*** in the darkness

And the darkness ***has not*** overcome it

And ***the Word became flesh***

The Word ***dwelt among us***

From ***his fullness***

We have

We have ***all received***

We have all received, ***grace*** upon ***grace***

Grace and truth ***came through*** Jesus Christ

He has made God, the only God, his Father ***known***

[Murmur and mumble the words. Phrase by phrase. Word by word. Syllable by syllable. Take pleasure in making the sounds of the words, getting the feel of the meaning. Experience pleasurable anticipation of taking in what will make you more yourself, the self that God made in his own image and likeness. The self that God made for intimate communion with him. The self that God created for good works, that you should walk in them. Eat God's words. Let God's words become a joy and the delight of your heart.]

Journal:

The **Word**. God **said**, "Let there be light, and there was light." All things were made through him, the Word. What do you discover about wisdom, the Word, and Jesus Christ from these Scripture texts?

What is the significance of the Word of God becoming flesh?

What is the darkness that has not, cannot overcome the life that is the light of men?

From his fullness <u>we have all received</u>, grace upon grace. Are you aware of the grace upon grace that you have received?

Col 2:8-10 - See to it that no one takes you captive by philosophy and empty deceit, according to human tradition, according to the elemental spirits of the world, and not according to Christ. For <u>***in him*** the whole fullness of deity dwells bodily, and you have been filled ***in him***</u>, who is the head of all rule and authority.

Matt 3:11-12 - "I baptize you with water for repentance, but he who is coming after me is mightier than I, whose sandals I am not worthy to carry. <u>He will baptize you with the Holy Spirit and with fire</u>.

From his fullness ***we have all*** received

See to it [Beware]

See to it that ***no one takes you captive***

By ***philosophy and empty deceit***

According to ***human tradition***

According to the ***elemental spirits of the world***

Instead, let yourself ***be taken captive***

According to Christ

For **in him**

The ***whole fullness of deity*** dwells bodily

And you ***have been*** filled ***in him*** [made complete]

Who is the head of ***all rule and authority***

He will baptize you with ***the Holy Spirit and with fire***

[Murmur and mumble the words. Phrase by phrase. Word by word. Syllable by syllable. Take pleasure in making the sounds of the words, getting the feel of the meaning. Experience pleasurable anticipation of taking in what will make you more yourself, the self that God made in his own image and likeness. The self that God made for intimate communion with him. The self that God created for good works, that you should walk in them. Eat God's words. Let God's words become a joy and the delight of your heart.]

Journal:

What is the danger that you are warned to be alert to in these Scripture texts?

You have been filled in him. What does this mean?

Col 2:9-10 - All of God lives in Christ's body, and God has made you complete in Christ. Christ is in charge of every ruler and authority. (God's Word)

Col 2:3 - in [Christ] are hidden all the treasures of wisdom and knowledge.

"The Lord possessed me at the beginning of his work, the first of his acts of old.

Ages ago I was set up, at the first, before the beginning of the earth. When there were no depths I was brought forth, when there were no springs abounding with water. Before the mountains had been shaped, before the hills, I was brought forth, before he had made the earth with its fields, or the first of the dust of the world.

When he established the heavens, I was there; when he drew a circle on the face of the deep, when he made firm the skies above, when he established the fountains of the deep, when he assigned to the sea its limit, so that the waters might not transgress his command, when he marked out the foundations of the earth, then I was beside him, like a master workman, and I was daily his delight, rejoicing before him always, rejoicing in his inhabited world and delighting in the children of man. (Prov 8:21-31)

Gen 1:1-3 - In the beginning, God created the heavens and the earth. The earth was without form and void, and darkness was over the face of the deep. And the Spirit of God was hovering over the face of the waters. And God said, "Let there be light," and there was light.

John 1:1-5 - In the beginning was the Word, and the Word was with God, and the Word was God. He was in the beginning with God. All things were made through him, and without him was not any thing made that was made. In him was life, and the life was the light of men. The light shines in the darkness, and the darkness has not overcome it.

John 1:14-18 - And the Word became flesh and dwelt among us, and we have seen his glory, glory as of the only Son from the Father, full of grace and truth. (John [the Baptist] bore witness about him, and cried out, "This was he of whom I said, 'He who comes after me ranks before me, because he was before me.'") And from his fullness we have all received, grace upon grace. For the law was given through Moses; grace and truth came through Jesus Christ. No one has ever seen God; the only God, who is at the Father's side, he has made him known.

Matt 3:11-12 - "I baptize you with water for repentance, but he who is coming after me is mightier than I, whose sandals I am not worthy to carry. He will baptize you with the Holy Spirit and with fire.

[Pause. Breathe. Inhale and exhale. Reflect. Listen.]

Give me life according to your word, God!

Journal:

What do you hear God saying to you in these Scripture texts? What do they reveal about God and about you? Converse with God about what you're hearing him say. Verbalize and describe your thoughts, memories that come to mind, questions and emotions, concerns, desires.

Is there a particular word or phrase that disturbs or soothes you?

Do the Scripture texts create a picture or an impression that draws you to linger in exploring and experiencing it?

Choose a word or a phrase from your meditation to write on a slip of paper to carry with you today. Refer to it often throughout the day to remind you of your conversation with God and to continue the conversation all day long. Throughout the day pause to become aware of your thoughts and feelings and will. Ask yourself, "What drives me in this moment? Life according to God's word? Or life according to someone else's word?"

Anticipate that God's words stirred your heart for a reason. He's conversing with you through them. Anticipate that God will bring his word to life in you, to bear fruit in your heart and mind and soul and body. Anticipate that God will reveal the secrets of your heart, for anything that is visible is light. And anticipate that God will cause his words to become a joy and the delight of your heart.

CONTEMPLATE

God is spirit, and those who worship him must worship in spirit and truth. Seek him. Feel your way to him. Reach out. Find him.

You exist in God's abounding grace. Only in God's abounding grace do you exist. In God's abounding grace you are you, the real you, able to worship God in spirit and truth.

2 Cor 9:8 - And ***God is able*** *to make all grace abound to you, so that having all sufficiency in all things at all times,* ***you may*** *abound in every good work.*

Anticipate that God's abounding grace, in which you exist and are, will flow around you and through you to enlighten and empower you to love as you have been loved so that you may abound in every good work this day.

47 - We Have All Received Grace Upon Grace

Pray: Ask God to prepare your heart and mind and soul to receive his words, to receive truth that will set you free, which will heal and perfect your understanding and knowledge of who God is and who you are.

Ps 119:25-32 - My soul clings to the dust; give me life according to your word! When I told of my ways, you answered me; teach me your statutes! Make me understand the way of your precepts, and I will meditate on your wondrous works. My soul melts away for sorrow; strengthen me according to your word! Put false ways far from me and graciously teach me your law! I have chosen the way of faithfulness; I set your rules before me. I cling to your testimonies, O Lord; let me not be put to shame! I will run in the way of your commandments when you enlarge my heart! (ESV)

[Murmur and mumble the words. Phrase by phrase. Word by word. Syllable by syllable. Pause. Breathe. Inhale and exhale. Reflect. Listen.]

Journal:

Note how this prayer stirs you today and what you hear God saying to you.

Col 2:3 - in [Christ] are hidden all the treasures of wisdom and knowledge.

John 1:14-18 - And the Word became flesh and dwelt among us, and we have seen his glory, glory as of the only Son from the Father, full of grace and truth. (John [the Baptist] bore witness about him, and cried out, "This was he of whom I said, 'He who comes after me ranks before me, because he was before me.'") And from his fullness we have all received, grace upon grace. For the law was given through Moses; grace and truth came through Jesus Christ. No one has ever seen God; the only God, who is at the Father's side, he has made him known.

From ***his fullness***

From his fullness ***we have all received***

Grace ***upon*** grace

He has made God, the only God, his Father ***known***

[Murmur and mumble the words. Phrase by phrase. Word by word. Syllable by syllable. Take pleasure in making the sounds of the words, getting the feel of the meaning. Experience pleasurable anticipation of taking in what will make you more yourself, the self that God made in his own image and likeness. The self that God made for intimate communion with him. The self that God created for good works, that you should walk in them. Eat God's words. Let God's words become a joy and the delight of your heart.]

Journal:

Who is your source of information about God? What is the foundation that your perceptions and beliefs about God are built upon?

Do you know the life that is in Christ Jesus? Are you aware that you have received grace upon grace? The natural person cannot know and accept the things of the Spirit of God.

If our source of information about God is not Jesus Christ, then we are fashioning an idol based on the philosophy and empty deceit according to human tradition and the elemental spirits of the world. If the foundation that we're building our life and future on is not Jesus Christ, then we are fashioning an idol. And our foreign god is wreaking havoc on our perception of who God is and who we are.

No one has ever seen God; the only God, who is at the Father's side, ***he has made him known***.

He has

He has ***made him known***.

Grace ***upon*** grace.

Graciousness. To please. To give pleasure or satisfaction. Especially the divine influence upon the heart, and its reflection in the life; including gratitude. Be well. Cheerful. Calmly happy. Well-off.[1]

Grace upon grace. The divine influence upon the heart. Grace upon grace. The reflection of the divine influence in the life.

[Murmur and mumble the words. Phrase by phrase. Word by word. Syllable by syllable. Take pleasure in making the sounds of the words, getting the feel of the meaning. Experience pleasurable anticipation of taking in what will make you more yourself, the self that God made in his own image and likeness. The self that God made for intimate communion with him. The self that God created for good works, that you should walk in them. Eat God's words. Let God's words become a joy and the delight of your heart.]

Journal:

Why have we all received grace upon grace?

Prov 8:29-31 - when he assigned to the sea its limit, so that the waters might not transgress his command, when he marked out the foundations of the earth, then I was beside him, like a master workman, and I was daily his delight, rejoicing [to laugh in pleasure, play] before him always, rejoicing in his inhabited world and delighting in the children of man.

I, wisdom

Like a ***master*** workman

I was daily ***his delight***

Rejoicing [to laugh in pleasure, play]

Rejoicing ***before him*** always

Rejoicing [to laugh in pleasure, play] in his inhabited world

Delighting [enjoyment, pleasure]

In the ***children of man***

[Murmur and mumble the words. Phrase by phrase. Word by word. Syllable by syllable. Take pleasure in making the sounds of the words, getting the feel of the meaning. Experience pleasurable anticipation of taking in what will make you more yourself, the self that God made in his own image and likeness. The self that God made for intimate communion with him. The self that God created for good works, that you should walk in them. Eat God's words. Let God's words become a joy and the delight of your heart.]

Journal:

Are you aware of how God and Jesus Christ feel about you? Are you aware that they delight in you? They take pleasure in you? They enjoy you?

What does God want from you in response?

Prov 8:32 "And now, O sons, listen to me: blessed are those who keep my ways.

Listen to me.

Keep my ways.

Hedge about as with thorns my ways. Guard, protect, attend to my ways.

By "keeping my ways" might Wisdom/Word/Jesus Christ mean that he wants us to laugh in pleasure and play before God along with him always?

How we've missed the mark! How we've failed to properly hedge about as with thorns that precious relationship with God. How we've failed to guard, protect and attend to that gracious intimacy. To laugh in pleasure and play before God. Do those words call forth a picture that arouses a lonesome homesickness in your core? Do you long for your true home?

Are you willing to pay the cost to find and know and commune with

Wisdom, to laugh with him in pleasure and play before God always? Are you willing to lose yourself, the self that you know and love, that has been created by leaning on your own understanding and based on the philosophy and empty deceit according to human tradition and the elemental spirits of the world? Are you willing to find yourself, the self that intimately communes with Wisdom?

Wisdom's advice to the children of men:

Prov 4:5-8 - Get wisdom; get insight; do not forget, and do not turn away from the words of my mouth. Do not forsake her, and she will keep you; love her, and she will guard you. The beginning of wisdom is this: Get wisdom, and whatever you get, get insight. Prize her highly, and she will exalt you; she will honor you if you embrace her.

[Murmur and mumble the words. Phrase by phrase. Word by word. Syllable by syllable. Take pleasure in making the sounds of the words, getting the feel of the meaning. Experience pleasurable anticipation of taking in what will make you more yourself, the self that God made in his own image and likeness. The self that God made for intimate communion with him. The self that God created for good works, that you should walk in them. Eat God's words. Let God's words become a joy and the delight of your heart.]

Journal:

Will you take wisdom's advice?

Col 2:3 - in [Christ] are hidden all the treasures of wisdom and knowledge.

John 1:14-18 - And the Word became flesh and dwelt among us, and we have seen his glory, glory as of the only Son from the Father, full of grace and truth. (John [the Baptist] bore witness about him, and cried out, "This was he of whom I said, 'He who comes after me ranks before me, because he was before me.'") And from his fullness we have all received, grace upon grace. For the law was given through Moses; grace and truth came through Jesus Christ. No one has ever seen God; the only God, who is at the Father's side, he has made him known.

Prov 8:29-31 - when he assigned to the sea its limit, so that the waters might not transgress his command, when he marked out the foundations of the earth, then I was beside him, like a master workman, and I was daily his delight, rejoicing [to laugh in pleasure, play] before him always, rejoicing in his inhabited world and delighting in the children of man.

[Pause. Breathe. Inhale and exhale. Reflect. Listen.]

Give me life according to your word, God!

Journal:

What do you hear God saying to you in these Scripture texts? What do they reveal about God and about you? Converse with God about what you're hearing him say. Verbalize and describe your thoughts, memories that come to mind, questions and emotions, concerns, desires.

Is there a particular word or phrase that disturbs or soothes you?

Do the Scripture texts create a picture or an impression that draws you to linger in exploring and experiencing it?

Choose a word or a phrase from your meditation to write on a slip of paper to carry with you today. Refer to it often throughout the day to remind you of your conversation with God and to continue the conversation all day long. Throughout the day pause to become aware of your thoughts and feelings and will. Ask yourself, "What drives me in this moment? Life according to God's word? Or life according to someone else's word?"

Anticipate that God's words stirred your heart for a reason. He's conversing with you through them. Anticipate that God will bring his word to life in you, to bear fruit in your heart and mind and soul and body. Anticipate that God will reveal the secrets of your heart, for anything that is visible is light. And anticipate that God will cause his words to become a joy and the delight of your heart.

CONTEMPLATE

God is spirit, and those who worship him must worship in spirit and truth. Seek him. Feel your way to him. Reach out. Find him.

You exist in God's abounding grace. Only in God's abounding grace do you exist. In God's abounding grace you are you, the real you, able to worship God in spirit and truth.

2 Cor 9:8 - And ***God is able*** *to make all grace abound to you, so that having all sufficiency in all things at all times,* ***you may*** *abound in every good work.*

Anticipate that God's abounding grace, in which you exist and are, will flow around you and through you to enlighten and empower you to love as you have been loved so that you may abound in every good work this day.

Resources:

[1]Grace: NT:5485<START GREEK>xa/ri$<END GREEK> charis (khar'-ece); from NT:5463; graciousness (as gratifying), of manner or act (abstract or concrete; literal, figurative or spiritual; especially the divine influence upon the heart, and its reflection in the life; including gratitude):

NT:5463<START GREEK>xai/rw<END GREEK> chairo (khah'-ee-ro); a primary verb; to be "cheerful", i.e. calmly happy or well-off; impersonally, especially as salutation (on meeting or parting), be well: (Biblesoft's New Exhaustive Strong's Numbers and Concordance with Expanded Greek-Hebrew Dictionary. Copyright © 1994, 2003, 2006, 2010 Biblesoft, Inc. and International Bible Translators, Inc.)

[2]Keep: OT:8104 <START HEBREW>rm^v*<END HEBREW> shamar (shaw-mar'); a primitive root; properly, to hedge about (as with thorns), i.e. guard; generally, to protect, attend to, etc.: (Biblesoft's New Exhaustive Strong's Numbers and Concordance with Expanded Greek-Hebrew Dictionary. Copyright © 1994, 2003, 2006, 2010

Biblesoft, Inc. and International Bible Translators, Inc.)

48 - In Christ Was Life

Pray: Ask God to prepare your heart and mind and soul to receive his words, to receive truth that will set you free, which will heal and perfect your understanding and knowledge of who God is and who you are.

Ps 119:25-32 - I'm feeling terrible — I couldn't feel worse! Get me on my feet again. You promised, remember? When I told my story, you responded; train me well in your deep wisdom. Help me understand these things inside and out so I can ponder your miracle-wonders. My sad life's dilapidated, a falling-down barn; build me up again by your Word. Barricade the road that goes Nowhere; grace me with your clear revelation. I choose the true road to Somewhere, I post your road signs at every curve and corner. I grasp and cling to whatever you tell me; God, don't let me down! I'll run the course you lay out for me if you'll just show me how. (MSG)

[Murmur and mumble the words. Phrase by phrase. Word by word. Syllable by syllable. Pause. Breathe. Inhale and exhale. Reflect. Listen.]

Journal:

Note how this prayer stirs you today and what you hear God saying to you.

Col 2:3 - in [Christ] are hidden all the treasures of wisdom and knowledge.

Gen 1:3 - And God said, "Let there be light," and there was light.

John 1:4-5 - In him [Word/Christ] was life, and the life was the light of men. The light shines in the darkness, and the darkness has not overcome it.

2 Cor 4:6-7 - For God, who said, "Let light shine out of darkness," has shone in our hearts to give the light of the knowledge of the glory of God in the face of Jesus Christ. But we have this treasure in jars of clay, to show that the surpassing power belongs to God and not to us.

In Christ

Are ***hidden***

In Christ are hidden ***all***

In Christ are hidden all ***the treasures***

In Christ are hidden all the treasures ***of wisdom and knowledge***.

But ***we have***

But we have this treasure ***in jars of clay***

All the treasures of wisdom and knowledge, such as prudence, sense, truth, life, favor, discretion, insight, strength, riches, enduring wealth, righteousness... All are hidden in Christ. We have this treasure in jars of clay!

[Murmur and mumble the words. Phrase by phrase. Word by word. Syllable by syllable. Take pleasure in making the sounds of the words, getting the feel of the meaning. Experience pleasurable anticipation of taking in what will make you more yourself, the self that God made in his own image and likeness. The self that God made for intimate communion with him. The self that God created for good works, that you should walk in them. Eat God's words. Let God's words become a joy and the delight of your heart.]

Journal:

How can you receive all the treasures of wisdom and knowledge that are hidden in Christ?

God

God ***has***

God...has ***shone*** [to beam, to radiate brilliancy[1]]

God...has shone ***in our hearts***

God...has shone in our hearts ***to give***

God...has shone in our hearts to give ***the light*** [illumination, explanation, enlightenment[2]]

God…has shone in our hearts to give the light ***of the knowledge of the glory of God***

In the face [presence, person, countenance, appearance[3]] of Jesus Christ.

[Murmur and mumble the words. Phrase by phrase. Word by word. Syllable by syllable. Take pleasure in making the sounds of the words, getting the feel of the meaning. Experience pleasurable anticipation of taking in what will make you more yourself, the self that God made in his own image and likeness. The self that God made for intimate communion with him. The self that God created for good works, that you should walk in them. Eat God's words. Let God's words become a joy and the delight of your heart.]

Journal:

What do you hear God revealing about the way to receive all the treasures of wisdom and knowledge that are hidden in Christ?

Let ***light shine***

Out of darkness

God has shone in our hearts ***to give*** the light of the knowledge [knowing, being aware of, perceiving, understanding[4]] of the glory of God.

God has shone ***in our hearts***

To give ***the light*** of the knowledge

Of the ***glory*** of God.

In the ***face of Jesus Christ***.

Jer 17:9 - The heart is deceitful above all things, and desperately sick; who can understand it?

Yet, in the very place that is deceitful above all things, God has shone. In that place which is desperately sick, God has radiated brilliancy to give light. In that place that we don't understand, God has shown light. Illumination. Knowing. Being aware of. Perceiving.

Understanding the glory of God.

[Murmur and mumble the words. Phrase by phrase. Word by word. Syllable by syllable. Take pleasure in making the sounds of the words, getting the feel of the meaning. Experience pleasurable anticipation of taking in what will make you more yourself, the self that God made in his own image and likeness. The self that God made for intimate communion with him. The self that God created for good works, that you should walk in them. Eat God's words. Let God's words become a joy and the delight of your heart.]

Journal:

What do you hear God saying to you in these Scripture texts?

Let light shine out of darkness. God <u>has shone</u> in our hearts to give the light of the knowledge of the glory of God in the face of Jesus Christ.

John 1:4-5 - In him [Christ] was life, and the life was the light of men. The light shines in the darkness, and the darkness has not overcome it.

In Christ

In Christ ***was life***.

And ***the life***

And the life was the ***light of men*** [to show or make known one's thoughts[5]]

The light ***shines in the darkness*** [dimness, obscurity, shadiness, of error[6]]

And the ***darkness has not overcome*** it.

[Murmur and mumble the words. Phrase by phrase. Word by word. Syllable by syllable. Take pleasure in making the sounds of the words, getting the feel of the meaning. Experience pleasurable anticipation of taking in what will make you more yourself, the self that God made in his own image and likeness. The self that God made for intimate communion with him. The self that God created for good works, that you should walk in them. Eat God's words. Let God's words become a joy and the delight of your heart.]

Journal:

What is the darkness that this Scripture text speaks of which cannot overcome the light that God has shone in our hearts to give the light of the knowledge of the glory of God in the face of Jesus Christ?

What does Scripture mean when it says, "In Christ was life, and the life was the light of men"?

Isa 42:16 - And I [God] will lead the blind in a way that they do not know, in paths that they have not known I will guide them. I will turn the darkness before them into light, the rough places into level ground. These are the things I do, and I do not forsake them.

Acts 26:22-23 - To this day I [Apostle Paul] have had the help that comes from God, and so I stand here testifying both to small and great, saying nothing but what the prophets and Moses said would come to pass: that the Christ must suffer and that, by being the first to rise from the dead, he would proclaim light both to our people and to the Gentiles."

Eph 5:13-14 - But when anything is exposed by the light, it becomes visible [to render apparent, external], for anything that becomes visible is light. Therefore it says, "Awake, O sleeper, and arise from the dead, and Christ will shine on you."

I [God] will lead ***the blind*** in a way that ***they do not know***

I [God] will guide ***the blind*** in paths that ***they have not known***

I [God] will ***turn the darkness*** before them into light

I [God] will ***turn the rough places*** into level ground

These are the things I [God] do, and ***I do not forsake them***

I [Apostle Paul] have had the ***help that comes from God***, and so I stand here ***testifying*** to what the prophets and Moses said would come to pass

The ***Christ must suffer***

By being the ***first to rise from the dead***

Christ would ***proclaim light*** both to our people [Israelites] and to the Gentiles

[Murmur and mumble the words. Phrase by phrase. Word by word. Syllable by syllable. Take pleasure in making the sounds of the words, getting the feel of the meaning. Experience pleasurable anticipation of taking in what will make you more yourself, the self that God made in his own image and likeness. The self that God made for intimate communion with him. The self that God created for good works, that you should walk in them. Eat God's words. Let God's words become a joy and the delight of your heart.]

Journal:

Describe what God has accomplished through Christ in whom was life, and life was the light of men.

Respond to God's statement, "I do not forsake them." Have you ever felt like God forsook you personally? Have you ever felt like God forsook humankind in general? How do you reconcile "your evidence" with God's statement, "I do not forsake them"?

Col 2:3 - in [Christ] are hidden all the treasures of wisdom and knowledge.

2 Cor 4:6-7 - For God, who said, "Let light shine out of darkness," has shone in our hearts to give the light of the knowledge of the glory of God in the face of Jesus Christ. But we have this treasure in jars of clay, to show that the surpassing power belongs to God and not to us.

Jer 17:9 - The heart is deceitful above all things, and desperately sick; who can understand it?

John 1:4-5 - In him [Christ] was life, and the life was the light of men. The light shines in the darkness, and the darkness has not overcome it.

Eph 5:13-14 - But when anything is exposed by the light, it becomes visible (to render apparent, external), for anything that becomes visible is light. Therefore it says, "Awake, O sleeper, and arise from the dead, and Christ will shine on you."

[Pause. Breathe. Inhale and exhale. Reflect. Listen.]

Give me life according to your word, God!

Journal:

What do you hear God saying to you in these Scripture texts? What do they reveal about God and about you? Converse with God about what you're hearing him say. Verbalize and describe your thoughts, memories that come to mind, questions and emotions, concerns, desires.

Is there a particular word or phrase that disturbs or soothes you?

Do the Scripture texts create a picture or an impression that draws you to linger in exploring and experiencing it?

Choose a word or a phrase from your meditation to write on a slip of paper to carry with you today. Refer to it often throughout the day to remind you of your conversation with God and to continue the conversation all day long. Throughout the day pause to become aware of your thoughts and feelings and will. Ask yourself, "What drives me in this moment? Life according to God's word? Or life according to someone else's word?"

Anticipate that God's words stirred your heart for a reason. He's conversing with you through them. Anticipate that God will bring his word to life in you, to bear fruit in your heart and mind and soul and body. Anticipate that God will reveal the secrets of your heart, for anything that is visible is light. And anticipate that God will cause his words to become a joy and the delight of your heart.

CONTEMPLATE

God is spirit, and those who worship him must worship in spirit and truth. Seek him. Feel your way to him. Reach out. Find him.

You exist in God's abounding grace. Only in God's abounding grace do you exist. In God's abounding grace you are you, the real you, able to worship God in spirit and truth.

*2 Cor 9:8 - And **God is able** to make all grace abound to you, so that having all sufficiency in all things at all times, **you may** abound in every good work.*

Anticipate that God's abounding grace, in which you exist and are, will flow around you and through you to enlighten and empower you to love as you have been loved so that you may abound in every good work this day.

Resources:

[1]Shine: NT:2989<START GREEK>la/mpw<END GREEK> lampo (lam'-po); a primary verb; to beam, i.e. radiate brilliancy (literally or figuratively):(Biblesoft's New Exhaustive Strong's Numbers and Concordance with Expanded Greek-Hebrew Dictionary. Copyright © 1994, 2003, 2006, 2010 Biblesoft, Inc. and International Bible Translators, Inc.)

[2]Light: NT:5462<START GREEK>fwtismo/$<END GREEK> photismos (fo-tis-mos'); from NT:5461; illumination (figuratively):

NT:5461<START GREEK>fwti/zw<END GREEK> photizo (fo-tid'-zo); from NT:5457; to shed rays, i.e. to shine or (transitively) to brighten up (literally or figuratively): (Biblesoft's New Exhaustive Strong's Numbers and Concordance with Expanded Greek-Hebrew Dictionary. Copyright © 1994, 2003, 2006, 2010 Biblesoft, Inc. and International Bible Translators, Inc.)

[3]Face: NT:4383<START GREEK>pro/swpon<END GREEK> prosopon (pros'-o-pon); from NT:4314 and ops (the visage, from NT:3700); the front (as being towards view), i.e. the countenance, aspect, appearance, surface; by implication, presence, person: (Biblesoft's New Exhaustive Strong's Numbers and Concordance with Expand-

ed Greek-Hebrew Dictionary. Copyright © 1994, 2003, 2006, 2010 Biblesoft, Inc. and International Bible Translators, Inc.)

[4]Knowledge: NT:1108 <START GREEK>gnw=si$<END GREEK> gnosis (gno'-sis); from NT:1097; knowing (the act), i.e. (by implication) knowledge: (Biblesoft's New Exhaustive Strong's Numbers and Concordance with Expanded Greek-Hebrew Dictionary. Copyright © 1994, 2003, 2006, 2010 Biblesoft, Inc. and International Bible Translators, Inc.)

[5]Light: NT:5457 <START GREEK>fw=$<END GREEK> phos (foce); from an obsolete phao (to shine or make manifest, especially by rays; compare NT:5316, NT:5346); luminousness (in the widest application, nat. or artificial, abstract or concrete, literal or figurative):

NT:5346 <START GREEK>fhmi/<END GREEK> phemi (fay-mee'); properly, the same as the base of NT:5457 and NT:5316; to show or make known one's thoughts, i.e. speak or say:

NT:5316 <START GREEK>fai/nw<END GREEK> phaino (fah'-ee-no); prolongation for the base of NT:5457; to lighten (shine), i.e. show (transitive or intransitive, literal or figurative): (Biblesoft's New Exhaustive Strong's Numbers and Concordance with Expanded Greek-Hebrew Dictionary. Copyright © 1994, 2003, 2006, 2010 Biblesoft, Inc. and International Bible Translators, Inc.)

[6]Darkness: NT:4653<START GREEK>skoti/a<END GREEK> skotia (skot-ee'-ah); from NT:4655; dimness, obscurity (literally or figuratively):

NT:4655<START GREEK>sko/to$<END GREEK> skotos (skot'-os); from the base of NT:4639; shadiness, i.e. obscurity (literally or figuratively):

NT:4639 <START GREEK>ski/a<END GREEK> skia (skee'-ah); apparently a primary word; "shade" or a shadow (literally or figuratively [darkness of error or an adumbration]): (Biblesoft's New Exhaustive Strong's Numbers and Concordance with Expanded Greek-Hebrew Dictionary. Copyright © 1994, 2003, 2006, 2010 Biblesoft, Inc. and International Bible Translators, Inc.)

49 - Awake, O Sleeper

Pray: Ask God to prepare your heart and mind and soul to receive his words, to receive truth that will set you free, which will heal and perfect your understanding and knowledge of who God is and who you are.

Ps 119:25-32 - My soul clings to the dust; give me life according to your word! When I told of my ways, you answered me; teach me your statutes! Make me understand the way of your precepts, and I will meditate on your wondrous works. My soul melts away for sorrow; strengthen me according to your word! Put false ways far from me and graciously teach me your law! I have chosen the way of faithfulness; I set your rules before me. I cling to your testimonies, O Lord; let me not be put to shame! I will run in the way of your commandments when you enlarge my heart! (ESV)

[Murmur and mumble the words. Phrase by phrase. Word by word. Syllable by syllable. Pause. Breathe. Inhale and exhale. Reflect. Listen.]

Journal:

Note how this prayer stirs you today and what you hear God saying to you.

Col 2:3 - in [Christ] are hidden all the treasures of wisdom and knowledge.

Isa 42:16 - And I [God] will lead the blind in a way that they do not know, in paths that they have not known I will guide them. I will turn the darkness before them into light, the rough places into level ground. These are the things I do, and I do not forsake them.

Acts 26:22-23 - To this day I [Apostle Paul] have had the help that comes from God, and so I stand here testifying both to small and great, saying nothing but what the prophets and Moses said would come to pass: that the Christ must suffer and that, by being the first to rise from the dead, he would proclaim light both to our people and to the Gentiles."

And I [God] ***will lead***

I ***will guide***

I ***will turn*** the darkness before them into light

I ***do not*** forsake them

I [Apostle Paul] have had the ***help that comes from God.***

Christ

By being

By being ***the first***

By being the first to ***rise from the dead***

Christ would proclaim ***light***

Both to our people ***and*** to the Gentiles.

[Murmur and mumble the words. Phrase by phrase. Word by word. Syllable by syllable. Take pleasure in making the sounds of the words, getting the feel of the meaning. Experience pleasurable anticipation of taking in what will make you more yourself, the self that God made in his own image and likeness. The self that God made for intimate communion with him. The self that God created for good works, that you should walk in them. Eat God's words. Let God's words become a joy and the delight of your heart.]

Journal:

Christ, being the first to rise from the dead, would proclaim light. How is this revelation tied to the Apostle John's statement that in Christ was the life, and life was the light of men (John 1:4)?

Are you aware that God has shone in your heart? Are you aware that God has shone in your heart to give light, to give enlightenment, to show or make known your thoughts? And his thoughts? Are you aware that God has shone in your heart to give the light of the knowledge of the glory of God? Knowing. Being aware of. Perceiving. Understanding.

Or are you still sleeping? Are you still dead? Are you still leaning on your own understanding? Are you still content to be independent? Are you still striving to have things your own way? Are you still under the influence of foreign gods, the elementary spirits of this world?

That Christ… by being the first to rise from the dead, he would proclaim light both to our people and to the Gentiles.

Awake, O sleeper, and arise from the dead, and Christ will shine on you (Eph 5:14)

[Murmur and mumble the words. Phrase by phrase. Word by word. Syllable by syllable. Take pleasure in making the sounds of the words, getting the feel of the meaning. Experience pleasurable anticipation of taking in what will make you more yourself, the self that God made in his own image and likeness. The self that God made for intimate communion with him. The self that God created for good works, that you should walk in them. Eat God's words. Let God's words become a joy and the delight of your heart.]

Journal:

How do we awake and arise from the dead?

We may not yet be aware, but God says <u>he has</u> shone in our hearts to give the light of the knowledge of the glory of God. He says the light <u>does shine</u> in the darkness. It shines in the deceitful, desperately sick heart. And he says the darkness has <u>not</u> overcome the light. Do you believe these statements about yourself and your fellow human beings? Record your response.

Ps 138:8 - The Lord <u>will</u> fulfill his purpose for me; your steadfast love, O Lord, endures forever. Do not forsake the work of your hands. (ESV)

Prov 21:30 - There is <u>no</u> wisdom, understanding, or advice that can succeed against the Lord. (NCV)

Col 2:3 - in [Christ] are hidden all the treasures of wisdom and knowledge.

Isa 42:16 - And I [God] will lead the blind in a way that they do not know, in paths that they have not known I will guide them. I will turn the darkness before them into light, the rough places into level ground. These are the things I do, and I do not forsake them.

Acts 26:22-23 - To this day I [Apostle Paul] have had the help that comes from God, and so I stand here testifying both to small and great, saying nothing but what the prophets and Moses said would come to pass: that the Christ must suffer and that, by being the first to rise from the dead, he would proclaim light both to our people and to the Gentiles."

[Pause. Breathe. Inhale and exhale. Reflect. Listen.]

Give me life according to your word, God!

Journal:

What do you hear God saying to you in these Scripture texts? What do they reveal about God and about you? Converse with God about what you're hearing him say. Verbalize and describe your thoughts, memories that come to mind, questions and emotions, concerns, desires.

Is there a particular word or phrase that disturbs or soothes you?

Do the Scripture texts create a picture or an impression that draws you to linger in exploring and experiencing it?

Choose a word or a phrase from your meditation to write on a slip of

paper to carry with you today. Refer to it often throughout the day to remind you of your conversation with God and to continue the conversation all day long. Throughout the day pause to become aware of your thoughts and feelings and will. Ask yourself, "What drives me in this moment? Life according to God's word? Or life according to someone else's word?"

Anticipate that God's words stirred your heart for a reason. He's conversing with you through them. Anticipate that God will bring his word to life in you, to bear fruit in your heart and mind and soul and body. Anticipate that God will reveal the secrets of your heart, for anything that is visible is light. And anticipate that God will cause his words to become a joy and the delight of your heart.

CONTEMPLATE

God is spirit, and those who worship him must worship in spirit and truth. Seek him. Feel your way to him. Reach out. Find him.

You exist in God's abounding grace. Only in God's abounding grace do you exist. In God's abounding grace you are you, the real you, able to worship God in spirit and truth.

*2 Cor 9:8 - And **God is able** to make all grace abound to you, so that having all sufficiency in all things at all times, **you may** abound in every good work.*

Anticipate that God's abounding grace, in which you exist and are, will flow around you and through you to enlighten and empower you to love as you have been loved so that you may abound in every good work this day.

50 - I Incline My Heart

Pray: Ask God to prepare your heart and mind and soul to receive his words, to receive truth that will set you free, which will heal and perfect your understanding and knowledge of who God is and who you are.

Ps 119:25-32 - I'm feeling terrible — I couldn't feel worse! Get me on my feet again. You promised, remember? When I told my story, you responded; train me well in your deep wisdom. Help me understand these things inside and out so I can ponder your miracle-wonders. My sad life's dilapidated, a falling-down barn; build me up again by your Word. Barricade the road that goes Nowhere; grace me with your clear revelation. I choose the true road to Somewhere, I post your road signs at every curve and corner. I grasp and cling to whatever you tell me; God, don't let me down! I'll run the course you lay out for me if you'll just show me how. (MSG)

[Murmur and mumble the words. Phrase by phrase. Word by word. Syllable by syllable. Pause. Breathe. Inhale and exhale. Reflect. Listen.]

Journal:

Note how this prayer stirs you today and what you hear God saying to you.

Eph 5:13-14 - But when anything is exposed by the light, it becomes visible, for anything that becomes visible is light. Therefore it says, "Awake, O sleeper, and arise from the dead, and Christ will shine on you."

But when ***anything***

When anything ***is exposed***

When anything is exposed ***by the light*** [by Christ Jesus, the life, the light]

When anything is exposed by the light, ***it becomes visible***

For anything that becomes visible ***is*** light.

[Murmur and mumble the words. Phrase by phrase. Word by word. Syllable by syllable. Take pleasure in making the sounds of the words, getting the feel of the meaning. Experience pleasurable anticipation of taking in what will make you more yourself, the self that God made in his own image and likeness. The self that God made for intimate communion with him. The self that God created for good works, that you should walk in them. Eat God's words. Let God's words become a joy and the delight of your heart.]

Journal:

Are you resisting having your heart exposed by the light so that it becomes visible? Why?

Do you realize that you are dead if your heart is not exposed by the light?

For anything that becomes visible ***is*** light

Therefore it says

Awake

Awake, ***O sleeper***

And arise ***from the dead***

And Christ ***will*** shine on you.

Can we wake ourselves up? Can we make ourselves arise from the dead?

Which life is this passage referring to when it urges you to arise from the dead?

John 12:25-26 - Whoever loves his life loses it, and whoever hates [to detest, love less] his life in this world will keep it for eternal life. If anyone serves me, he must follow me; and where I am, there will my servant be also. If anyone serves me, the Father will honor him.

2 Cor 4:16-18 - So we do not lose heart. Though our outer nature is wasting away [rot thoroughly, ruin, decay, pervert], our inner nature is being renewed [renovate, make fresh or sound again as though new] day by day. For this slight momentary affliction is preparing for us an eternal weight of glory beyond all comparison, as we look not to the things that are seen but to the things that are unseen. For the things that are seen are transient, but the things that are unseen are eternal.

How do we participate in our inner nature being renewed?

Prov 6:20-22 - My son, keep your father's commandment, and forsake not your mother's teaching. Bind them on your heart always; tie them around your neck. When you walk, they will lead you; when you lie down, they will watch over you; and when you awake, they will talk with you.

My son, ***keep*** [guard, protect, maintain, obey]

Keep your ***father's*** [God's] ***commandment***

Forsake not [do not reject, let alone]

Your ***mother's*** [God's] ***teaching*** [precept or statute]

Bind them [in love, in covenant, in alliance]

On your ***heart*** always

Tie them around your ***neck*** [as in rumination, to chew, to turn over in your mind; meditate]

When you ***walk***

They will ***lead you***

When you ***lie down***

They will ***watch over you***

And when you ***awake***

They will ***talk with you***

[Murmur and mumble the words. Phrase by phrase. Word by word. Syllable by syllable. Take pleasure in making the sounds of the words, getting the feel of the meaning. Experience pleasurable anticipation of taking in what will make you more yourself, the self that God made in his own image and likeness. The self that God made for intimate communion with him. The self that God created for good works, that you should walk in them. Eat God's words. Let God's words become a joy and the delight of your heart.]

Guard, protect, maintain, do not reject, do not let alone your father's commandment and mother's teaching. Bind them on your heart always in love, in covenant, in alliance, and chew them, meditate.

How can you comply with this instruction?

Ps 119:25-32 - My soul clings to the dust; give me life according to your word! When I told of my ways, you answered me; teach me your statutes! Make me understand the way of your precepts, and I will meditate on your wondrous works. My soul melts away for sorrow; strengthen me according to your word! Put false ways far from me and graciously teach me your law! I have chosen the way of faithfulness; I set your rules before me. I cling to your testimonies, O Lord; let me not be put to shame! I will run in the way of your commandments when you enlarge my heart! (ESV)

My soul ***clings***

My soul clings ***to the dust***

Give me life

Give me life ***according to your word!***

Prov 30:5 - Every word of God proves true; he is a shield to those who take refuge in him.

2 Cor 4:7-11 - But we have this treasure in jars of clay, to show that the surpassing power belongs to God and not to us. We are afflicted in every way, but not crushed; perplexed, but not driven to despair; persecuted, but not forsaken; struck down, but not destroyed; always carrying in the body the death of Jesus, so that the life of Jesus may also be manifested in our bodies.

My soul clings to the ***dust***

We have ***this treasure*** in jars of clay

The surpassing power ***belongs to God*** and not to us

Give me life according to ***your word***!

When I told of my ways, you answered me

Teach me your statutes!

Make me understand the way of your precepts

And ***I will meditate*** on your wondrous works

My soul melts away ***for sorrow***

Strengthen me ***according to your word***!

Put false ways far from me

And ***graciously teach me*** your law!

I have chosen the way of faithfulness

I set your rules before me

I cling to your testimonies, O Lord

Let me not be put to shame!

I will run in the way of your commandments

When

When you enlarge my heart!

Ps 119:32 - <u>I will eagerly pursue</u> your commandments **because you** *continue to increase my understanding. (God's Word)*

Ps 119:32 - <u>I run in the path</u> of your commands, **for you have** *set my heart free. (NIV)*

[Murmur and mumble the words. Phrase by phrase. Word by word. Syllable by syllable. Take pleasure in making the sounds of the words, getting the feel of the meaning. Experience pleasurable anticipation of taking in what will make you more yourself, the self that God made in his own image and likeness. The self that God made for intimate communion with him. The self that God created for good works, that you should walk in them. Eat God's words. Let God's words become a joy and the delight of your heart.]

Journal:

My soul clings to the dust. How is this statement related to the statement that we have this treasure (life, light, Word, wisdom, knowledge, understanding, power…) in jars of clay?

Describe the difference between life when your soul clings to the dust and when God gives life according to his word.

When I told of my ways. Have you told God of your ways?

Note the requests the psalmist makes of God and also the commitments and actions that he himself takes on while acknowledging that he relies completely upon God's grace and power.

Using the psalmist's prayer as a guide, write your own personal prayer uniting your will and desire and activity with God's regarding your life.

Eph 5:13-14 - But when anything is exposed by the light, it becomes visible, for anything that becomes visible is light. Therefore it says, "Awake, O sleeper, and arise from the dead, and Christ will shine on you."

John 12:25-26 - Whoever loves his life loses it, and whoever hates [to detest, love less] his life in this world will keep it for eternal life. If anyone serves me, he must follow me; and where I am, there will my servant be also. If anyone serves me, the Father will honor him.

2 Cor 4:16-18 - So we do not lose heart. Though our outer nature is wasting away [rot thoroughly, ruin, decay, pervert], our inner nature is being renewed [renovate, make fresh or sound again as though new] day by day. For this slight momentary affliction is preparing for us an eternal weight of glory beyond all comparison, as we look not to the things that are seen but to the things that are unseen. For the things that are seen are transient, but the things that are unseen are eternal.

Ps 119:36-37 - *Incline my heart* to your testimonies, and not to selfish gain! Turn my eyes from looking at worthless things; and give me life in your ways.

Ps 119:112 - *I incline my heart* to perform your statutes forever, to the end.

[Pause. Breathe. Inhale and exhale. Reflect. Listen.]

Give me life according to your word, God!

Journal:

What do you hear God saying to you in these Scripture texts? What do they reveal about God and about you? Converse with God about what you're hearing him say. Verbalize and describe your thoughts, memories that come to mind, questions and emotions, concerns, desires.

Is there a particular word or phrase that disturbs or soothes you?

Do the Scripture texts create a picture or an impression that draws you to linger in exploring and experiencing it?

Choose a word or a phrase from your meditation to write on a slip of paper to carry with you today. Refer to it often throughout the day to remind you of your conversation with God and to continue the conversation all day long. Throughout the day pause to become aware of your thoughts and feelings and will. Ask yourself, "What drives me

in this moment? Life according to God's word? Or life according to someone else's word?"

Anticipate that God's words stirred your heart for a reason. He's conversing with you through them. Anticipate that God will bring his word to life in you, to bear fruit in your heart and mind and soul and body. Anticipate that God will reveal the secrets of your heart, for anything that is visible is light. And anticipate that God will cause his words to become a joy and the delight of your heart.

CONTEMPLATE

God is spirit, and those who worship him must worship in spirit and truth. Seek him. Feel your way to him. Reach out. Find him.

You exist in God's abounding grace. Only in God's abounding grace do you exist. In God's abounding grace you are you, the real you, able to worship God in spirit and truth.

*2 Cor 9:8 - And **God is able** to make all grace abound to you, so that having all sufficiency in all things at all times, **you may** abound in every good work.*

Anticipate that God's abounding grace, in which you exist and are, will flow around you and through you to enlighten and empower you to love as you have been loved so that you may abound in every good work this day.

51 - When You Awake, They Will Talk With You

Pray: Ask God to prepare your heart and mind and soul to receive his words, to receive truth that will set you free, which will heal and perfect your understanding and knowledge of who God is and who you are.

Ps 119:25-32 - My soul clings to the dust; give me life according to your word! When I told of my ways, you answered me; teach me your statutes! Make me understand the way of your precepts, and I will meditate on your wondrous works. My soul melts away for sorrow; strengthen me according to your word! Put false ways far from me and graciously teach me your law! I have chosen the way of faithfulness; I set your rules before me. I cling to your testimonies, O Lord; let me not be put to shame! I will run in the way of your commandments when you enlarge my heart! (ESV)

[Murmur and mumble the words. Phrase by phrase. Word by word. Syllable by syllable. Pause. Breathe. Inhale and exhale. Reflect. Listen.]

Journal:

Note how this prayer stirs you today and what you hear God saying to you.

Prov 6:20-22 - My son, keep your father's commandment, and forsake not your mother's teaching. Bind them on your heart always; tie them around your neck. When you walk, they will lead you; when you lie down, they will watch over you; and when you awake, they will talk with you.

2 Cor 4:16-18 - So we do not lose heart. Though our outer nature is wasting away [rot thoroughly, ruin, decay, pervert], our inner nature is being renewed [renovate, make fresh or sound again as though new] day by day. For this slight momentary affliction is preparing for us an eternal weight of glory beyond all comparison, as we look not to the things that are seen but to the things that are unseen. For the things that are seen are transient, but the things that are unseen are eternal.

Guard, protect, maintain, do not reject, do not let alone your father's commandment and your mother's teaching. Bind them on your heart always in love, in covenant, in alliance, and chew them, meditate.

And ***when***

When you ***awake***

They will ***talk with you***

So we ***do not lose heart***

Though our ***outer nature*** is wasting away

Our inner nature

Our inner nature is ***being renewed***

Day by day

For this slight momentary affliction is ***preparing for us an eternal weight of glory*** beyond all comparison

As we ***look not to the things that are seen***

But to the ***things that are unseen***

For the things that are ***seen are transient***

But the things that are ***unseen are eternal***

[Murmur and mumble the words. Phrase by phrase. Word by word. Syllable by syllable. Take pleasure in making the sounds of the words, getting the feel of the meaning. Experience pleasurable anticipation of taking in what will make you more yourself, the self that God made in his own image and likeness. The self that God made for intimate communion with him. The self that God created for good works, that you should walk in them. Eat God's words. Let God's words become a joy and the delight of your heart.]

Journal:

Are the afflictions that we experience in our everyday lives designed to wake us up?

Are God and Christ Jesus, the Wisdom and Word and Light of God always working, day by day, in aiding the wasting away of our outer nature while renewing our inner nature even if we're asleep, dead, and completely unaware of the grace that they are filling us with?

Is it this light (life) that God has shone in our hearts, but seems to be hidden within each of us, which wisdom strongly admonishes us to seek and find? Know. Be aware of. Perceive. Understand. The knowledge of the glory of God in the face of Jesus Christ.

Awake, O sleeper

And ***arise*** from the dead

What does one who has awakened do?

Ps 119:146-148 - I call to you; save me, that I may observe your testimonies. I rise before dawn and cry for help; I hope in your words. My eyes are awake before the watches of the night, that I may meditate on your promise.

Prov 2:1-6 - My child, listen to what I say and remember what I command you. Listen carefully to wisdom; set your mind on understanding. Cry out for wisdom, and beg for understanding. Search for it like silver, and hunt for it like hidden treasure. Then you will understand respect for the Lord, and you will find that you know God. Only the Lord gives wisdom; he gives knowledge and understanding. (NCV)

Prov 4:5-8 - Get wisdom; get insight; do not forget, and do not turn away from the words of my mouth. Do not forsake her, and she will keep you; love her, and she will guard you. The beginning of wisdom is this: Get wisdom, and whatever you get, get insight. Prize her highly, and she will exalt you; she will honor you if you embrace her.

God's call:

Listen to what I say

Remember what I command you

Listen ***carefully*** to wisdom

Set your mind on understanding

Cry out for wisdom

Beg for understanding

Search for it like silver

Hunt for it like hidden treasure

Then you will ***understand respect*** for the Lord

Then you will find that you ***know God***

Get wisdom

Get insight

Do not forget, and ***do not turn away*** from the words of my mouth

Do not forsake her [wisdom], and she will keep you

Love her, and she will guard you

Prize her highly, and she will exalt you

She will honor you if you ***embrace her***

The awakened one's response:

I ***call to you***; save me

That I may ***observe*** your testimonies.

I rise before dawn and ***cry for help***

I ***hope*** in your words

My eyes are ***awake*** before the watches of the night

That I may ***meditate*** on your promise

[Murmur and mumble the words. Phrase by phrase. Word by word. Syllable by syllable. Take pleasure in making the sounds of the words, getting the feel of the meaning. Experience pleasurable anticipation of taking in what will make you more yourself, the self that God made in his own image and likeness. The self that God made for intimate communion with him. The self that God created for good works, that you should walk in them. Eat God's words. Let God's words become a joy and the delight of your heart.]

Journal:

Does waking up seem to be a full-time occupation?

Note all the actions that these Scripture texts urge you to participate in regarding wisdom. All are actions that you will begin to practice as you awake, and God inclines your heart to his word, and as you incline your heart to his word. Which action will you start with?

Do you regularly practice what these Scripture texts urge you to do? Describe your activity or practice as you seek and strive to comply with the advice given in these texts.

How does your practice impact you? Does it awaken you from the dead? Does it show and make known your thoughts and God's thoughts? Does it cause you to love Wisdom? To prize Wisdom and insight? To embrace them? Does your practice give you pleasure and satisfaction as you become aware of the divine influence upon your heart, and its reflection in your life?

Prov 6:20-22 - My son, keep your father's commandment, and forsake not your mother's teaching. Bind them on your heart always; tie them around your neck. When you walk, they will lead you; when you lie down, they will watch over you; and when you awake, they will talk with you.

2 Cor 4:16-18 - So we do not lose heart. Though our outer nature is wasting away [rot thoroughly, ruin, decay, pervert], our inner nature is being renewed [renovate, make fresh or sound again as though new] day by day. For this slight momentary affliction is preparing for us an eternal weight of glory beyond all comparison, as we look not to the things that are seen but to the things that are unseen. For the things that are seen are transient, but the things that are unseen are eternal.

Ps 119:146-148 - I call to you; save me, that I may observe your testimonies. I rise before dawn and cry for help; I hope in your words. My eyes are awake before the watches of the night, that I may meditate on your promise.

[Pause. Breathe. Inhale and exhale. Reflect. Listen.]

Give me life according to your word, God!

Journal:

What do you hear God saying to you in these Scripture texts? What do they reveal about God and about you? Converse with God about what you're hearing him say. Verbalize and describe your thoughts, memories that come to mind, questions and emotions, concerns, desires.

Is there a particular word or phrase that disturbs or soothes you?

Do the Scripture texts create a picture or an impression that draws you to linger in exploring and experiencing it?

Choose a word or a phrase from your meditation to write on a slip of paper to carry with you today. Refer to it often throughout the day to remind you of your conversation with God and to continue the conversation all day long. Throughout the day pause to become aware of your thoughts and feelings and will. Ask yourself, "What drives me in this moment? Life according to God's word? Or life according to someone else's word?"

Anticipate that God's words stirred your heart for a reason. He's conversing with you through them. Anticipate that God will bring his word to life in you, to bear fruit in your heart and mind and soul and body. Anticipate that God will reveal the secrets of your heart, for anything that is visible is light. And anticipate that God will cause his words to become a joy and the delight of your heart.

CONTEMPLATE

God is spirit, and those who worship him must worship in spirit and truth. Seek him. Feel your way to him. Reach out. Find him.

You exist in God's abounding grace. Only in God's abounding grace do you exist. In God's abounding grace you are you, the real you, able to worship God in spirit and truth.

2 Cor 9:8 - And ***God is able*** *to make all grace abound to you, so that having all sufficiency in all things at all times,* ***you may*** *abound in every good work.*

Anticipate that God's abounding grace, in which you exist and are, will flow around you and through you to enlighten and empower you to love as you have been loved so that you may abound in every good work this day.

52 - My Heart Says "Your face, Lord, Do I Seek."

Pray: Ask God to prepare your heart and mind and soul to receive his words, to receive truth that will set you free, which will heal and perfect your understanding and knowledge of who God is and who you are.

Ps 119:25-32 - My soul clings to the dust; give me life according to your word! When I told of my ways, you answered me; teach me your statutes! Make me understand the way of your precepts, and I will meditate on your wondrous works. My soul melts away for sorrow; strengthen me according to your word! Put false ways far from me and graciously teach me your law! I have chosen the way of faithfulness; I set your rules before me. I cling to your testimonies, O Lord; let me not be put to shame! I will run in the way of your commandments when you enlarge my heart! (ESV)

[Murmur and mumble the words. Phrase by phrase. Word by word. Syllable by syllable. Pause. Breathe. Inhale and exhale. Reflect. Listen.]

Journal:

Note how this prayer stirs you today and what you hear God saying to you.

Hurt, anger, fear, and frustration encapsulated me like a shroud after my father's death in a tragic accident when I was ten years old. An Aunt, trying desperately to console me, told me that God took Daddy to be with him in heaven.

The only detail my childish mind grabbed hold of was that God took Daddy away from me. And the only reason I could come up with as to why God would do such a thing to me, was that God was angry with me and was punishing me, though I had no idea what I'd done wrong. My view of God, of myself, and of the world changed.

From that day forward, everything that I saw and heard and experienced was seen and interpreted through the dark shadow of my painful circumstances. That shroud distorted light, life and truth. But I didn't know that my vision and hearing and thinking and perceptions were warped.

I began to work hard at making myself good, so God wouldn't take away anyone or anything else that I loved. I buried my grief and distrust, for if I voiced it, surely God would punish me further. I built facades to hide my inadequacies and ugliness from others, though I was intimately familiar with each and every one of them. I saw God as an angry, vengeful bully, who this wretched, misfit could never please. Trying to be good and stay out of his way seemed to me to be my best chance of escaping more heartache. What misery one buries herself in when she leans on her own understanding and does not trust in the Lord!

I thought I was an innocent victim of God's bullying ways. On one hand, maybe I was an innocent victim. But on another, I can now see that by hearing every word of God and interpreting every experience through my shroud, I judged God and his Word as being untrue, at least where I was concerned. I regularly challenged the words I heard or read for myself in the Bible. I constantly accused, "Yes, but what about… a good god, a just god, a loving god… wouldn't…" and I'd fill in my accusation with a personal experience or a world event that seemed to contradict what God said about himself.

That shroud which wound itself around me and confined me was a delusion, darkness, a lie, a life that wasn't real. But I didn't know it. It certainly looked and felt real to me, and very painful.

I finally encountered the truth, the person, Christ Jesus the Messiah, God is salvation, for the first time on the day my friend, Debbie, asked me to read a Scripture text. I finally began to wake up! That day, I met the Word who had become flesh, the living Word, the active Word, who gave life to all the written words that I'd heard but not understood all my life.

Ps 103:13 - As a father shows compassion to his children, so the Lord shows compassion to those who fear him.

For the first time my darkened mind asked, "Could I be wrong about God? Might God be like my Daddy? Compassionate? Might God be someone I longed to hang out with, to laugh in pleasure and play with?"

On that day, the tiniest pinprick of light penetrated the burial cloth that veiled the truth from me! And my eye and heart has focused unwaveringly on it ever since, as I've sought to understand and experience what it is to fear God and to lose my life, so I could find life.

All the while my own understanding indicted God as a bully, a vengeful, punishing God, He was not punishing me, but working to save me! He was causing my outer nature to waste away, while renewing my inner nature, even while I was completely oblivious that I even had an inner nature.

Truly, the darkness in me, the darkness of my misunderstanding had not overcome the life that is the light of men! Truly, every word of God proves true! While leaning on my own understanding I thought I was alone, abandoned, forsaken, unloved. But not for one nanosecond had God ever failed to practice steadfast love, justice, and righteousness in me and on my behalf.

Prov 3:5-12 - Trust in the Lord with all your heart, and do not lean on your own understanding. In all your ways acknowledge him, and he will make straight your paths. Be not wise in your own eyes; fear the Lord, and turn away from evil. It will be healing to your flesh and refreshment to your bones. Honor the Lord with your wealth and with the firstfruits of all your produce; then your barns will be filled with plenty, and your vats will be bursting with wine. My son, do not despise the Lord's discipline or be weary of his reproof, for the Lord reproves him whom he loves, as a father the son in whom he delights.

Trust [refuge, be confident or sure]

Trust in the Lord with ***all*** your heart

And do not lean on ***your own*** understanding

In ***all*** your ways acknowledge him [to know by seeing]

And ***he will*** make straight your paths

Be not wise in ***your own*** eyes

Fear the Lord, and ***turn away*** from evil [that which spoils, and makes good for nothing]

It will be ***healing*** <u>to your flesh</u> and ***refreshment*** <u>to your bones</u>

Honor the Lord with ***your wealth*** and with the firstfruits of all your produce

Do not despise the Lord's discipline

Do not be weary of his reproof

For the Lord reproves him whom ***he loves***

As a father the son in whom ***he delights***

[Murmur and mumble the words. Phrase by phrase. Word by word. Syllable by syllable. Take pleasure in making the sounds of the words, getting the feel of the meaning. Experience pleasurable anticipation of taking in what will make you more yourself, the self that God made in his own image and likeness. The self that God made for intimate communion with him. The self that God created for good works, that you should walk in them. Eat God's words. Let God's words become a joy and the delight of your heart.]

Journal:

According to this Scripture text, what does God want from you? And how will he respond to you?

Rev 3:19 - 'As many as I love, I do convict [bring to a realization one's guilt] and chasten [train, educate, discipline]; be zealous [feel heat, ardor], then, and reform; (YLT)

Reform. Think differently. Denoting accompaniment. Relation. Exercise the mind. Comprehend. Heed.[1]

Think differently. It's the heart where life and light are found and experienced. Accompaniment. Relation. In him. Not alone. Never alone.

Col 2:3 - in [Christ] are hidden all the treasures of wisdom and knowledge.

Prov 8:35 - For whoever finds me finds life and obtains favor from the Lord,

How do we accomplish what God asks of us?

The man whom God described as a man after his own heart expressed it this way:

Ps 27:8 - You have said, "Seek my face." My heart says to you, "Your face, Lord, do I seek."

You [God]

You ***have said***

Seek

Seek ***my face***.

My ***face.*** [Not my mighty right arm.]

Seek my face.

My

My ***heart***

My heart says to ***you*** [Lord]

Your face

Your face, ***Lord***,

Your face, Lord, do ***I seek***.

[Murmur and mumble the words. Phrase by phrase. Word by word. Syllable by syllable. Take pleasure in making the sounds of the words, getting the feel of the meaning. Experience pleasurable anticipation of taking in what will make you more yourself, the self that God made in his own image and likeness. The self that God made for intimate communion with him. The self that God created for good works, that you should walk in them. Eat God's words. Let God's words become a joy and the delight of your heart.]

Journal:

Will you set your heart to seek the Lord? To tread or frequent; to follow for pursuit or search; to seek or ask; specifically to worship.

Heb 13:20-21 - Now may the God of peace who brought again from the dead our Lord Jesus, the great shepherd of the sheep, by the blood of the eternal covenant, equip you with everything good that you may do his will, working in us that which is pleasing in his sight, through Jesus Christ, to whom be glory forever and ever. Amen.

Now may the God of peace who brought again ***from the dead*** our Lord Jesus

Our Lord Jesus, the great shepherd of the sheep, ***by the blood of the eternal covenant***,

May the ***God of peace***...

Equip you

Equip you ***with everything good*** that you may do his will

Working in us

Working in us that which is ***pleasing in his sight***

Through Jesus Christ, to whom be glory forever and ever. Amen.

Journal:

As you seek God's face, will you trust that *he* will stir a passion within you to do his will? Will you trust that *he will* equip you that you may do his will, that *he will* work in you that which is pleasing in his sight, through Jesus Christ?

The grace of the Lord Jesus Christ and the love of God and the fellowship of the Holy Spirit be with you all (2 Cor 13:14).

Prov 3:5-12 - Trust in the Lord with all your heart, and do not lean on your own understanding. In all your ways acknowledge him, and he will make straight your paths. Be not wise in your own eyes; fear the Lord, and turn away from evil. It will be healing to your flesh and refreshment to your bones. Honor the Lord with your wealth and with the firstfruits of all your produce; then your barns will be filled with plenty, and your vats will be bursting with wine. My son, do not despise the Lord's discipline or be weary of his reproof, for the Lord reproves him whom he loves, as a father the son in whom he delights.

Rev 3:19 - 'As many as I love, I do convict and chasten; be zealous [feel heat, ardor], then, and reform; (YLT)

Ps 27:8 - You have said, "Seek my face." My heart says to you, "Your face, Lord, do I seek."

Heb 13:20-21 - Now may the God of peace who brought again from the dead our Lord Jesus, the great shepherd of the sheep, by the blood of the eternal covenant, equip you with everything good that you may do his will, working in us that which is pleasing in his sight, through Jesus Christ, to whom be glory forever and ever. Amen.

[Pause. Breathe. Inhale and exhale. Reflect. Listen.]

Give me life according to your word, God!

Journal:

What do you hear God saying to you in these Scripture texts? What do they reveal about God and about you? Converse with God about what you're hearing him say. Verbalize and describe your thoughts, memories that come to mind, questions and emotions, concerns, desires.

Is there a particular word or phrase that disturbs or soothes you?

Do the Scripture texts create a picture or an impression that draws you to linger in exploring and experiencing it?

Choose a word or a phrase from your meditation to write on a slip of paper to carry with you today. Refer to it often throughout the day to remind you of your conversation with God and to continue the conversation all day long. Throughout the day pause to become aware of your thoughts and feelings and will. Ask yourself, "What drives me in this moment? Life according to God's word? Or life according to someone else's word?"

Anticipate that God's words stirred your heart for a reason. He's conversing with you through them. Anticipate that God will bring his word to life in you, to bear fruit in your heart and mind and soul and body. Anticipate that God will reveal the secrets of your heart, for anything that is visible is light. And anticipate that God will cause his words to

become a joy and the delight of your heart.

CONTEMPLATE

God is spirit, and those who worship him must worship in spirit and truth. Seek him. Feel your way to him. Reach out. Find him.

You exist in God's abounding grace. Only in God's abounding grace do you exist. In God's abounding grace you are you, the real you, able to worship God in spirit and truth.

2 Cor 9:8 - And ***God is able*** *to make all grace abound to you, so that having all sufficiency in all things at all times,* ***you may*** *abound in every good work.*

Anticipate that God's abounding grace, in which you exist and are, will flow around you and through you to enlighten and empower you to love as you have been loved so that you may abound in every good work this day.

Resources:

[1]Reform: NT:3340 <START GREEK>metanoe/w<END GREEK> metanoeo (met-an-o-eh'-o); from NT:3326 and NT:3539; to think differently or afterwards, i.e. reconsider (morally, feel compunction):

NT:3326<START GREEK>meta/<END GREEK> meta (met-ah'); a primary preposition (often used adverbially); properly, denoting accompaniment; "amid" (local or causal); modified variously according to the case (genitive case association, or accusative case succession) with which it is joined; occupying an intermediate position between NT:575 or NT:1537 and NT:1519 or NT:4314; less intimate than NT:1722 and less close than NT:4862):

NT:3539 <START GREEK>noie/w<END GREEK> noeo (no-eh'-o) or noieo (noy-eh'-o); from NT:3563; to exercise the mind (observe), i.e. (figuratively) to comprehend, heed:

NT:575 <START GREEK>a)po/<END GREEK> apo (apo'); a primary particle; "off," i.e. away (from something near), in various senses (of place, time, or relation; literal or figurative):

NT:1537 <START GREEK>e)k<END GREEK> ek (ek) or ex (ex); a primary preposition denoting origin (the point whence action or motion proceeds), from, out (of place, time, or cause; literal or figurative; direct or remote):

NT:1519<START GREEK>ei)$<END GREEK> eis (ice); a primary preposition; to or into (indicating the point reached or entered), of place, time, or (figuratively) purpose (result, etc.); also in adverbial phrases:

NT:4314 <START GREEK>pro/$<END GREEK> pros (pros); a strengthened form of NT:4253; a preposition of direction; forward to, i.e. toward (with the genitive case the side of, i.e. pertaining to; with the dative case by the side of, i.e. near to; usually with the accusative case the place, time, occasion, or respect, which is the destination of the relation, i.e. whither or for which it is predicated):

NT:1722 <START GREEK>e)n<END GREEK> en (en); a primary preposition denoting (fixed) position (in place, time or state), and (by implication) instrumentality (medially or constructively), i.e. a relation of rest (intermediate between NT:1519 and NT:1537); “in,” at, (up-) on, by, etc.:

NT:4862 <START GREEK>su/n<END GREEK> sun (soon); a primary preposition denoting union; with or together (but much closer than NT:3326 or NT:3844), i.e. by association, companionship, process, resemblance, possession, instrumentality, addition, etc.: (Biblesoft's New Exhaustive Strong's Numbers and Concordance with Expanded Greek-Hebrew Dictionary. Copyright © 1994, 2003, 2006, 2010 Biblesoft, Inc. and International Bible Translators, Inc.)

For Further Exploration

I have found the following references insightful into contemplation and centering prayer.

Open Mind, Open Heart 20th Anniversary Edition, Thomas Keating, The Continuum International Publishing Group, 2006

Centering Prayer and Inner Awakening, Cynthia Bourgeault, Crowley Publications, 2004

www.ingramcontent.com/pod-product-compliance
Lightning Source LLC
LaVergne TN
LVHW020040110826
845155LV00029B/570

* 9 7 8 1 8 9 3 4 7 8 3 4 3 *